Node.js Recipes

Cory Gackenheimer

Apress·

Node.js Recipes

ISBN-13 (pbk): 978-1-4302-6058-5

ISBN-13 (electronic): 978-1-4302-6059-2

President and Publisher: Paul Manning
Lead Editor: Louise Corrigan
Technical Reviewers: Tom Ashworth and Adriaan De Jonge
Editorial Board: Steve Anglin, Mark Beckner, Ewan Buckingham, Gary Cornell, Louise Corrigan, Morgan Ertel, Jonathan Gennick, Jonathan Hassell, Robert Hutchinson, Michelle Lowman, James Markham, Matthew Moodie, Jeff Olson, Jeffrey Pepper, Douglas Pundick, Ben Renow-Clarke, Dominic Shakeshaft, Gwenan Spearing, Matt Wade, Tom Welsh
Coordinating Editor: Christine Ricketts
Copy Editor: Christine Dahlin
Compositor: SPi Global
Indexer: SPi Global
Artist: SPi Global
Cover Designer: Anna Ishchenko

Distributed to the book trade worldwide by Springer Science+Business Media New York, 233 Spring Street, 6th Floor, New York, NY 10013. Phone 1-800-SPRINGER, fax (201) 348-4505, e-mail orders-ny@springer-sbm.com, or visit www.springeronline.com. Apress Media, LLC is a California LLC and the sole member (owner) is Springer Science + Business Media Finance Inc (SSBM Finance Inc). SSBM Finance Inc is a Delaware corporation.

For information on translations, please e-mail rights@apress.com, or visit www.apress.com.

Apress and friends of ED books may be purchased in bulk for academic, corporate, or promotional use. eBook versions and licenses are also available for most titles. For more information, reference our Special Bulk Sales–eBook Licensing web page at www.apress.com/bulk-sales.

Any source code or other supplementary materials referenced by the author in this text is available to readers at www.apress.com. For detailed information about how to locate your book's source code, go to www.apress.com/source-code/.

For Mel and our children.

Contents at a Glance

Contents

About the Author

Cory Gackenheimer is a software engineer from Indiana. He studied Physics at Purdue University where he worked with image analysis software for nanoscale environments. His software experience has led him to utilize many different technologies including C#, C++, Visual Basic, SQL Server, Cassandra, and, of course, JavaScript. When he first encountered Node.js, he realized that the possibility of utilizing the ubiquitous language of the web on the server was both efficient and revolutionary. Since then, he has spent a considerable amount of time learning and building applications with Node.js. Aside from hacking on code, he enjoys spending time with his family, running, and cycling.

About the Technical Reviewers

Adriaan de Jonge is Principal Consultant for Xebia IT Architects in the Netherlands. Adriaan specializes in DevOps, Continuous Delivery, and Agile Architecture. He wrote two books, "Essential App Engine" and "jQuery, jQuery UI and jQuery Mobile," published by Addison-Wesley in 2011 and 2012, respectively. He is currently writing a manager's guide to Continuous Delivery. In the past, Adriaan wrote several articles for IBM developerWorks.

Tom Ashworth is a JavaScript developer from Brighton in the United Kingdom. He's been writing all kind of applications with Node as long as it has been around, in combination with front-end technologies like AngularJS and Backbone, as well as many open source projects.

He's worked as a freelancer, at Buffer, Left Logic, and now Twitter. Around the web you'll find him as @phuu and at phuu.net.

Acknowledgments

This book would not be possible without the encouragement of my friends and family. For the long hours and late nights of researching, writing, and editing that my family so graciously allotted me I will always be grateful.

I also owe a great deal to the technical reviewers of this book, Tom and Adriaan. Their feedback was always superb. All of the editors who worked on this book, especially Louise and Christine, were a tremendous help in moving this project along and responding to my queries.

CHAPTER 1

■ ■ ■

Understanding Node.js

Node.js is a server-side framework useful for building highly scalable and fast applications. Node.js is a platform that is built on v8, the JavaScript runtime that powers the Chrome browser designed by Google. Node.js is designed to be great for intensive I/O applications utilizing the nonblocking event-driven architecture. While Node.js can serve functions in a synchronous way, it most commonly performs operations asynchronously. This means that as you develop an application, you call events with a callback registered for handling the return of the function. While awaiting the return, the next event or function in your application can be queued for execution. Once the first function completes, its callback event is executed and handled by the function call that invoked the callback. This event-driven processing is described in Node.js's very own definition:

> Node.js is a platform built on Chrome's JavaScript runtime for easily building fast, scalable network applications. Node.js uses an event-driven, non-blocking I/O model that makes it lightweight and efficient, perfect for data-intensive real-time applications that run across distributed devices.

Applications written in Node.js are written in JavaScript, the ubiquitous language of the web platform. Because of the accessibility of JavaScript to many experienced developers and newcomers alike, the Node.js platform and community have taken off and have become critical parts of the development landscape for many companies and developers.

This book is about Node.js. In particular this book is designed as a recipe book, which aims to provide a large set of useful and high-quality examples of what Node.js is capable of accomplishing. This book is geared for a developer who has some experience with JavaScript and at least some exposure to Node.js. By reading this book, you will gain an understanding of many of the highly utilized modules, both those native to Node.js and those written by third-party contributors, that are the main targets for Node.js developers.

This first chapter is a departure from the recipe format that will follow in the rest of the book. It is broken down to get a developer up and running from scratch with installation and it gives an overview of how to function within the Node.js platform. You will get an idea of how to install Node.js and understand many of the common paradigms and the basic workflow to get a Node.js application running. As you will see, a considerable amount of time is spent covering how Node.js works. Once you have read this chapter, you should be well equipped to dive into the recipes in the chapters that follow.

1-1. Installing Node.js on Your Machine

There are several ways in which an install of Node.js can happen, and they vary slightly across different operating systems. The three primary methods to install Node.js are via a binary installer, via a package manager, or by compiling the source code.

To install Node.js on your machine via a binary installer, you first need the installer. Currently the only installers that are available for Node.js are for Windows and Macintosh OS X. To find these installers, you need to go to http://nodejs.org/download/. Here you will find your choice of installer to download as shown in Figure 1-1.

1

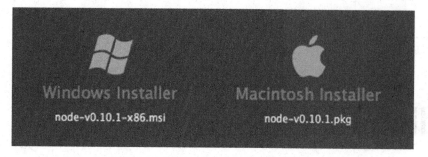

Figure 1-1. *Platform-specific installers available for download*

Windows

On Windows, first download the .msi installer package. When you open the file, you will begin your walkthrough with the Setup Wizard, shown in Figure 1-2.

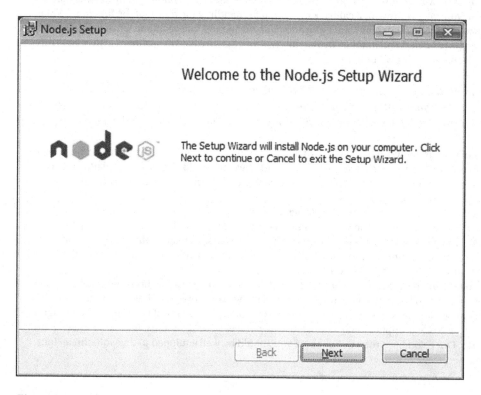

Figure 1-2. *Beginning the install*

As in most Windows applications, you will be presented with a default location to which you can install the application files. This destination, however, can be overwritten and is presented to you as in Figure 1-3.

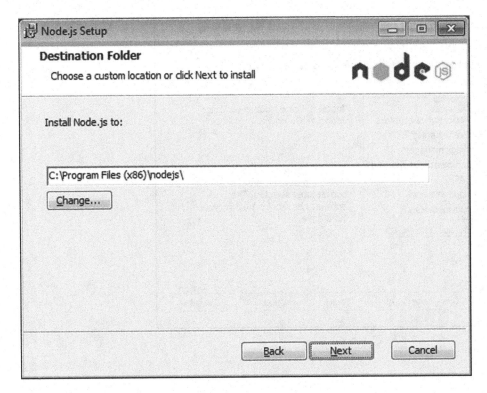

Figure 1-3. *You can choose to use or overwrite the default file location*

The last step before finalizing your install on Windows is to set up any custom configurations that you may want for your Node.js installation. For example you could not add Node.js to your path; perhaps you want to test multiple versions and will explicitly call the executable during your testing phase. This custom step is shown in Figure 1-4.

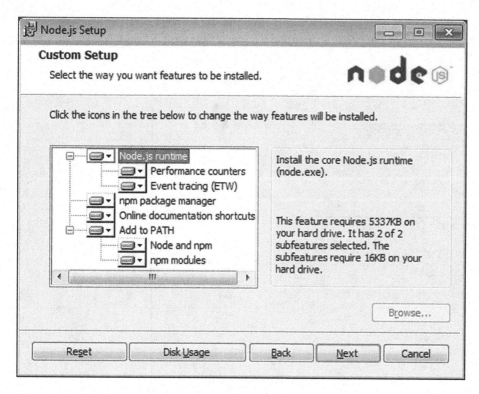

Figure 1-4. *Custom setup*

OS X

The installer on a Macintosh is very similar to the Windows setup. First, download the .pkg file. When you open this, it will walk you through the standard installer that runs on OS X. This presents as you see in Figure 1-5.

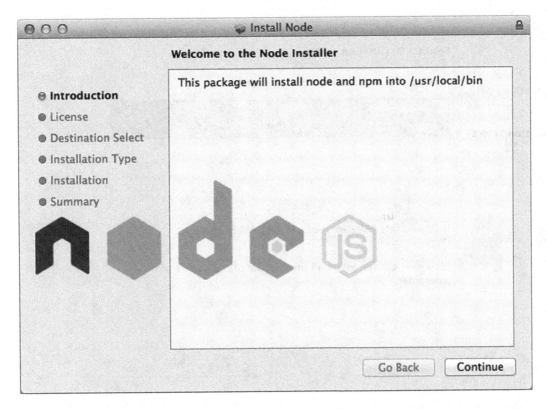

Figure 1-5. *Installing on OS X*

Sometimes when installing Node.js, you want only a subset of the potential users to be able to access it. This functionality is built into the OS X installer, presenting you with the option of how you would like Node.js installed, as shown in Figure 1-6.

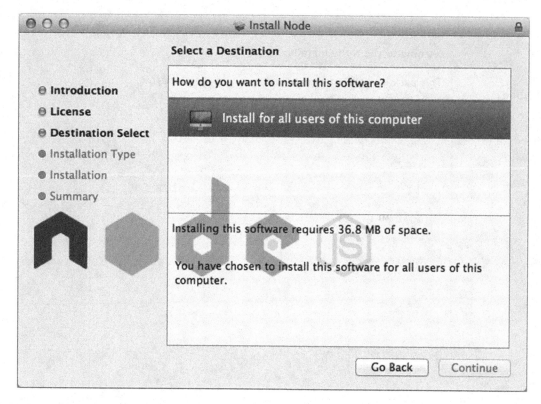

Figure 1-6. *Installing for specified users*

Just as on Windows, you can customize the installation. Click the Custom Install button and then set your configuration accordingly as shown in Figure 1-7. For example, you may wish not to install npm, in favor of doing a more customized npm install, which we will outline in the next section.

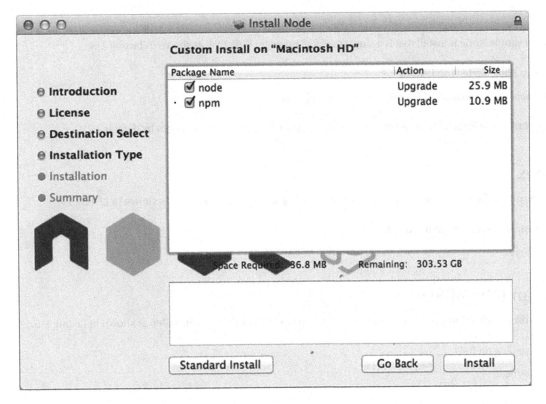

Figure 1-7. *A custom Node.js install on OS X*

There are, of course, many platforms that are not Macintosh or Windows, but you would still like to not have to download and compile Node.js from sources. The solution for this is to find a package manager that will install Node.js for you. There are several package management systems that vary across platforms, each with its own style for fetching new packages.

Ubuntu and Linux Mint

The package for Ubuntu and Linux Mint requires that a few components be installed onto your machine before you can install Node.js. To meet these prerequisites you must first run the code shown in Listing 1-1.

Listing 1-1. Ensuring Prerequisites Are Installed

```
sudo apt-get install python-software-properties python g++ make
```

You can then proceed with the installation by adding the repository that hosts Node.js, updating your sources, and installing with the commands shown in Listing 1-2.

Listing 1-2. Installing Node.js on Ubuntu and Linux Mint

```
sudo add-apt-repository ppa:chris-lea/node.js
sudo apt-get update
sudo apt-get install nodejs
```

Fedora

Fedora 18 has a simple Node.js install that is a single package manager directive, as shown in Listing 1-3.

Listing 1-3. Installing Node.js on Fedora

```
sudo yum --enablerepo=updates-testing install nodejs npm
```

In future versions of Fedora, Node.js should be integrated within the operating system by default.

Arch Linux

For Arch Linux, utilize the pacman package manager by targeting the "nodejs" package, as shown in Listing 1-4.

Listing 1-4. Installing via pacman on Arch Linux

```
pacman -S nodejs
```

FreeBSD and OpenBSD

An installation on Berkeley Software Distribution (BSD) platforms utilizes the ports installer, as shown in Listing 1-5.

Listing 1-5. Installing on BSD

```
/usr/ports/www/node
```

openSUSE

When using openSUSE you can install Node.js using the zypper command-line package management tool, as shown in Listing 1-6.

Listing 1-6. Using zypper to install Node.js on openSUSE

```
sudo zypper ar http://download.opensuse.org/repositories/devel:/languages:/nodejs/openSUSE_12.1/
NodeJSBuildService
sudo zypper in nodejs nodejs-devel
```

Many developers prefer utilizing package managers on OS X and even Windows as opposed to utilizing the installers. Node.js can also be installed via these package managers.

Windows

Using the Chocolatey package manager, simply install with the chocolatey command, as shown in Listing 1-7.

Listing 1-7. installing Node.js on Windows with Chocolately

```
cinst nodejs
```

OS X

Whether you utilize MacPorts or Homebrew for your package manager on Macintosh, you can install Node.js in either case as shown in Listings 1-8 and 1-9.

Listing 1-8. MacPorts

```
port install nodejs
```

Listing 1-9. Homebrew

```
brew install node
```

At this point you should have Node.js installed on your machine by using the method of your choosing on your preferred platform. Next, you need to make sure you have a way to discover and manage Node.js packages.

1-2. Installing the npm Package Manager

Many programming languages and platforms depend on the use of third-party modules to extend the utility of the platform. Node.js is no different in that it is greatly extended by the use of the package manager: npm. npm originated separately from Node.js itself and is still maintained as an independent project. However, due to its growing popularity and acceptance, it has been built and deployed with the Node.js binary installs since Node.js version 0.6.3. This means that installing npm is as simple as grabbing the latest version of Node.js as outlined in the previous section. So if you have used one of the binary installers, npm is already available to you. You can, of course, as shown in the previous section, choose to omit npm from your install. If it appears npm is not available, you can run the `make install` command and you will soon have it.

There are, as you might expect, less simple ways to install npm. These would be useful if you want to debug npm or test a certain functionality that is not readily available in the default npm install. To get into the "fancy" installs, you must first locate the install.sh shell script, which is located at `https://npmjs.org/install.sh`.

This installation shell script contains many tools for invoking npm in a way that meets your specific needs. For instance, if you wish to create a debug mode instance of npm you could invoke install.sh, as shown in Listing 1-10.

Listing 1-10. npm debug Install

```
npm_debug=1 sh install.sh
```

You could also set configuration parameters with the npm install script, shown in Listing 1-11.

Listing 1-11. Additional Configuration Parameters for npm

```
npm_config_prefix=/my/path sh install.sh
```

Of course, you could build a patch for npm, in which case you will be best served to download from the GitHub source and build it yourself. This requires running the make command in the folder that you have downloaded the npm source to (see Listing 1-12).

Listing 1-12. Installing npm Manually

```
make install
```

With npm installed your machine is now set up to utilize the packages and modules that are easily accessed through this package utility.

1-3. Understanding CommonJS Modules

Because Node.js is a framework in which programs are written in JavaScript, it carries with it some of the perceived limitations that JavaScript has as well. One of these items that is missing is the concept of a robust standard library, like one might find in a language like C++. Because of this, there are many variations and ways for including modules within a JavaScript application. In the browser world, for example, this could be anything from simple `<script>` tag ordering to script loaders to module loaders. For Node.js, a simple and robust module loading system is used quite heavily though is not required. This modular system is known as CommonJS and represents the methods utilized for sharing; it includes standard and third-party modules within your Node.js application.

CommonJS is a community-driven initiative that will bring a standard library-loading functionality to the JavaScript community as a whole. What CommonJS actually represents is a set of specification proposals that will aim to create a standardized system of module loaders. The concept of CommonJS modules is straightforward and involves two parts. First, a creator of a CommonJS module should come up with a reusable piece of JavaScript and export a specific objects or objects from this reusable JavaScript. Second, a consumer of the module will require the exported objects from the module, which will then load into the application. The basic module contract as outlined in the specification (`http://commonjs.org/specs/modules/1.0/`) is as follows:

Module Context

1. In a module, there is a free variable "require", which is a function.

    a. The "require" function accepts a module identifier.

    b. "require" returns the exported API of the foreign module.

    c. If there is a dependency cycle, the foreign module may not have finished executing at the time it is required by one of its transitive dependencies; in this case, the object returned by "require" must contain at least the exports that the foreign module has prepared before the call to require that led to the current module's execution.

    d. If the requested module cannot be returned, "require" must throw an error.

2. In a module, there is a free variable called "exports" that is an object that the module may add its API to as it executes.

3. Modules must use the "exports" object as the only means of exporting.

Module Identifiers

1. A module identifier is a string of "terms" delimited by forward slashes.

2. A term must be a CamelCase identifier: ".", or "..".

3. Module identifiers may not have file-name extensions like ".js".

4. Module identifiers may be "relative" or "top-level." A module identifier is "relative" if the first term is "." or "..".

5. Top-level identifiers are resolved off the conceptual module namespace root.

6. Relative identifiers are resolved relative to the identifier of the module in which "require" is written and called.

You can now examine what a simple implementation of a CommonJS module would look like. Assume you create a file called "describe.js," which will export a string of text that responds with a description of the module shown in Listing 1-13.

Listing 1-13. describe.js Exporting a Description of Itself

```
/**
* Describe module
*/
exports.describe = function() {
        return 'I am a CommonJS Module';
};
```

This module does not require any other modules to function; all that it does is export the describe function, which returns a string description. But this is very uninteresting and if you wish to include this module within your applications elsewhere, you need to install that module in your code. To do this, use the CommonJS require( ) function, as shown in Listing 1-14.

Listing 1-14. Requiring the describe Module

```
var describeModule = require('./describe.js');
```

Now you have a reference to your describe module, but what does that mean? What happens when you call require( )? When you call require( ), Node.js will locate the resource and read and parse the file, granting you access to the exported API of the module. When Node.js loads the file into your application, it will automatically isolate the module into its own scoped namespace to prevent global names colliding in a disastrous thunder of crying. Because Node.js has loaded this resource for you, you can call exported functionality from this resource (see Listing 1-15).

Listing 1-15. Reference an Exported Function from a Required Module

```
var describeModule = require('./describe.js');

console.log(describeModule.describe());
```

CommonJS modules are not entirely about exporting functionality either. They can be used to create an API that builds on functionality with the module's file but leaves that functionality private to the module itself. Imagine you have a more robust module where only a certain portion of your module needs to be exposed; you can easily create a method for this "private" functionality and still see it in the exported solution, as in Listing 1-16.

Listing 1-16. "Private" Methods in Exported Modules

```
/**
* Desc module with private method
*/
var _getType = function() {
        return 'CommonJS Module';
};

exports.describe = function() {
        return 'I am a ' + _getType();
};
```

You will see more about authoring and consuming CommonJS modules later, but, for now, the important takeaway is how this all works. CommonJS modules export functionality, and only the explicitly exported functionality is exported. Other functions or methods may live with the CommonJS modules, but they are limited to the private scope of the module itself and not to the application that accesses the module. This can result in very clean APIs for your application if you are careful and structure your CommonJS modules appropriately.

Understanding how Node.js implements the CommonJS methodology for module loading helps you to think creatively about the structure and API of your application, allows for code sharing and reuse, and makes your application code cleaner and easier to follow.

1-4. Writing Modules for Your Application

Now that you understand what CommonJS is and how it pertains to Node.js as a module loader, you can begin to think about how you will build your own modules for your application. If you decide not to build modules for your application, you will quickly see your application code grow unwieldy and cause you maintenance nightmares, with heterogeneous data structures, objects, and callbacks strewn throughout what will become a monolithic Node.js application.

When you begin thinking about writing your modules, the first thing that should come to mind is a simple division of tasks. If your application requires a user to authenticate against a server in order to access content, you will likely want to create a module for your user data. This could hold the session state, user information, authentication protocols, and more. If you include this chunk of user-specific data at the heart of your Node.js application, you will regret having to navigate past or around this code every time you see it. Listing 1-17 shows how these data might look when your application lacks modules.

Listing 1-17. Messy Code with Exportable Features

```
/**
* User authentication code not in its own module
*/

var db = require('./db.js');

app.on('/createUser', function(req, res) {
  var user = req.username,
    pwd = req.password,
    email = req.email;

  db.lookup('user', {username: user }, function(err, data) {
    if (err) {
      return;
    }
    // Didn't find a user by that name
    if (data.userid === null) {
      createSalt(10, function(err, salt) {
        if (err) {
          return;
        }
        createHash(pwd, salt, function(err, hash) {
          db.create('user', {username: user, password: pwd, email: email }, function(err, user) {
            if (err) {
              return;
```

```
            } else {
                user.isauthenticated = true;
                app.users.push[user];
                res.send(user);
            }
        });
    });

    });
    }
  });

});

function createSalt(depth, callback) {
  // do salting here
  if (err) {
    return callback(err);
  };
  callback();
};

function createHash(password, salt, callback) {
  // hashify
  if (err) {
    return callback(err);
  }
  callback();
}
```

The code above is an example of a request from the client to create a new user. This has to pass through various parts of the application before you can create a user successfully. It must first check the database to ensure the username has not been claimed. Then it must create a salt and hash the password with that salt. Then it must store that user information in the database and transmit the new user object to the application. This by itself does not seem entirely unwieldy, but you can imagine as part of a large project you would like to move this outside of the main application into its own module. We can eliminate a large portion of the code by creating an authentication module to hold the createSalt and createHash methods. These new methods are shown in Listing 1-18.

Listing 1-18. Exporting the Salt and Hash Methods

```
/**
 * Authentication module
 */

exports.createSalt = function(depth, callback) {
  //do salty things
  if (err) {
    return callback(err);
  }
  callback();
}
```

```
exports.createHash = function(password, salt, callback) {
  //hashification
  if (err) {
    return callback(err);
  }
  callback();
}
```

We eliminated two large functions from our main code by placing them into a module. Next we create a user module that will handle all the user-related things in Listing 1-19.

Listing 1-19. User Module

```
/**
* User module
*/

var db = require('./db.js');
var auth = require('./auth.js');

exports.create = function(req, res, callback) {
  var user = req.username,
    pwd = req.password,
    email = req.email;

  db.findOrCreate('user', {username: user});
  db.lookup('user', {username: user }, function(err, data) {
    if (err) {
      return callback(err);
    }
    // Didn't find a user by that name
    if (data.userid === null) {
      auth.createSalt(depth, function(err, salt) {
        if (err) {
          return callback(err);
        }
        auth.createHash(pwd, salt, function(err, hash) {
          db.create('user', {username: user, password: pwd, email: email }, function(err, user) {
            if (err) {
              return callback(err);
            } else {
              user.isauthenticated = true;
              return callback(user);
            }
          });
        });

      });
    }
  });
};
```

This is now outside of the application, so our original handler for createUser is now reduced to the concise information shown in Listing 1-20.

Listing 1-20. Main Application with Required User Module

```
/**
* User Authentication code within its own module
*/
var user = require('./user.js');

app.on('/createUser', user.create(function(err, user){
  if (err) {
    return;
  }
  app.users.push[user];
}));
```

This example outlines a generalist approach to reducing your code into manageable portions by using modularization. It is important to remember some of the basic rules of CommonJS modules when writing them. You can create your modules based on whatever guidelines you see fit, but you must use the exports variable in order to expose any methods of your module to whatever portion of code you wish to see it in. You will also need to design a logical place for your module in order to load it, since the require function needs an identifier to find the module. For many cases this can be a local relative path within the structure of your Node.js application, or a more globalized package if you use an npm module. Of course, use cases will vary, but as a rule of thumb, if the code is getting in your way, you should be able to extract it to its own module.

1-5. Requiring Modules in Your Application

As you build a Node.js application, you will almost inevitably need to utilize a set of modules, like those created in the previous section, in your application. To do this you will use the CommonJS module-loading require function. This function will find the module by name in the file system and load its exported API. This sounds very simple, but to really understand what happens when you load a module you must understand how the modules are retrieved.

Node.js utilizes a complex strategy when it attempts to load a module. The very first place that is checked when loading a module is the module cache, so if you have previously loaded a module, you will have access to it already. If Node.js cannot find a cached module, precedence is then given to the Node.js native modules, such as crypto, http, fs, etc. If a native module is not found by the identifier passed to require(), then Node.js will perform a file-system search for the identifier that was passed to it.

The file-system lookup for Node.js modules is a little bit more complex than looking for a native or cached module by name. When you require a module in Node.js the identifier can be in several forms, and the lookup performed can change accordingly.

The first scenario that Node.js encounters when you are attempting to load a non-native module is if you provide an identifier with a file extension, such as require('aModule.js');. Node.js will try to load only that file, in the base path that you are requiring from, unless you have prefixed your require with a relative path as in require('./modules/aModule.js');. In that case, your Node.js will attempt to load your module from within the path you designate. When loading a module in Node.js, the file extension is optional. This allows a more concise way of writing your modules but also gives Node.js a more ambiguous path to parse. To load a module that does not provide an extension the first thing Node.js will do is try to load the file with each of the extensions: .js, .json, .node. If Node.js has not resolved a file based on implicitly appending the extensions to the module identifier, it is assumed that the identifier is a path relative to the base. Once it is assumed that this is a path, Node.js will parse the path and first search for package.json and load that if it exists. If it does not, the next thing that Node.js assumes is that there must be an "index" file in the path, and again it tries to load this file with the extensions implicitly added. At this point,

Node.js either has a file that it can load (in which case it will add that module to the module cache) or it cannot find the module and will throw an error.

To visualize these scenarios, let's create a hypothetical application with a folder structure that looks like the outline in Listing 1-21.

Listing 1-21. Outlining a Nested Application

```
myApp/
        -main.js
        -aModule.js
        -subfolder/
                bModule.js
                index.js
```

You can assume that the application root is in the JavaScript file "main.js", which loads all the dependencies needed for our application, shown in Listing 1-22.

Listing 1-22. Loading Dependencies

```
/**
* main.js - module loading
*/

    // First we require 'http' which is a native Node.js Module
    var http = require('http'),

    // load a module with an extension Node.js has not trouble with this
    modA = require('./aModule.js'),

    // Load ambiguous filename from subdirectory load bModule.js fine
    modB = require('./subfolder/bModule'),

    // Load index.js from subdirectory
    sub = require('/subfolder/'),

    // not a file or native module
    // Error: Cannot find Module 'cheese'
    missing = require('cheese');
```

When requiring modules in Node.js, you have a lot of freedom as to how you decide to structure your application and your file names. These rules apply not only to locally created files and native Node.js modules but also to the modules that are loaded into your application via npm, which you will discover in detail in the following section.

1-6. Using npm Modules

You installed Node.js and npm. You also know how you should include CommonJS modules in your Node.js applications, but you do not want to have to reinvent the wheel each time you create an application. Also, you may know of a Node.js package that exists for a task you want to accomplish in your code. Enter the npm modules.

npm is a community-driven repository of Node.js packages and utilities that are published in such a way as to allow anyone access to them. The npm system has grown extremely quickly, keeping step with the growth of Node.js in general throughout its development. Currently there are more than twenty-five thousand npm packages available, according to the npm site at `https://npmjs.org`. With that many packages, it can easily become difficult to identify the packages that fit your needs. To find a package, use the search functionality, which is a Google site search, on `https://npmjs.org/`, shown in Figure 1-8.

Figure 1-8. *npm Search on* `https://npmjs.org/`

Alternatively you can utilize the built-in search mechanism within npm itself. This is run on the command line of your terminal (see Listing 1-23).

Listing 1-23. Command-Line npm Search

```
npm search <term(s) or package name>
```

When you perform the search command, npm will first cache a local index of all packages and will then search the package names, descriptions, authors, and keywords for the packages. The results are returned in a table that shows the package name, description, author, date of publication, version, and keywords. This can be useful for determining which package you want to use. To view detailed information about a package, run the npm view command, shown in Listing 1-24.

Listing 1-24. Detailed View of a Package

```
npm view <package name>
```

Once you have discovered the package you wish to install and have viewed the details about the package, you can install it, also via the command line (see Listing 1-25).

Listing 1-25. Installing via the Command Line

```
npm install <package name>
```

Running the npm install command will download the package and place it in a directory in your application. This directory is named "node_modules" and will usually reside in the same directory as your package definition file named package.json. This folder helps to define your npm package. This means that if you have a file that requires this npm module, it will look to this directory to find it. This is also the case for files within subdirectories as well, meaning that, within a package, npm-installed modules will be installed and referenced from this directory. This prevents too many subdirectories from containing a "node_modules" directory referencing a single module and cluttering your application structure.

Contrary to many package managers (i.e., Python's easy_install) that download packages to a central shared directory, npm installs modules locally, relative to the package itself. However, there is also a global flag that can be set when you install a package from npm. By setting the package to install globally, it will be accessible by any application for that user, as it is installed in the $HOME directory ($USERPROFILE on Windows). To install globally, simply add the flag to your install command, as shown in Listing 1-26.

Listing 1-26. Globalizing a Package Install

```
npm install -g <package name>
# or
npm install --global <package name>
```

The node_modules directory is a special case in Node.js's module-lookup routine, which was outlined in the previous section. A module lookup does not jump directly from looking for a native Node.js module to then searching the directory structure for the file name. If Node.js does not recognize the module as a native module, it will then check the node_modules directory to see if the module is located there, before continuing through the loading waterfall.

Because this is part of the loading path for modules, there is not really any difference to requiring an npm module versus a module that you author yourself, which allows you to reference it in the same way.

1-7. Getting Started with npm and Dependency

Using npm has many advantages when you are developing a robust Node.js application. As you have seen, it is incredibly easy to discover, retrieve, and include any published npm package within your application. There are even simpler ways of determining how your application is structured and what npm modules are included with your application. This is done via the npm package management files that live within your application directory. These files are named package.json and include all of the details needed to completely manage the remote dependencies of your application.

Let us examine in detail precisely what package.json is and how it works in your Node.js application. First, package.json contains JavaScript Object Notation (JSON), which is what is parsed by Node.js and npm in order to read the details of your application. When this file is parsed it can help load dependencies, serve application metadata, start and stop your application, and list authors and contributors, code repositories, development dependencies, and much more. Let's discover what all the various fields for package.json could be and what they tell npm and Node.js. Some of these fields should be included in all your package.json files, whereas others are really more useful when you are publishing your package to the npm registry, which will be covered in a later chapter.

name

The name field is required in package.json. Without it, your application cannot be installed. One rule for the name is that it needs to be a URL-safe name. If you publish your package, the name will become a part of a URL for locating the package and therefore must be capable of being parsed as a URL. It is also what other modules will utilize when they require your module. This means that utilizing a ridiculously long name is not recommended because it is highly unlikely anyone will want to type an extraordinarily long package name (like the one in Listing 1-27).

Listing 1-27. A Ridiculously Long Package Name

```
var poppins = require('supercalifragilisticexpialidocious');
```

However, you may need to craft a creatively particular name because the npm module names must be unique throughout the entire npm registry. Also do not include "js" or "node" in the name. It is assumed that the file is JavaScript and you can add the "node" as part of the "engines" directive, which you will see later.

version

The version field is also required. This manages which version is installed, and it is utilized with the "name" field in your package.json file to determine a completely unique identifier. Each time you make a change to your package, you should bump the version number. Version numbers can take various forms: some common forms are simply numeric (0.0.1, or v0.0.1). Sometimes developers like to place a qualifier on the version number, such as 0.0.2-alpha, 0.0.2beta, or 0.0.2-42. These all denote different versions and fit into a hierarchy that is parsed by node-semver, the npm semantic versioner.

description

The description field is simply a text description of the package; terms in the description are searchable via the npm search.

keywords

Keywords are also used in an npm search; these help other developers target your package.

homepage

This field is where you can place the URL of your package or project's homepage.

bugs

This points developers to a place (an issue tracker or e-mail address) to find or submit bugs so they can help you make your project even more amazing.

license

This field describes the license that your code will be under. This can be simple like MIT, BSD, or GPL, or you can use a custom license with a type and URL of the license file.

author, contributors

These sections hold the names, e-mails, and URLs for the persons who are responsible for the package.

files

This field can be vital to good dependency management in your package.json file. This field lists the files that you want to include with your package. This can also contain a list of the folders that need to be bundled with the package. You can load a directory of files and then exclude certain ones with an .npmignore file within the directory, which specifies which files to ignore.

main

This field tells the module loader which module to load when the package is required within a Node.js application. This should be the module identifier for that module.

bin

This field controls where npm will install any executable files that will either live in the node_modules/.bin/ directory or will be symbolically linked globally. This is precisely the way that npm itself installs the command-line interface for npm. The bin field takes a key field, which will be the linked command, and a value, which is the script that will be linked to that key. For example, the bin field looks like what is shown in Listing 1-28.

Listing 1-28. bin Field in package.json

```
{"bin": {"program": "./path/to/program"}}
```

repository

This field indicates where the central repository is located. The repository holds the code for your Node.js package. This field takes a type, denoting the version control type, such as git or svn, and a URL argument in order to locate your code.

config

This field can be utilized for configuration options that persist with your package. You could set a configured port number, tell the application to run in production mode, or set the username to associate in the npm registry.

dependencies

This is a very important field when you design your package.json file: it holds information vital to the success of your application. Because there are various versions of other packages available, this field will list those that you have presumably tested with your Node.js application and know will work correctly. Dependencies can not only outline what npm libraries your application depends on but also target the specific versions of those items. There are multiple methods for which you can specify the version you are targeting. This can be done either by explicit listing of the exact version number, defining a range explicitly, implicitly defining a range with comparison operators, listing a URL, a tilde versioning system, and "X version ranges" (see Listing 1-29).

Listing 1-29. Managing Dependencies in package.json files

Explicit Listing of Version Number for a Dependency

```
"package": "0.0.1"
"package": "=0.0.1"
```

Dependencies can also be managed by providing a set of versions via a range

```
"package": "0.0.1 - 0.0.3"
"package": ">=0.0.1
```

Package ranges are also listed in the dependency section of your file by comparison operators such as

```
"package": ">0.0.1"
"package": "<0.0.1"
"package": ">=0.0.1"
"package": "<=0.0.1"
```

Ranges can also be represented with an "x" placeholder that will allow any numeral in the place of the "x"

```
"package":  "0.1.x"
"package":  "0.0.x"
```

Packages as URLs must point to a tarball or a git endpoint that can be checked out (

```
tarball
"package": "https://example.com/package.tar.gz"
```

```
Git
"package": "git://github.com/organization/source.git"
```

Tilde ranges represent a subset of ranges that must be at least equal to the version listed with the tilde, but not greater than the next major version

```
"package": "~0.8.4"
Is equivalent to:
"package": ">=0.8.4 <0.9.0"
```

There are variants of dependencies that can be a part of your package.json file as well. These are devDependencies, optionalDependencies, and bundledDependencies.

devDependencies

devDependencies, as you might expect, are dependencies that will be downloaded if npm install is called, utilizing the development flag --dev. This would be useful if the development branch utilizes a framework that is not needed when installing the production version.

bundledDependencies

The bundledDependencies flag denotes what items are to be bundled when publishing the package.

optionalDependencies

optionalDependencies are dependencies that need to be handled in your application if they are or are not present. If you have a section of code that would optionally rely on a certain package, you must account for that if the package is listed in the optionalDependencies hash, as in Listing 1-30.

Listing 1-30. optionalDependencies in Practice

```
try {
    var optional = require('optional');
} catch(err) {
    optional = null;
}

if (optional) {
    optional.doThing();
} else {
    doThingWithoutOptionalPackage();
}
```

Engines

You can specify engines within your package.json file as well. This means that if you know that your application will only work on Node.js or npm within a certain version range, set this here. The values for engines follow the same values as the dependencies (see Listing 1-31).

Listing 1-31. Defining Engines

```
"engines": {
    "node": "0.8.x",
    "npm": "*"
}
```

OS and CPU

If you are aware that certain aspects of your application will only perform on a given operating system, or you are only targeting a specific operating system, then you can add the specific values within your package.json file as well. This also applies if you have a certain CPU you are targeting, such as 64-bit machines, which can be seen in Listing 1-32.

Listing 1-32. Defining Architectures for Your Application

```
"os" : ["linux", "darwin", "!win32"],
"cpu": ["!arm", "x64" ]
```

preferGlobal

If the package that you are maintaining is best run as a global package, or you would prefer it to be installed as global, set this flag to true and it will set a console warning message if it is chosen to be installed locally by the user.

Putting together all the fields in your package.json file helps to dictate the configuration and dependencies required to run your Node.js application. This makes your package extremely portable, and setup on a new machine is usually straightforward. When you put together even a simple app, you will be able to gain valuable information about your application by examining the package.json file. Managing all of these settings can seem cumbersome when you are building an application. Fortunately, if you have already built an application in Node.js you can retroactively create a valid package.json file by running the command `npm init`, which will produce a file that may be similar to the package shown in Listing 1-33.

Listing 1-33. Initialized Application via npm init

```
{
  "name": "squirrel",
  "version": "0.0.1",
  "private": true,
  "scripts": {
    "start": "node app"
  },
  "dependencies": {
    "express": "3.0.0rc4",
    "ejs": "*",
    "feedparser": ""
  },
```

```
    "gitHead": "e122...",
    "description": "A sample app to parse through your RSS feeds",
    "main": "app.js",
    "devDependencies": {},
    "repository": {
      "type": "git",
      "url": "ssh://git@bitbucket.org/username/squirrel.git"
    },
    "keywords": [
      "rss"
    ],
    "author": "cory gackenheimer",
    "license": "MIT"
}
```

When you examine the above package.json skeleton, generated by `npm init`, you notice that not every field available is included in the file. This is okay, but what this file does indicate is the name and version of your application. More important, however, it dictates dependencies, so when you execute `npm install` from the root of your application, npm will install the prescribed version of express, ejs, and feedparser, in order to resolve the dependencies listed in package.json.

1-8. Installing a Node.js Version Manager

If you are going to spend any amount of time developing Node.js applications, you will inevitably encounter a new version of Node.js. This is because the development of Node.js is moving at an incredible pace. As of this writing the current stable release version is 0.10.x. This release holds the stabilized APIs that are suitable for production environments. There is also a secondary, experimental build, which is currently at version 0.11.x. The experimental build is not suitable for production because it holds new features as they are being created for upcoming versions. It may be the case that you are developing a package for the current stable version, but you also would like to ensure it will continue to work with Node.js API changes in upcoming releases. If this is the case, you are going to need to install multiple versions of Node.js. There are two ways to accomplish this sort of version management. First, you can go to the Node.js web site, download Node.js, and install the version you are targeting. Second, and more elegant, you can use a version management tool.

Once you have decided to use a Node.js version management tool, you have a choice between different tools. There are currently three predominant variations of Node.js version management tools: nvm, n, and nave. Each of these tools is slightly different and may offer options that suit your particular use case better.

Node Version Manager, or nvm, created by Tim Caswell, is an installable shell script that will download and install multiple versions of Node.js that you specify. To install the nvm utility you need to get the install script, which is also a shell script. There are three ways to get and install this script: cURL, Wget, or a manual install.

To install manually, you first need to get the nvm.sh file that is located at the project's repository on GitHub (https://github.com/creationix/nvm). It can be downloaded from that location directly, or fetched at git clone git://github.com/creationix/nvm.git ~/nvm.

Then you need to run the shell script that was just downloaded to the nvm directory:

```
~/nvm/nvm.sh
```

Luckily there is an even easier way that you can install nvm if you use cURL (see Listing 1-34) or Wget (see Listing 1-35): you can download the shell script and have an nvm alias added to your ~/.bash_profile or ~/.profile file.

Listing 1-34. Using cURL

```
curl https://raw.github.com/creationix/nvm/master/install.sh | sh
```

Listing 1-35. Using Wget

```
wget -qO- https://raw.github.com/creationix/nvm/master/install.sh | sh
```

Installing other Node.js version management tools is just as straightforward. A similar script to nvm is a tool called nave, which was developed by Isaac Schlueter, and is packaged as Virtual Environment for Node. Nave runs a shell script, just as nvm does; however, it is installable via npm.

```
npm install –g nave
```

The last version management utility that will be covered is also installed via npm, npm install –g n, and is also similar in functionality to the other tools.

These tools are built to make working with more than one version of node extremely easy and intuitive. They each have their own divergent features that set them apart, so that you as a developer may find the right tool for the job. In the next section you will see an in-depth look into the workflow and options available for each of these version management tools.

1-9. Using Multiple Versions of Node.js on Your Machine

As you might imagine, developing a Node.js application takes time. You might begin a project while Node.js is on a given version and all the packages work seamlessly with it. However, you may find that, for one reason or another, you need to upgrade (or downgrade) the version of Node.js that you are using with your application. To do this with your application and to utilize multiple Node.js instances on your machine, you can use one of the Node.js versioning tools. While each tool provides similar functionality, their APIs are slightly different and do contain certain features unique to each tool.

nvm

Installation for nvm follows the pattern nvm install <version>, as shown in Listing 1-36. The version that you specify can be written explicitly or as a shortened version that will install the latest provided version.

Listing 1-36. nvm Install

```
$ nvm install v0.8.23
$ nvm install 0.8.23
$ nvm install 0.8
```

The install script finds the appropriate version number, goes to the appropriate location in the https://nodejs.org/dist/ directory, and installs the specified version of Node.js on your machine. The script does not alter your path in order for it to be utilized globally. To do this, specify the version you wish to use with the command use (see Listing 1-37).

Listing 1-37. nvm Use

```
$ nvm use 0.10.1
```

If you do not know the specific version of Node.js that you would like to install or use, you can list the remote versions of Node.js that are available by executing the nvm ls-remote command. This will list all versions available for download. If you have multiple versions installed on your machine already, you can utilize the nvm ls command to show the list of Node.js versions that are currently available on your machine.

nvm allows you to specify a particular version, separate from the installed version you are using, to run your application with. For example, you could enter nvm run 0.6 server.js. This would run your application (server.js) with the latest installed version of Node.js 0.6.x, even if the version set with the use command is completely different.

With nvm you can also set an alias for a version by running nvm alias <name> <version>. The use case for this could be similar to the run command, but if you want to test a build more than once against your application, you might find it cumbersome to type the run command. For this an alias is very useful, such as nvm alias dev 0.11.0, which would allow you to test out new features in Node.js version 0.11.0 with a simpler command (dev server.js, instead of nvm run 0.11.0 server.js).

Of course, by installing multiple versions via nvm, you may end up with a housekeeping nightmare. Too many versions could pose an issue when trying to maintain some order. These issues are resolved with the nvm uninstall <version> command and the nvm unalias <alias> command. These uninstall a specified version of Node.js and remove the specified alias from your machine, respectively.

nave

nave is not very dissimilar from nvm. In fact nave credits nvm for inspiration. There are a few differences with the implementations and underlying shell scripts that do vary enough to note. It is important to understand that nave is presented as a Node.js virtual environment provider, versus a version manager. First, nave install <version> expects the version parameter to be an exact version of Node.js, with the exception of fetching the latest, or latest stable version, which would look like nave install latest and nave install stable, respectively.

The virtual environment portion of nave is based around the use command. This command takes either a version number by itself, a version number followed by a Node.js program parameter, or a name followed by a version number, as shown in Listing 1-38.

Listing 1-38. Nave Use

Nave use version, this will open a subshell utilizing the version specified

```
$ nave use <version>
```

Providing a version with a program target, it will run the program in a subshell using the specified version

```
$ nave use <version> <program>
```

This will provide an alias based on the specified version

```
$ nave use <name> <version>
```

To set the main version to use for development, the command is nave usemain <version>. You can also remove an installed instance by running nave uninstall <version>. Similar to this is the nave clean <version> command. The clean command does not uninstall the version, but it does remove the source code for the specified version. nave also provides a set of listing commands, ls and ls-remote operate, in the same manner as the nvm ls and ls-remote commands by providing a list of local or remote versions of Node.js that are available. The nave script provides an additional ls-all command, which will list both local and remote Node.js versions available to you as a developer. If you are curious as to which version of Node.js is the latest, simply run the nvm latest command.

n

The Node.js versioning tool n is different in implementation and its API than nvm and nave, but it still serves the primary purpose of allowing you to install multiple versions of Node.js. With n, you can specify an exact version of Node.js by using the command n <version>. This is less lenient than nvm, which allows you to pick a major revision, and it will install the latest of that version. Where this does differ is that you can specify the latest (see Listing 1-39), or the latest stable release (see Listing 1-40), and n will fetch it for you.

Listing 1-39. Fetch the Latest Version

```
$ n latest
```

Listing 1-40. Fetch the Latest Stable Version

```
$ n stable
```

What these commands do is go to the https://nodejs.org/dist/ site and search for the latest version (the highest number available for retrieving the latest or the highest even-numbered release available for latest stable). To move to a previous version that you had installed, simply use the n prev command.

To view the locally installed versions of Node.js that are available, and to select one to use, simply type the command n. The n command by itself will list test versions, along with any flags you have specified to run with that version. In order to specify a flag, or configuration option, you simply provide it as a parameter after your n <version> command, as shown in Listing 1-41.

Listing 1-41. Pass the debug Parameter to This Version of node

```
n latest --debug
```

The n bin <version> command will output the path to that binary installation that is on your machine. If the specified version is not present on your machine, n will let you know it is not installed. The bin command is very handy if you want to target a specific version directly without using the use command, which is run as n use <version> [args...]

To uninstall, or remove Node.js using n, the command is n rm <version list>. You will notice that this command takes a list of versions, meaning that you can remove multiple versions of Node.js from your system in a single bound.

Summary

In this chapter you reviewed the multiple ways to get Node.js installed on your machine. You also saw the basics of implementing and using CommonJS modules within your Node.js application, including utilizing the npm Node.js package management tool. The following chapters will begin to have a recipe-centric format. This format divides many of the interesting Node.js topics into a problem–solution approach. This means that you will start with a definition of a problem you might encounter when building a Node.js application, and you will then read about a solution to that problem. You can read through these chapters, see how certain portions of Node.js work, and be able to find these solutions again easily when returning to the book as a desk reference.

CHAPTER 2

■ ■ ■

Networking with Node.js

Node.js is designed to function well in a networked environment. Its nonblocking, event-driven architecture allows for the use of highly scalable, networked applications. In this chapter you will discover many of the implementation details surrounding Node.js and its networking capabilities. In particular the recipes you will see will cover these topics:

- Setting up a server

- Creating connections to your server

- Configuring server defaults

- Creating a client

- Using sockets to communicate between servers

- Retrieving details about connected servers

- Controlling socket details

Once you have read this chapter, you should have the capability not only to build a simple networked application but also perhaps to have a robust solution to incorporate into your workflow.

2-1. Setting Up a Server
Problem

You need to set up a server to provide a networked Node.js application.

Solution

In Node.js, the standard solution for building a networked application that serves data between endpoints is to utilize a built-in Node.js module called net. This module provides all you need to set up a Node.js TCP server. To set up a network server, you must first require the module (see Listing 2-1).

Listing 2-1. Requiring the net Module

```
var net = require('net');
```

After requiring this module, creating the server happens with the createServer() method. This method takes an optional parameter, which will set default options on the server, and a connectionListener argument, which will listen for connections to your server. To truly enable your newly created server, you will need to tell your server on which port to listen. This is accomplished by a call to the `listen()` method that is provided by the net module. A fully operational server is shown in Listing 2-2.

Listing 2-2. A Simple TCP Server

```
var net = require('net');

var server = net.createServer(function(connectionListener) {
    console.log('connected');

    //Get the configured address for the server
    console.log(this.address());

        //get connections takes callback function
    this.getConnections(function(err, count) {
        if (err) {
            console.log('Error getting connections');
        } else {
            console.log('Connections count: ' + count);
        }
    });

    connectionListener.on('end', function() {
        console.log('disconnected');
    });
    //Write to the connected socket
    connectionListener.write('heyyo\r\n');
});

server.on('error', function(err) {
    console.log('Server error: ' + err);
});
server.on('data', function(data) {
    console.log(data.toString());
});

/**
* listen()
*/
server.listen(8181, function() {
    console.log('server is listening');
});
```

Now you have created a simple server. Assuming you have named your server file `server.js`, you can easily run it with node `server.js`.

How It Works

Let us examine this server in more detail. First, you recall how Node.js modules are loaded as described in Chapter 1. This is how the native Node.js module net is loaded, `require('net');`. The server is created via the module's exported `createServer()` method, which instantiates an internal server object within the net module as shown in Listing 2-3.

Listing 2-3. net Module createServer Method

```
exports.createServer = function() {
  return new Server(arguments[0], arguments[1]);
};
```

This method takes two arguments, so it must be that within the server function, there is some sort of determination as to which argument represents the options object that is optionally passed into the createServer() method, which is the connection listener. If you investigate a little further into this function, you see that what Node.js uses to determine these arguments is a simple check of their properties. If it is determined that the type of the first argument is a function, then it cannot be that the first argument is the options object, making the first argument the connection listener. Alternatively, if the first argument is not a function, it is assumed to be the options object, and the second argument–if it is a function–is used as the connection listener.

The connection listener, like many functions in Node.js programming, is a simple callback. Once the server object in the net module has identified it as a function, it is passed as the callback to a server connection listener, which takes the form similar to server.on('connection', connectionListener);. This will now pass any new connection back to your listener in your application. This logic is shown in Listing 2-4.

Listing 2-4. Determining the Server Options and Connection Listener

```
var self = this;

var options;

if (typeof arguments[0] == 'function') {
  options = {};
  self.on('connection', arguments[0]);
} else {
  options = arguments[0] || {};

  if (typeof arguments[1] == 'function') {
    self.on('connection', arguments[1]);
  }
}
```

A new connection happens after the server you have created begins to listen on a port. The port is determined by the first argument that you pass to the listen() function of your server. The listen() function can also take a path, if your server is to listen on a UNIX path, or any connectable handle object. In the example server in Listing 2-2, the port was set as 8181. The second parameter was a callback, which is executed once the server successfully begins to listen to the port, or path, where it is defined. The listen() event also assumes a host. The host can be any IPv4 address, but if it is omitted, Node.js will assume you are targeting the localhost. You now have a simple server that will listen on a port of your choosing.

As you can see in the server you created in Listing 2-2, you can also gain some insight into the current configuration of your server. First, you can retrieve the information about the address on which the server is listening. This information is fetched by calling the server.address() method. This will return an object that shows the address, family, and port of the server (see Listing 2-5).

Listing 2-5. server.address()

```
{
  address: '127.0.0.1',
  family: 'IPv4',
  port: 8181
}
```

In addition to retrieving the server address, you can also get the count of the number of connections to your server. This is done by calling the getConnections() method within your code. The getConnections() function takes a callback function that should accept two arguments: an error argument and a count argument. This will allow you both to check for an error when getting connections and to get the current count of connections to the server. This is shown in the connectionListener callback within the server created in Listing 2-2.

The server object in the net module of Node.js is an event emitter, which is a common paradigm in Node.js programming. An event emitter provides a common language in which an object can register, remove, and listen for events that are either generated by the system or customized by the developer. The server object exposes several events, some of which you have already seen, such as the connection and listening events. The connection event happens each time a new socket connects to the server, whereas the listening event, as you have seen, is emitted once the server begins to listen. Two other events that are a base for the net.Server object are close and error. The error event is emitted when the server encounters an error. The error event also emits the close event immediately after the error is emitted. The close event simply shuts down the server; however, it will wait until each of the connected socket's connections end.

2-2. Creating Connections to Your Server
Problem

You need to create a connection to a networked server.

Solution

In order to build a connection to your server, you need to know the port or UNIX path on which is it listening. Once you know this, you can create a connection via Node.js. For this you will once again use the Node.js native net module, which exposes a createConnection method for connecting to a remote (or local) instance.

To utilize the net module to connect to a server via Node.js, you, once again, must set the connection to the net module via a CommonJS require as shown in Listing 2-6.

Listing 2-6. Importing the net Module for Connections

```
var net = require('net');
```

Then the next step is to call the createConnection method passing in the port or UNIX path on which to connect. Optionally, you can also pass the host if you need to specify an IP address. Now we can create a connectListener that logs the connection to the console, as shown in Listing 2-7.

Listing 2-7. Creating a Connection to Your Server

```
var net = require('net');
// createConnection
var connection = net.createConnection({port: 8181, host:'127.0.0.1'},
// connectListener callback
    function() {
        console.log('connection successful');
});
```

How It Works

In this section you created a connection to a TCP server. This was done with Node.js's net module. This contained the createConnection function, which is the same as the connect() function. The connect method first checks the arguments that you passed to it. It will evaluate which options are set.

Checking the arguments sent is done by first checking if the first argument is an object, then subsequently parsing that object if it is indeed an object. If the first argument is not an object, it is evaluated to see if it is a valid pipe name, in which case it will be set as the UNIX path option. If it is not the name of a pipe, it will default to a port number. The final check of the parameters is for the optional callback argument, which is evaluated by checking to see if the last parameter passed to the connect() function is a function itself. This whole process is run in a function called normalizeConnectArgs, shown in Listing 2-8.

Listing 2-8. Extracting createConnection Arguments

```
function normalizeConnectArgs(args) {
  var options = {};

  if (typeof args[0] === 'object') {
    // connect(options, [cb])
    options = args[0];
  } else if (isPipeName(args[0])) {
    // connect(path, [cb]);
    options.path = args[0];
  } else {
    // connect(port, [host], [cb])
    options.port = args[0];
    if (typeof args[1] === 'string') {
      options.host = args[1];
    }
  }

  var cb = args[args.length - 1];
  return (typeof cb === 'function') ? [options, cb] : [options];
}
```

Next, the net module creates a new socket object, passing in the newly normalized connect arguments. This socket has a method on its prototype called connect.

This connect method on the socket is called, passing to it the normalized arguments as well. The connect method will try to create a new socket handle and connect to the path or port and host combination that was specified in the arguments. If the host is not specified for a given port, then it is assumed that the host being targeted is the localhost, or 127.0.0.1. Where this gets interesting is that, if a hostname or IP address is provided in the arguments, Node.js will require the dns module and perform a DNS lookup to locate the host. This again will default to the localhost if the lookup returns null without an error, as shown in Listing 2-9.

Listing 2-9. Socket.prototype.connect's Method to Resolve Path, Port, and Host

```
/* ... */
if (pipe) {
    connect(self, options.path);

  } else if (!options.host) {
    debug('connect: missing host');
    connect(self, '127.0.0.1', options.port, 4);
```

```
  } else {
    var host = options.host;
    debug('connect: find host ' + host);
    require('dns').lookup(host, function(err, ip, addressType) {
      // It's possible we were destroyed while looking this up.
      // XXX it would be great if we could cancel the promise returned by
      // the lookup.
      if (!self._connecting) return;

      if (err) {
        // net.createConnection() creates a net.Socket object and
        // immediately calls net.Socket.connect() on it (that's us).
        // There are no event listeners registered yet so defer the
        // error event to the next tick.
        process.nextTick(function() {
          self.emit('error', err);
          self._destroy();
        });
      } else {
        timers.active(self);

        addressType = addressType || 4;

        // node_net.cc handles null host names graciously but user land
        // expects remoteAddress to have a meaningful value
        ip = ip || (addressType === 4 ? '127.0.0.1' : '0:0:0:0:0:0:0:1');

        connect(self, ip, options.port, addressType, options.localAddress);
      }
    });
  }
/* ... */
```

As can be seen in the listing, the result of discovering the path, port, or port and host is to call the function connect(). This function simply connects the socket handle to the path or port and host. Once the connection request has connected, the connectListener callback is called as the code for the connect function shown in Listing 2-10.

Listing 2-10. function connect( ) Implementation in the net Module

```
function connect(self, address, port, addressType, localAddress) {

  assert.ok(self._connecting);

  if (localAddress) {
    var r;
    if (addressType == 6) {
      r = self._handle.bind6(localAddress);
    } else {
      r = self._handle.bind(localAddress);
    }

    if (r) {
```

```
      self._destroy(errnoException(process._errno, 'bind'));
      return;
    }
  }

  var connectReq;
  if (addressType == 6) {
    connectReq = self._handle.connect6(address, port);
  } else if (addressType == 4) {
    connectReq = self._handle.connect(address, port);
  } else {
    connectReq = self._handle.connect(address, afterConnect);
  }

  if (connectReq !== null) {
    connectReq.oncomplete = afterConnect;
  } else {
    self._destroy(errnoException(process._errno, 'connect'));
  }
}
```

This was the function in Listing 2-8 where you logged "connection successful" to the console. As you will see in Section 2-4 there is much more to listening and connecting a client than simply logging a string to the console, but first you will examine the various ways in which to configure your server and the default settings that accompany the configuration options.

2-3. Configuring Server Defaults

Problem

You are creating a server in Node.js and you need to control the accessible defaults for the server.

Solution

When you create any type of networked server, you often find that the default configuration might need to be tweaked to meet your specific needs. Aside from setting the host and port for a TCP server, you might like to be able to set the maximum number of connections, or control what the system backlog queue length for pending connections is configured as in your server. Many of these settings have default values on your server.

Naturally, one of the simplest parts of your server that you can control is the port and host where the server will be listening. These are set when calling the listen() method on your server. The listen method (as seen in Section 2-1) also takes the listener callback, but a third parameter that is optionally placed before this callback is the backlog setting, which limits your server's connection queue length. Putting these defaults into place, you can see what the listen() function will look like in Listing 2-11.

Listing 2-11. Setting the listen() Defaults

```
server.listen(8181, '127.0.0.1', 12, function() {
        // listen on 127.0.0.1:8181
        // backlog queue capped at 12
        console.log('server is listening');
});
```

Another default to consider is the option set when calling the `createServer()` method, which allows for a half-open connection and which defaults to false but is set in the method as shown in Listing 2-12.

Listing 2-12. allowHalfOpen: true

```
var server = net.createServer({ allowHalfOpen: true }, function(connectionListener) {
/* connection Listener stuffs */
});
```

Setting a maximum number of connections to your server can also be quite useful in your Node.js application. If you wish to limit this, you must explicitly set the number, as it defaults to undefined. This is best set in the `connectionListener` callback, as shown in Listing 2-13.

Listing 2-13. Setting a Maximum Number of Connections to Your Server

```
var server = net.createServer({ allowHalfOpen: true }, function(connectionListener) {
        console.log('connected');

        //get maxConnections - default undefined
        console.log(this.maxConnections);

        // set maxConnections to 4
        this.maxConnections = 4;

        // check set maxConnections is 4
        console.log(this.maxConnections);
});
```

How It Works

Setting and overriding server defaults happens by checking them against the default settings; then they are overwritten. What happens when you pass a backlog argument to the `listen()` method in Node.js? First, the default value that is passed into the backlog argument is 511. The value 511 is passed because of how the backlog size is determined by the operating system kernel.

> // Use a backlog of 512 entries. We pass 511 to the listen( ) call because
> // the kernel does: backlogsize = roundup_pow_of_two(backlogsize + 1);
> // which will thus give us a backlog of 512 entries.

This is interesting to know. Because you set the backlog queue to be capped at 12 in the `server.listen()` example from Listing 2-11, you can now know that this will be calculated to be 16. This is because the value you set, 12, is incremented by one, then rounded up to the nearest power of 2, which is 16. It should be noted that in the example `server.listen` from Listing 2-11, you set the value of the host address as 127.0.0.1, which is IPv4. However, Node.js just as easily handles IPv6 connections, so you could change your default server listen to use IPv6, as shown in Listing 2-14.

Listing 2-14. Configuring a Server Using IPv6

```
server.listen(8181, '::1', 12, function() {
    console.log(server.address());
});
```

Subsequently the server.address() function will log the new host and also the family will now be IPv6 instead of IPv4.

```
{ address: '::1', family: 'IPv6', port: 8181 }
```

Allowing a half-open connection was an option you set in Listing 2-12, { allowHalfOpen: true }. This sets the connection to allow for what you may find to be a more finely grained control of your server's connection. This will allow a connection to send the TCP FIN packet, the packet that requests a termination of the connection but does not automatically send the response FIN packet to the connection.

This means that you will leave one half of the TCP connection open, allowing the socket to remain writable but not readable. To officially close the connection, you must explicitly send the FIN packet by calling the .end() method on the connection.

You also saw how you could set a limit to the maximum number of connections to your server via Node.js and the net module's maxConnections setting. This, by default, is undefined, but in Listing 2-13 it was set to a low number of 4. This means your connections are limited to 4, but what happens when you connect, or attempt to connect, to a server that has a maximum number of connections set? You can see what the Node.js source does to this setting in Listing 2-15.

Listing 2-15. Node.js Handles the maxConnections Setting

```
if (self.maxConnections && self._connections >= self.maxConnections) {
    clientHandle.close();
    return;
}
```

This gives you a little more insight into why maxConnections defaults to undefined. This is because if it isn't set, there is no need for Node.js to bother with this section of code. However, if it is set, a simple check will see if the current number of connections on the server is greater than or equal to the maxConnections setting, and it will close the connection. If you have a Node.js client connection you wish to connect (which you will read more about in Section 2-4), but the number of connections exceeds this limit, you will see the connection's close event emitted, and you can handle it appropriately, as shown in Listing 2-16.

Listing 2-16. Handling the close Event on a Connection Handle

```
connection.on('close', function() {
    console.log('connection closed');
});
```

If, on the other hand, you have simply hit the server endpoint via Telnet (telnet ::1 8181), the response will be "connection closed by foreign host," as shown in Figure 2-1.

```
gack~: telnet ::1 8181
Trying ::1...
Connected to localhost.
Escape character is '^]'.
Connection closed by foreign host.
```

Figure 2-1. Telnet connection closed

2-4. Creating a Client
Problem

You want to create a client that connects to a networked server by using Node.js.

Solution

Creating a functional Node.js client extends from the concepts you learned about in Section 2-2. That is to say that a client is simply a connection to a server endpoint. Earlier you saw how to initiate a connection; in this section you will learn how to take that connected socket and understand the events that can be associated with it.

Let us make an assumption that we will connect our client to a simple Node.js server, similar to that which you created in Section 2-1. However, this server will receive a message from the client and also write a message to the client. This message will be a simple text message that shows a count of the current connections to the server. This server is shown in Listing 2-17.

Listing 2-17. Simple Node.js Server to Echo Back to the Client

```
var net = require('net');

var server = net.createServer(function(connectionListener) {
        //get connection count
        this.getConnections(function(err, count) {
                if (err) {
                        console.log('Error getting connections');
                } else {
                        // send out info for this socket
                        connectionListener.write('connections to server: ' + count + '\r\n');
                }
        });

        connectionListener.on('end', function() {
                console.log('disconnected');
        });

        //Make sure there is something happening
        connectionListener.write('heyo\r\n');

        connectionListener.on('data', function(data) {
                console.log('message for you sir: ' + data);
        });

        // Handle connection errors
        connectionListener.on('error', function(err) {
                console.log('server error: ' + err);
        });
});

server.on('error', function(err) {
        console.log('Server error: ' + err);
});
```

```
server.on('data', function(data) {
        console.log(data.toString());
});

server.listen(8181, function() {
        console.log('server is listening');
});
```

First, you see that, when creating a connected client using the net module in Node.js, you need to register the underlying events that can be emitted via the Node.js event emitter. In the example client you will create, these events are set to listen for data, end, and error. These events take a callback, which can be used to process the data transmitted via these events. This takes the example of the server shown in Section 2-2 and turns it into something that looks like what you see in Listing 2-18.

Listing 2-18. Client with Socket Events

```
var net = require('net');

// createConnection
var connection = net.createConnection({port: 8181, host:'127.0.0.1'},
// connectListener callback
        function() {
                console.log('connection successful');
                this.write('hello');
});

connection.on('data', function(data) {
        console.log(data.toString());
});

connection.on('error', function(error) {
        console.log(error);
});

connection.on('end', function() {
        console.log('connection ended');
});
```

As you see, there are many options for registering event listeners on a client. These events are gateways to determining the state of a server or to processing a response buffer from a server. These can help you to determine the state and information sent from a networked client in your Node.js application.

Also present in the client (see Listing 2-18) is the simplest form of communication to the server that you can send: the write() method on a socket. The socket in this case is the one that you created when you instantiate your connection. This simply sends a string, "hello," to the server once the connection is established. This is handled on the client via the connectionListener's data event binding.

```
connectionListener.on('data', function(data) {
        console.log('message for you sir: ' + data);
});
```

If you have everything running properly, you will see the client interacting with your server in the console output as shown in Listings 2-19 and 2-20.

Listing 2-19. Server Interaction on the Command Line

```
$ node server.js
server is listening
message for you sir: hello
```

Listing 2-20. Client Communicating with the Server

```
$ node client.js
Connection successful
Heyo
```

How It Works

As you investigate how this client connects and communicates with your server, you again see that we have created a connection to a server using the net module that is native to Node.js. This module carries with it the ability to communicate smoothly between TCP servers and clients. In the example you created in Listing 2-17, you created a connection that listened on a port and a host as described in Section 2-2. Once you created this connection, which you set to the variable 'client', it takes three arguments. These are exposed because the client is actually a representation of a TCP socket.

Regardless, the socket is created when you implement the net.createConnection() method. This means that you now have access to the options and events that are passed between sockets. This can be demonstrated by looking at the Node.js source for these sockets. In Node.js, the net socket is a representation of a stream. This means that to understand the code that is executing when connection.end happens you can see it is really a representation of the socket.end method, as shown in Listing 2-21.

Listing 2-21. Socket.end Method

```
Socket.prototype.end = function(data, encoding) {
  stream.Duplex.prototype.end.call(this, data, encoding);
  this.writable = false;
  DTRACE_NET_STREAM_END(this);

  // just in case we're waiting for an EOF.
  if (this.readable && !this._readableState.endEmitted)
    this.read(0);
  return;
};
```

You can see from Listing 2-21 that you have access to the socket that is in reality a stream. The 'end' method calls the end to this stream and immediately sets the stream to not be writable. The end event is triggered when the other end of the stream sends the FIN packet, which you saw in the previous sections. There you examined the half-open socket connection; however, in this case, the socket is no longer writable. Then there is one last round of checks to see if there is still a readable entity in the stream, which it reads before it returns, finalizing the "end" of the socket.

In Listings 2-19 and 2-20 you saw the server was started with the command node server.js. This immediately produces the .listen() callback, which prints the message "server is listening" to your console. You then start the client (node client.js) and you invoke the connectListener callback that prints "Connection successful" in your console. This connection also initiates a Socket.write() from the server and a Socket.write() from the client. You will learn more about utilizing sockets to communicate in the next section, but for now you really need to understand that the end result of Socket.write is that each socket sends its data along the socket. This results in producing the "hello" message from the client on the server and the "heyo" message on the client via the server.

If you examine the data event, the event that handles the receipt of the data for your client, you see it is emitted each time data are received. When you listen for this event, which you register with client.on('data'...), you will be able to see data that are transmitted from your server. Data, in Node.js, is transmitted as a buffer or a string. It is emitted as a buffer by default, but if you set the socket.setEncoding() function, you will see that the data are transmitted as a string. In this solution you sent this data via the Socket.write() method, which defaults to sending the data with UTF-8 encoding. The data event is triggered in the stream module of Node.js. The stream module is triggered from the socket.write() method in the net module within Node.js as in Listing 2-22.

Listing 2-22. Triggering the Streams Module from socket.write( )

```
if (typeof chunk !== 'string' && !Buffer.isBuffer(chunk))
    throw new TypeError('invalid data');
  return stream.Duplex.prototype.write.apply(this, arguments);
```

Once you have worked your data into the stream interface, you meander it through the module until you find yourself where the readable stream exists. Stream.Readable is an instance of a readable stream that has a function, emitDataEvents . This is the "data" that will be read into the server that you send from your client. This lets an event listener, which is registered on the data event, actually go through the readable event on the stream, emitting the stream.read() as the "data" returned .on('data'). This section of the source can be viewed in Listing 2-23.

Listing 2-23. Emitting the Data Event from the Stream Module

```
stream.readable = true;
stream.pipe = Stream.prototype.pipe;
stream.on = stream.addListener = Stream.prototype.on;

stream.on('readable', function() {
  readable = true;

  var c;
  while (!paused && (null !== (c = stream.read())))
    stream.emit('data', c);

  if (c === null) {
    readable = false;
    stream._readableState.needReadable = true;
  }
});
```

This section of the code highlights the main point about transferring data as streams. You can see that within the emitDataEvents() method the stream listens for its own readable event. Once the readable event registers, then the stream.read() event is called, passing the data to the variable "c." Then the stream emits the data event, while passing the argument "c."

The other event listener that was created for the Node.js client in this section was registered on the error event. This event is emitted when the socket encounters an error. A great example of this is that, if you have your client connected to the server, you will get an error when the connection to the server fails. If you shut down the server, the error you will receive is a connection reset. This will be an object that looks like Listing 2-24.

Listing 2-24. Error: Connection Reset

```
{ [Error: read ECONNRESET] code: 'ECONNRESET', errno: 'ECONNRESET', syscall: 'read' }
```

You now should be able to build a networked client in a Node.js environment. The process of communicating via sockets will be covered in more detail in Section 2-5.

2-5. Using Sockets to Communicate Between Servers
Problem

You want to build a networked application in Node.js and utilize sockets to communicate between instances.

Solution

Sockets are native to the Node.js net module. This means that if you wish to utilize sockets, you need to require the net module in your script. You will then create a new instance of a socket by calling the `Socket()` constructor. Then to connect a socket, you simply create a connection with the `socket.connect()` method, directing the socket to which port and host you wish to connect (see Listing 2-25).

Listing 2-25. Creating a Socket Connection

```
var net = require('net');

var socket = new net.Socket();

socket.connect(/* port */ 8181, /*host*/ '127.0.0.1' /, *callback*/ );
```

Assuming there is a connection that can be made on port 8181 of the localhost, you now have a socket connected to this server. At this point, there is nothing but a connected stream via this socket. Any data transmitted will be lost. Now let us take a closer look at a socket connection to a simple server to share messages between each other. To do this you can create a simple server (Listing 2-26) that will listen for the socket and its data as well as send a response back to the sockets.

Listing 2-26. Server to Communicate to Sockets

```
var net = require('net');

var server = net.createServer(connectionListener);

server.listen(8181, '127.0.0.1');

function connectionListener(conn) {
        console.log('new client connected');
        //greet the client
        conn.write('hello');

        // read what the client has to say and respond
        conn.on('readable', function() {
                var data = JSON.parse(this.read());
                if (data.name) {
                        this.write('hello ' + data.name);
                }
        });

        //handle errors
        conn.on('error', function(e) {
                console.log('' + e);
        });
}
```

This server will listen for a connection, and then greet the new connection with a "hello" via the socket stream. It will also listen for data from the socket, which is expected to be a JSON object in this case. You can then parse the data from the "readable" stream and return a response with the data parsed.

The socket connection, shown in Listing 2-27, shows how you can create this socket that will connect to the server from Listing 2-26 and send communication between the two.

Listing 2-27. Socket Connection

```
var net = require('net');

var socket = new net.Socket(/* fd: null, type: null, allowHalfOpen: false */);

socket.connect(8181, '127.0.0.1' /*, connectListener  replaces on('connect') */);

socket.on('connect', function() {
        console.log('connected to: ' + this.remoteAddress);
        var obj = { name: 'Frodo', occupation: 'adventurer' };
        this.write(JSON.stringify(obj));
});

socket.on('error', function(error) {
        console.log('' + error);
        // Don't persist this socket if there is a connection error
        socket.destroy();
});

socket.on('data', function(data) {
        console.log('from server: ' + data);
});
socket.setEncoding('utf-8'); /* utf8, utf16le, ucs2, ascii, hex */

socket.setTimeout(2e3 /* milliseconds */ , function() {
        console.log('timeout completed');
        var obj = { name: 'timeout', message: 'I came from a timeout'};
        this.write(JSON.stringify(obj));
});
```

Putting the server and the client server together–running the server first, so that your socket has an endpoint to connect to–you are able to successfully communicate with the socket connections. The initiating server console will look like Listing 2-28 while the client server output will look like Listing 2-29.

Listing 2-28. Server Output

```
$ node server.js
new client connected
```

Listing 2-29. Connected Socket Output

```
$ node socket.js
Connected to: 127.0.0.1
From server: hellohello Frodo
Timeout completed
From server: hello timeout
```

How It Works

A net.Socket connection, as you have seen, is a Node.js object that represents a TCP or UNIX socket. In Node.js this means that it implements a duplex stream interface. A duplex stream in node represents two event emitters, objects that publish events in Node.js. The two event emitters that make up duplex streams are readable streams and writable streams, which you can see from the Node.js duplex stream source in Listing 2-30.

Listing 2-30. Duplex Stream Calls Readable and Writable Streams

```
function Duplex(options) {
  if (!(this instanceof Duplex))
    return new Duplex(options);

  Readable.call(this, options);
  Writable.call(this, options);

  if (options && options.readable === false)
    this.readable = false;

  if (options && options.writable === false)
    this.writable = false;

  this.allowHalfOpen = true;
  if (options && options.allowHalfOpen === false)
    this.allowHalfOpen = false;

  this.once('end', onend);
}
```

The readable streams interface will take in data from a stream buffer and emit it as a data event on the socket. The writable streams, on the other hand, will emit data in the form of a write, or an end, event. Together these make up a socket. The socket has a few interesting properties and methods, some of which you utilized in Listings 2-26 and 2-27 to create your socket communication servers.

In the first server instance, within the connectionListener callback, the conn argument was passed. Because a net.Server object is really a socket that will listen for connections, this conn argument represents the socket you want to work with. The very first thing this server does is emit a greeting to the connection. This happens with conn.write('hello'); which is a socket.write() method.

The socket.write() method takes one required argument, the data that are to be written, and two optional arguments. These optional arguments are encoding, which can be used to set the encoding type of the socket. The encoding defaults to utf8 but other valid values are utf-8, utf16le, ucs2, ascii, and hex.

Next, in the server's connectionListener the socket was bound to the readable event. This readable event is from the stream module. This event is triggered each time that the stream sends data that are ready to be read. The way to retrieve the data that are sent via the readable event is to call the read() event to read the data. In the example from Listing 2-26, you expect the data to be a JSON string, which you can then parse to reveal the JSON object. This is then used to emit another message back to the connection via the write() method.

The final event binding in place on the server is a handling of errors by binding to the error event on the connection. Without this, the server will crash anytime an error occurs on the connection. This could be a killed connection, or any other error, but regardless of the type of error, there is nothing better to place on your Node.js code (or any code for that matter) than great error-handling capabilities.

Now look at the socket connections you made in Listing 2-27. This shows the other side of our communication story. It starts with the instantiation of a new net.Socket(). In the example, there are no arguments passed to the constructor function. The constructor can take an options object that has keys of fd, type, and allowHalfOpen.

fd is the file descriptor, or what the socket handle should be; this defaults to null. The type key also defaults to a null value but can take the values tcp4, tcp6, or unix to determine the type of the socket you wish to instantiate. Again, as you have seen in previous sections, the allowHalfOpen option can be set to allow the socket to remain open once the initial FIN packet is transferred.

In order to connect the socket, you call the connect() event on the socket, with the host and port specified. This initializes the TCP or UNIX socket handle, beginning the connection. The host argument is optional, as is a callback function that was omitted in the example. The callback in the example was replaced, because the callback function on the connect function is the same as the socket.on('connect', ...) event listener, which is bound to the socket in our example listening for the connection to be established.

Inside of the connect event callback, the first thing your solution does is to gain a little knowledge about the connection by logging the remoteAddress() of the socket. You will see more about getting information about connected servers in the following section of this chapter. After this information, you create an object with some information, make it a string using the JSON.stringify method, then send it along the socket with the write() method. The object must be encoded as a string; if not, the write method will fail, as shown in Listing 2-31.

Listing 2-31. socket.write from Node.js net Module

```
Socket.prototype.write = function(chunk, encoding, cb) {
  if (typeof chunk !== 'string' && !Buffer.isBuffer(chunk))
    throw new TypeError('invalid data');
  return stream.Duplex.prototype.write.apply(this, arguments);
};
```

The socket is then bound to the error event. This event will handle all errors from the socket, but one thing that is noteworthy here is that once the error is handled, via the callback provided to the on('error') listener, the socket.destroy(); method is invoked. The destroy method provides a useful and graceful way to prevent any further I/O activity from happening and to close a socket. It goes through the closing of the socket handle, emitting any error callbacks as necessary during the destroy process. Finally, the close event is emitted after the handle is closed, as shown in Listing 2-32.

Listing 2-32. Closing a Socket within socket.destroy()

```
Socket.prototype._destroy = function(exception, cb) {
  debug('destroy');

  var self = this;

  function fireErrorCallbacks() {
    if (cb) cb(exception);
    if (exception && !self.errorEmitted) {
      process.nextTick(function() {
        self.emit('error', exception);
      });
      self.errorEmitted = true;
    }
  };

  if (this.destroyed) {
    debug('already destroyed, fire error callbacks');
    fireErrorCallbacks();
    return;
  }
```

```
  self._connecting = false;

  this.readable = this.writable = false;

  timers.unenroll(this);

  debug('close');
  if (this._handle) {
    if (this !== process.stderr)
      debug('close handle');
    var isException = exception ? true : false;
    this._handle.close(function() {
      debug('emit close');
      self.emit('close', isException);
    });
    this._handle.onread = noop;
    this._handle = null;
  }

  fireErrorCallbacks();
  this.destroyed = true;

  if (this.server) {
    COUNTER_NET_SERVER_CONNECTION_CLOSE(this);
    debug('has server');
    this.server._connections--;
    if (this.server._emitCloseIfDrained) {
      this.server._emitCloseIfDrained();
    }
  }
};
```

After the error handler for your socket, the socket is bound to the data event. This event will produce the data from a readable stream sent from the connection, essentially calling the stream.read( ) method and emitting that as the data event. This provides a useful place to parse and process the information sent from the connection.

As you saw above, for the write( ) method on the socket, there is the option to set the encoding for the data that are sent via the socket buffer. This can be configured for the entire socket by setting the setEncoding(<type>) parameter on the socket. In the example above, it was set to the default for strings of utf-8 but could be changed to any of the valid types of encoding. Changing this setting to each of the valid types causes different output, as shown in Listing 2-33.

Listing 2-33. Variations on Encoding

```
# utf8
connected to: 127.0.0.1
from server: hello
from server: hello Frodo
timeout completed
from server: hello timeout

# hex
connected to: 127.0.0.1
from server: 68656c6c6f
```

```
from server: 68656c6c6f2046726f646f
timeout completed
from server: 68656c6c6f2074696d656f7574

# ucs2
connected to: 127.0.0.1
from server: 敨荣
from server: 桯泆潭被渆潤
timeout completed
from server: 敨荣棩敓睃

# ascii
connected to: 127.0.0.1
from server: hello
from server: hello Frodo
timeout completed
from server: hello timeout

# utf16le
connected to: 127.0.0.1
from server: hello
from server: hello Frodo
timeout completed
from server: hello timeout
```

Finally, you saw that the socket can "wait" by using the setTimeout function. The setTimeout takes a parameter that dictates the number of milliseconds you choose to wait, and a callback. In the example application, this was used to send a message to the connection, from the socket on a two-second delay. For the callback to work (shown in Listing 2-34), the number of milliseconds must be greater than zero, finite, and not a number (NaN). If this is the case, then Node.js will add this callback to the list of timers and emit the timeout event once the timeout has occurred.

Listing 2-34. socket.setTimeout

```
Socket.prototype.setTimeout = function(msecs, callback) {
  if (msecs > 0 && !isNaN(msecs) && isFinite(msecs)) {
    timers.enroll(this, msecs);
    timers.active(this);
    if (callback) {
      this.once('timeout', callback);
    }
  } else if (msecs === 0) {
    timers.unenroll(this);
    if (callback) {
      this.removeListener('timeout', callback);
    }
  }
};
```

There are other events and parameters on a net.Socket that were not covered in the socket example from Listing 2-27. These are outlined in Table 2-1 below.

Table 2-1. Socket Parameters and Events

Socket Parameter or Event	Description
socket.end([data],[encoding])	This event sends the FIN packet to the connected end of the socket, basically closing half the connection. The server can still send data if allowHalfOpen is set. You can specify data to send and an encoding, but both of those parameters are optional.
socket.pause()	This does exactly as you might expect: it pauses data being sent on the socket.
socket.resume()	This resumes the data transmission on a socket.
socket.setNoDelay([noDelay])	This determines whether or not the TCP connection will buffer data before sending the data off. This is known as the "Nagle algorithm" and the noDelay boolean parameter defaults to true.
socket.setKeepAlive([enable], [initialDelay])	This will enable or disable the keepalive functionality of the socket. This means there will be a keepalive probe sent after the last data packet is received and the initialDelay time, which defaults to zero. The enable boolean parameter defaults to false.
socket.unref()	Calling this on the socket will check the Node.js event system, and if the socket is the only remaining socket in this system, it will be allowed to exit.
socket.ref()	This, once set on a socket, will prevent the event system in Node.js from letting the program exit if it's the only socket remaining. This is the opposite of the default behavior, which would let the program exit if it is the only remaining socket.
socket.remotePort	This is the port to which the socket is connected.
socket.localAddress	This is the address from which the socket originated.
socket.localPort	This is the port from which the socket originates.
socket.bytesRead	This gathers the number of bytes read from the data transmission.
socket.bytesWritten	This indicates the amount of bytes written.

These properties and events will be covered in more detail in the final two sections of this chapter in which you will discover how to retrieve details about connected servers and how to control these properties and details within the sockets themselves.

2-6. Retrieving Details About Connected Servers
Problem

You want to be able to fetch details about the connected servers and sockets in your Node.js application.

Solution

To retrieve details about your connected servers, you need to employ the knowledge about the net.Server and net.Socket modules that you were presented with in the previous sections. There are many details that you may be interested in knowing about a connection, but one that may be of interest is gathering the number of bytes transmitted and received between connections. This is handled with the socket.bytesRead and socket.bytesWritten properties. These could be valuable for any number of reasons, but many utilize it for benchmarking and logging progress in their applications. Listing 2-35 creates a server with a looping connection that tallies up the total number of bytes written and read during the Node.js's process execution.

Listing 2-35. Tallying Bytes

```
var net = require('net');

var PORT = 8181,
        totalRead = 0,
        totalWritten = 0,
        connectionCount = 0;

var server = net.Server(connectionListener);

function connectionListener(conn) {
        //tally the bytes on end
        conn.on('end', function() {
                totalRead += conn.bytesRead;
        });
}

server.listen(PORT);

//Connect a socket
var socket = net.createConnection(PORT);

socket.on('connect', function() {
        // plan on writing the data more than once
        connectionCount++;

        // My = 2 Bytes
        socket.write('My', function () {
                // Precious = 8 Bytes
                socket.end('Precious');
        });
});

// tally the bytes written on end
socket.on('end', function() {
        totalWritten += socket.bytesWritten;
});

socket.on('close', function() {
        // Each time we should get +=10 bytes Read and Written
        console.log('total read: ' + totalRead);
        console.log('total written: ' + totalWritten);
        // We're gonna do this a few times
        if (connectionCount < 5) {
                socket.connect(PORT);
        } else {
                server.close();
        }
});
```

You now have access to the amount of bytes that are being sent between your server and your connections. This is terrific, but now you want to be able to reveal the details of where this server resides and where the sockets are coming from. To do this, you use the socket properties, `remoteAddress`, and `remotePort` (Listing 2-36). You can add these into the example above by adding a line in the `connectionListener` callback function and another line in the `socket.on('connect')` event.

Listing 2-36. Adding Some Address and Port Sniffers

```
console.log(socket.remoteAddress + ":" + socket.remotePort);
```

How It Works

Getting information about connected servers is actually quite easy. These data points that tell you how many bytes have been sent or received can be quite valuable when creating a Node.js application. How does Node.js build these data and present them to the net module for your consumption? If you examine the net module source code you will find that the bytesRead value is always set to zero when a new socket handle is created, as you might expect. This value is then incremented by the length of the buffer that is read during the buffer handle's onread function (shown in Listing 2-37).

Listing 2-37. onread Event–Increments bytesRead by Length

```
function onread(buffer, offset, length) {
  var handle = this;
  var self = handle.owner;
  assert(handle === self._handle, 'handle != self._handle');

  timers.active(self);

  var end = offset + length;
  debug('onread', process._errno, offset, length, end);

  if (buffer) {
    debug('got data');

    // read success.
    // In theory (and in practice) calling readStop right now
    // will prevent this from being called again until _read() gets
    // called again.

    // if we didn't get any bytes, that doesn't necessarily mean EOF.
    // wait for the next one.
    if (offset === end) {
      debug('not any data, keep waiting');
      return;
    }

    // if it's not enough data, we'll just call handle.readStart()
    // again right away.
    self.bytesRead += length;
```

```
    // Optimization: emit the original buffer with end points
    var ret = true;
    if (self.ondata) self.ondata(buffer, offset, end);
    else ret = self.push(buffer.slice(offset, end));

    if (handle.reading && !ret) {
      handle.reading = false;
      debug('readStop');
      var r = handle.readStop();
      if (r)
        self._destroy(errnoException(process._errno, 'read'));
    }

  } else if (process._errno == 'EOF') {
    debug('EOF');

    if (self._readableState.length === 0)
      self.readable = false;

    if (self.onend) self.once('end', self.onend);

    // push a null to signal the end of data.
    self.push(null);

    // internal end event so that we know that the actual socket
    // is no longer readable, and we can start the shutdown
    // procedure. No need to wait for all the data to be consumed.
    self.emit('_socketEnd');
  } else {
    debug('error', process._errno);
    // Error
    self._destroy(errnoException(process._errno, 'read'));
  }
}
```

Fetching the bytesWritten value is not quite as straightforward as incrementing a value by the length parameter that is passed into the onread function. In fact, as can be seen in Listing 2-38, the bytesWritten parameter is generated by reading the chunk length of a buffer, or the actual byte length itself.

Listing 2-38. bytesWritten

```
Socket.prototype.__defineGetter__('bytesWritten', function() {
  var bytes = this._bytesDispatched,
      state = this._writableState,
      data = this._pendingData,
      encoding = this._pendingEncoding;

  state.buffer.forEach(function(el) {
    if (Buffer.isBuffer(el.chunk))
      bytes += el.chunk.length;
```

```
    else
      bytes += Buffer.byteLength(el.chunk, el.encoding);
  });

  if (data) {
    if (Buffer.isBuffer(data))
      bytes += data.length;
    else
      bytes += Buffer.byteLength(data, encoding);
  }

  return bytes;
});
```

The remoteAddress and remotePort parameters come from the socket handle itself. These represent an abstraction (Listing 2-39) on top of the Node.js handle's getpeername object, which holds an address and a port parameter. This makes it simple for Node.js to define a getter for the remotePort and remoteAddress parameters.

Listing 2-39. getpeername Method and the remoteAddress and remotePort Properties

```
Socket.prototype._getpeername = function() {
  if (!this._handle || !this._handle.getpeername) {
    return {};
  }
  if (!this._peername) {
    this._peername = this._handle.getpeername();
    // getpeername() returns null on error
    if (this._peername === null) {
      return {};
    }
  }
  return this._peername;
};

Socket.prototype.__defineGetter__('remoteAddress', function() {
  return this._getpeername().address;
});

Socket.prototype.__defineGetter__('remotePort', function() {
  return this._getpeername().port;
});
```

You have seen how well Node.js defines properties on the server and sockets that support networked applications, making them easy to retrieve and to work with. Gaining these details about connected services can provide much-needed information when you develop a Node.js application.

■ ■ ■

## CHAPTER 3

Using the File System

In many instances within an application, you will want to work with the file system. Node.js makes this straightforward by creating a wrapper around standard file I/O operations that are present on the operating system. In Node.js these capabilities are centered around one of the Node.js native modules, fs. This chapter will provide examples of how to utilize the file-system module in your Node.js application. In this chapter you will learn how to perform these actions:

- Retrieve directory structures
- Navigate directories
- Manipulate directory structures
- Watch directories for modifications
- Read and write files
- Move and link files
- Alter file permissions
- Watch files for modifications

■ **Note** The file-system module contains many methods that not only are asynchronous but also have a synchronous counterpart. These synchronous methods are included in many of the solutions in the chapter to demonstrate how they can be utilized. It should be noted, however, that unless absolutely necessary the synchronous versions should be avoided as it is generally not best practice to utilize them. This is because the synchronous versions will block the entire process until they have completed, which will potentially wreak all manner of havoc on your application.

3-1. Retrieving Directory Structures
Problem

You want to access the structure of a directory, or a set of directories, from within your Node.js application.

Solution

To get a grasp of the Node.js utilities for retrieving a directory structure, you must first require the file-system module by using `require('fs')` in your code. You then want to get some information about the directory that you are targeting. Let us assume you want to print all the information pertaining to the current directory from your Node.js application. First, you can target the current directory, the directory from which the Node.js script is executed, as shown in Listing 3-1.

Listing 3-1. Target the Current Directory for Node.js

```
var fs = require('fs');
var out;

console.log(__dirname);
//read current directory asynchronously
fs.realpath(__dirname, function(err, /* [cache], */ path) {
    if (err) {
        console.log(err);
        return;
    }

    console.log('realpath async: ' + path);
});
out = fs.realpathSync(__dirname);
console.log('real path sync: ' + out);

fs.stat(__dirname, function(err, stat) {
    if (err) return;
    var isDir = false;

    fs.readdir(__dirname, function(err, contents) {
        if (err) return;
        contents.forEach(function(f) {
            console.log('contents: ' + f);
        });

    });
});

//get list of what's in the directory
out = fs.readdirSync(__dirname);
console.log('readdir sync: ' + out);
```

What results does this solution present? It produces a list, based in the current working directory, of what is contained within that directory. This list looks like what follows in Listing 3-2.

Listing 3-2. Output from Listing 3-1

```
$ node 3-1-1.js
/home/cgack/Dropbox/book/code/Ch03
real path sync: /home/cgack/Dropbox/book/code/Ch03
readdir sync: 3-1-1.js,3-1-2.js
contents: 3-1-1.js
contents: 3-1-2.js
realpath async: /home/cgack/Dropbox/book/code/Ch03
```

While that solution is effective for running your code in an attempt to get the directory structure of where your application is instantiated, it makes it difficult to parse the structure of arbitrary directories and directories relative to where you invoke your Node.js script. This can be solved by refactoring Listing 3-1 slightly to allow for a command-line parameter as shown in Listing 3-3.

Listing 3-3. Refactoring the Directory Digest

```
var fs = require('fs');
var out;
var args;
//Normalize the arguments
args = process.argv.splice(2);

args.forEach(function(arg) {
    console.log(arg);
    //read current directory asynchronous
    fs.realpath(arg, function(err, /* [cache], */ path) {
        if (err) {
            console.log(err);
            return;
        }

        console.log('realpath async: ' + path);
    });
    out = fs.realpathSync(arg);
    console.log('real path sync: ' + out);

    fs.stat(arg, function(err, stat) {
        if (err) return;

        fs.readdir(arg, function(err, contents) {
            if (err) return;
            contents.forEach(function(f) {
                console.log('contents: ' + f);
            });

        });
    });

    //get list of what's in the directory
    out = fs.readdirSync(arg);
    console.log('readdir sync: ' + out);

});
```

You can see that this solution offers a little more. It takes a list of arguments, normalizes them, and then loops through the directories provided, producing an output. This means that you can pass two relative paths to your Node.js application, and it will loop through and produce a result similar to the output in Listing 3-4.

Listing 3-4. Multiple Paths Output

```
$ node 3-1-2.js ...
.
real path sync: /home/cgack/Dropbox/book/code/Ch03
readdir sync: 3-1-1.js,3-1-2.js
..
real path sync: /home/cgack/Dropbox/book/code
readdir sync: 2-6-2.js,Ch01,Ch02,Ch03
contents: 3-1-1.js
contents: 3-1-2.js
contents: 2-6-2.js
contents: Ch01
contents: Ch02
contents: Ch03
realpath async: /home/cgack/Dropbox/book/code
```

How It Works

Now you examine how all of this works. You see that, in general, the difference between calling on a static, hard-coded directory and allowing a command-line argument to be passed into your command is the added benefit of flexibility. Let's start with the code that reads the directory information, and then you can examine the differences in implementation.

The Node.js file-system module presents a plethora of useful wrappers around the standard POSIX commands, which are semiubiquitous across platforms (some operating systems vary in implementation). The commands that are utilized in this section are readdir, stat, and realpath.

The Node.js implementation of readdir is a simple command to read a directory. You will note, however, that there are two separate calls of the readdir in the solution. One is to readdir ()and the other to readdirSync (). The readdirSync is the synchronous implementation of the file-system directory read, implemented as shown in Listing 3-5.

Listing 3-5. readdirSync

```
fs.readdirSync = function(path) {
  nullCheck(path);
  return binding.readdir(pathModule._makeLong(path));
};
```

This simply checks if the path exists, then returns that path. The alternative version of this call is asynchronous (Listing 3-6) and accepts a callback, as you might expect. The callback accepts two arguments: an error parameter and another that holds the information of the path.

Listing 3-6. readdir ()

```
fs.readdir = function(path, callback) {
  callback = makeCallback(callback);
  if (!nullCheck(path, callback)) return;
  binding.readdir(pathModule._makeLong(path), callback);
};
```

Similar to readdir, the Node.js function named realpath has both synchronous and asynchronous forms. The realpath function returns the absolute pathname for the provided path. So this is essentially two ways to gather information of the current directory. The function realpath retrieves the absolute path, and readdir retrieves information about its contents. Readdir can only retrieve a list of files or directories that are present in a directory, so in order to find out more details about a directory you need something different. This different method is stat (). stat() will gather all the information it can about the named file and you will see it used in more detail in subsequent sections, but in this case it is used as an entry point before you readdir on a path.

Now what about the two different versions of the example provided? One was based on a static path, which was in fact a Node.js global variable called __dirname. The __dirname variable is relative to each module, and it represents the path to the Node.js script that is currently executing. So when you use this in Listing 3-1, you are telling Node.js, and the file-system modules you invoke, to utilize the path to the Node.js module as the path argument for each file-system invocation.

This is rather limiting, so you see that in Listing 3-3 the module was opened up to utilize a set of command-line arguments that are passed to the module Node.js. This is utilizing the global process object that contains a list of the arguments in the argv element. In the listing, you see that these arguments are normalized to remove the first two parameters–'node <file>'–and then parse the rest of the arguments as an array. This array is then utilized as the path arguments for each of the Node.js file-system methods, giving much more versatility to the initial implementation of the directory information retrieval code.

3-2. Navigating Through Directories

Problem

In many applications in which you work with the file system, you may want to traverse the directory structure in some form or another.

Solution

Traversing the directory structure of your machine with your Node.js application is accomplished by using the fs module. This solution begins where the solution for Section 3-1 left off, in that it starts by reading a directory and then it will move throughout the directory accordingly. The parsing of the directory structure is recursive and results in an array containing the files and directories contained within. This Node.js application is shown in Listing 3-7.

Listing 3-7. Traversing Directories

```
var fs = require('fs');
var out;
var args;

/**
* To parse directory structure given a starting point - recursive
*/
function traverseDirectory(startDir, usePath, callback) {
    if (arguments.length === 2 && typeof arguments[1] === 'function') {
        callback = usePath;
        usePath = false;
    }
    //Hold onto the array of items
    var parsedDirectory = [];
    //start reading a list of whats contained
    fs.readdir(startDir, function(err, dirList) {
```

```
            if (usePath) {
                startDir = fs.realpathSync(startDir);
            }
            if (err) {
                return callback(err);
            }
            //keep track of how deep we need to go before callback
            var listlength = dirList.length;

            if (!listlength) {
                return callback(null, parsedDirectory);
            }
            //loop through the directory list
            dirList.forEach(function(file) {
                file = startDir + '/' + file;
                fs.stat(file, function(err, stat) {
                    //note the directory or file
                    parsedDirectory.push(file);
                    //recursive if this is a directory
                    if (stat && stat.isDirectory()) {
                        //recurse
                        traverseDirectory(file, function(err, parsed) {
                            // read this directory into our output
                            parsedDirectory = parsedDirectory.concat(parsed);
                            //check to see if we've exhausted our search
                            if (!--listlength) {
                                callback(null, parsedDirectory);
                            }
                        });
                    } else {
                        //check to see if we've exhausted the search
                        if (!--listlength) {
                            callback(null, parsedDirectory);
                        }
                    }
                });
            });
        });
    });
}

//Normalize the arguments
args = process.argv.splice(2);
//loop through the directories
args.forEach(function(arg) {

    // use provided path
    traverseDirectory(arg, function(err, result) {
        if (err) {
            console.log(err);
        }
        console.log(result);
    });
```

```
        //use full path
        traverseDirectory(arg, true, function(err, result) {
            if (err) {
                console.log(err);
            }
            console.log(result);
        });

});
```

This traversal results in a console output that looks something like that shown in Listing 3-8.

Listing 3-8. Output of Traversal

```
gack~/Dropbox/book/code/Ch03: node 3-2-1.js.
[ './3-1-1.js',
  './3-1-2.js',
  './3-2',
  './3-2-1.js',
  './3-2/file.txt',
  './3-2/sub directory',
  './3-2/sub directory/file.txt' ]
[ '/Users/gack/Dropbox/book/code/Ch03/3-1-1.js',
  '/Users/gack/Dropbox/book/code/Ch03/3-1-2.js',
  '/Users/gack/Dropbox/book/code/Ch03/3-2',
  '/Users/gack/Dropbox/book/code/Ch03/3-2-1.js',
  '/Users/gack/Dropbox/book/code/Ch03/3-2/file.txt',
  '/Users/gack/Dropbox/book/code/Ch03/3-2/sub directory',
  '/Users/gack/Dropbox/book/code/Ch03/3-2/sub directory/file.txt' ]
```

How It Works

This solution works by first taking a lesson from Section 3-1 and providing the arguments via the command line, which are then normalized. This directs the application which paths to use when beginning the traversal of the directory structure, which is handled in the function traverseDirectory.

The traverseDirectory function accepts a path (or starting directory), an optional flag to translate the starting path to a full path, and a callback function. The optional usePath flag is determined by checking if there are only two parameters passed in and that the second parameter is a function, indicating that the callback was supplied.

```
if (arguments.length === 2 && typeof arguments[1] === 'function') {
        callback = usePath;
        usePath = false;
}
```

The usePath flag is an option that, if set, will then parse the directory provided to the traverseDirectory method using the fs.realpath function. So this would convert a path provided as ',' representing the current working directory, to the actual path for your application (i.e. '/home/username/apps/').

The actual traversal through the directory structure begins with a call to fs.readdir, which, as you saw in Section 3-1, provides a callback with a list of what resides in the directory. Then a check is made on this returned list to ensure that there is information in the directory available to parse. If no result exists, the function exits with the provided callback. Alternatively, if there are results in the directory listing, you store the length of that array (listlength) to keep track of the remaining items to be parsed from the directory tree.

You then loop through the directory list array, applying the function fs.stat to each item it contains. The fs.stat function returns an fs.stat object detailing information about a file on the file system. The traverseDirectory function then stores the file (or directory) on which the fs.stat object was invoked into the output array parsedDirectory. The stat object is then checked to see if the result is a directory via the stat.isDirectory function. If the result is true, then the traverseDirectory function is called, passing in that directory–recursively parsing the directory. If the stat is not a directory, the function assumes it is a file, but, regardless if it is a file or not, the directory list length variable is decremented and checked to see if there are any entries remaining, if (!–listlength). In the case where there are not any entries remaining, the function returns the callback passing the parsedDirectory array. The results are passed on to the callback function, which, in this example, logs them to the console.

3-3. Manipulating the Directory Structure
Problem

You want to manipulate the structure of your directories by adding and removing directories via your Node.js application.

Solution

This solution takes two forms and will be described in two parts. The first part is the removal of directories. In Node.js this is as simple as calling the file-system module's make directory or make directory synchronous functions, fs.mkdir and fs.mkdirSync. Both of these functions are shown in a single example, Listing 3-9.

Listing 3-9. Creating Directory Synchronous and Asynchronous Functions

```
var fs = require('fs'),
        dirExists = false;

//Normalize the arguments
args = process.argv.splice(2);
//loop through named args
args.forEach(function(arg) {
        //mkdirSync - manually handle errors
        try {
                fs.mkdirSync(arg);
        } catch(err) {
                handleError(err);
        }

        //mkdir async
        fs.mkdir(arg, function(err) {
                if (err) handleError(err);
        });
*/

});
```

```
function handleError(err) {
        console.log(err);
        if (err.code === 'EEXIST') {
                console.log('That directory already exists');
        } else {
                console.log('An error occurred creating the directory');
        }
}
```

The second part of the solution for manipulating the structure of your directories involves the Node.js methods for removing existing directories. The removal code (shown in Listing 3-10) is essentially the reversal of the creation, with a slight difference in the handling of exceptions.

Listing 3-10. Removing Directories

```
var fs = require('fs'),
        dirExists = false;

//Normalize the arguments
args = process.argv.splice(2);
//loop through named args
args.forEach(function(arg) {
        //rmdir sync
        try {
                fs.rmdirSync(dir);
        } catch(err) {
                handleError(err);
        }
        //rmdir async
        fs.rmdir(arg, function(err) {
                if (err) handleError(err);
        });

});

function handleError(err) {
        console.log(err);
        if (err.code === 'ENOENT') {
                console.log('That directory does not exist');
        } else if (err.code === 'ENOTEMPTY') {
                console.log('Cannot remove directory because it is not empty');
        } else {
                console.log('An error occurred removing the directory');
        }
}
```

How It Works

The creation of directories happens with the mkdir function. The mkdir function also accepts a callback function with an error argument only. The error thrown when the directory already exist has the code EEXIST, so in the example this is handled explicitly in the handleError function. The synchronous version of mkdir (i.e., mkdirSync) does not provide an error callback, so in the example you see that it is creating inside of a try-catch, where the catch provides the same error handler as the asynchronous callback. Both the synchronous and asynchronous functions accept an optional second argument that dictates the mode with which the directory will be created, defaulting to 0777. If you want to restrict permissions you could alter the creation mode to anything (for example, 0755), restricting all but the user to read and execute permissions on the directory.

The removal of directories is similar to creation. The removal asynchronous function, rmdir, accepts a callback with an error argument. The common errors that are handled with this callback are EONENT and ENOTEMPTY. EONENT is thrown when the directory does not exist and you attempt to remove it from the directory structure. ENOTEMPTY is thrown when you attempt to remove a directory that is not empty. These are both handled via the handleError function. Later in this chapter you will see how to move and rename files, which will be necessary if you want to remove a folder that is not empty.

3-4. Watching a Directory for Modifications
Problem

You want to watch a directory for changes made to its structure during the process of running your Node.js application.

Solution

The solution to watching a directory structure follows the solution from Section 3-2, which traversed through a directory to read its contents into an array. For this solution you could do two things. One way could be to again traverse through the directory structure, caching the initial state of the directory and subdirectories. You will then set an interval for when you will check the directory structure again and compare the output of those two arrays. This is not the best solution because Node.js has a built-in utility within the file-system module that will create a file-system watcher object named fs.watch. The way in which this is implemented is shown in Listing 3-11.

Listing 3-11. Watching for Changes

```
/**
* Watching a directory
*/
var os = require('os'),
    fs = require('fs'),
    out,
    args;

/**
* To parse directory structure given a starting point - recursive
*/
function traverseDirectory(startDir, usePath, callback) {
    if (arguments.length === 2 && typeof arguments[1] === 'function') {
        callback = usePath;
        usePath = false;
    }
    //Hold onto the array of items
    var parsedDirectory = [];
    //start reading a list of what's contained
    fs.readdir(startDir, function(err, dirList) {
```

```
        if (usePath) {
            startDir = fs.realpathSync(startDir);
        }
        if (err) {
            return callback(err);
        }
        //keep track of how deep we need to go before callback
        var listlength = dirList.length;

        if (!listlength) {
            return callback(null, parsedDirectory);
        }
        //loop through the directory list
        dirList.forEach(function(file) {
            //WIndows is special
            file = startDir + (os.platform() === 'win32' ? '\\' : '/') + file;
            fs.stat(file, function(err, stat) {
                //note the directory or file
                parsedDirectory.push(file);
                //recursive if this is a directory
                if (stat && stat.isDirectory()) {
                    //recurse
                    traverseDirectory(file, function(err, parsed) {
                        // read this directory into our output
                        parsedDirectory = parsedDirectory.concat(parsed);
                        //check to see if we've exhausted our search
                        if (!--listlength) {
                            callback(null, parsedDirectory);
                        }
                    });
                } else {
                    //check if we've exhausted the search
                    if (!--listlength) {
                        callback(null, parsedDirectory);
                    }
                }
            });
        });
    });
}
//Normalize the arguments
args = process.argv.splice(2);
//loop through the directories
args.forEach(function(arg) {
    traverseDirectory(arg, true, function(err, result) {
        result.forEach(function(i) {
            fs.watch(i, filesystemListener);
        });
    });

});
```

```
function filesystemListener(e, f) {
    console.log(f + ': ' + e);
}
```

This solution is extremely powerful because it will also check the individual files for changes, with a call to a single function. However as you will see, the fs.watch method is unstable and may not perform as expected in your Node.js environment. Because of this, an alternative to watching for directory structure changes is shown in Listing 3-12.

Listing 3-12. Checking for Directory Structure Changes

```
function checkSame(err, result) {
    if (err) {
        console.log(err);
    }
    if (initialDir.length === 0) {
        initialDir = result;
    } else {
        secondaryDir = result;
        //let's compare these
        if (secondaryDir.length !== initialDir.length) {
            console.log('directory structure changed');
            clearInterval(checkInt);
        }

        secondaryDir.sort();
        initialDir.sort();

        for (var i=0, ii = secondaryDir.length; i < ii; i++) {
            if (secondaryDir[i] !== initialDir[i]) {
                if (secondaryDir.indexOf(initialDir[i]) < 0) {
                    console.log(initialDir[i] + ' removed');
                }
                if (initialDir.indexOf(secondaryDir[i]) < 0) {
                    console.log(secondaryDir[i] + ' added');
                }
                clearInterval(checkInt);
            }
        }
    }
}
var checkInt;
//Normalize the arguments
args = process.argv.splice(2);
//loop through the directories
args.forEach(function(arg) {
    checkInt = setInterval(traverseDirectory, 2e3, arg, true, checkSame);
});
```

How It Works

The example from Listing 3-11 shows the traversal of the directory tree with the addition of a very important function. The traverseDirectory function results in an array of file names and directory names. You then loop through these results, invoking the fs.watch function on each path. The fs.watch function is part of the file-system watching capabilities, which are covered later in Section 3-10.

Be warned that the fs.watch functionality is not always available across platforms, and (as of Node.js version 0.10.5) is still considered "unstable." Because of this the alternative implementation, shown in Listing 3-13, is more reliable across platforms and only looks for changes to the structure of the file system. Again this system utilizes the traverseDirectory function, but does so on an interval. This interval will parse the directory structure every two seconds, but you may want to adjust the interval if you are parsing a large directory tree that will take longer than that to recursively parse. After the first iteration, the array from the original parsing is compared to the array of the current parsing within the checkSame function. If a change is detected it is logged. Changes are detected first if the lengths of the arrays are different, meaning that the underlying structure has been modified (i.e., file deletion). The arrays are then both sorted, and then each item is checked to see if it still exists within the other result set.

Listing 3-13. Checking Directory Differences

```
if (secondaryDir.length !== initialDir.length) {
        console.log('directory structure changed');
        clearInterval(checkInt);
    }

    secondaryDir.sort();
    initialDir.sort();

    for (var i=0, ii = secondaryDir.length; i < ii; i++) {
        if (secondaryDir[i] !== initialDir[i]) {
            if (secondaryDir.indexOf(initialDir[i]) < 0) {
                console.log(initialDir[i] + ' removed');
            }
            if (initialDir.indexOf(secondaryDir[i]) < 0) {
                console.log(secondaryDir[i] + ' added');
            }
            clearInterval(checkInt);
        }
    }
}
```

Using this method when watching a directory for changes will produce a result that looks similar to the output in Listing 3-14, produced when changing a directory name from "that" to "this":

Listing 3-14. Noting Directory Structure Changes

```
$ node 3-4-1.js.
/home/cgack/book/code/Ch03/3-4/now/that removed
/home/cgack/book/code/Ch03/3-4/now/this added
```

3-5. Reading Files

Problem

In the process of building a Node.js application, you need to access and read a file from the file system.

Solution

Reading a file from the file system is fairly straightforward when utilizing the file-system module. The file-system module provides multiple ways in which you can read a file. In Listing 3-15, the solution displays the three main methods in which a file can be read in Node.js using the file system: readFile, readFileSync, and createReadStream.

Listing 3-15. Reading Files

```
/**
* Reading a file
*/
var fs = require('fs'),
        args;

args = process.argv.splice(2);

args.forEach(function(arg){
        //async read
        fs.readFile(arg, 'utf8', function(err, data) {
                if (err) console.log(err);
                console.log(data);
        });
        //synchronicity
        var file = fs.readFileSync(arg, 'utf8');
        console.log(file);
        //with a readable stream
        var readstrm = fs.createReadStream(arg, {flag: 'r', encoding: 'utf8'});

        readstrm.on('data', function(d) {

                console.log(d);
        });
});
```

How It Works

Reading a file in Node.js can take different forms. First, you can utilize the standard asynchronous function fs.readFile. This function will accept a file name (which is required), an optional options argument, and a callback (also required). The options argument is used to set the encoding (which will set the encoding for the file buffer as it is read), and added to the options object is the flag, which sets the flag with which the file is to be opened: this will always be 'r'.

The readFile function at its core makes a call to the function fs.open, which will open the file. The flag option, which is always set to 'r', means the file is to be opened for reading. In the case of readFile, the open method shown in Listing 3-16 will get the size of the file and then create a buffer matching that size. This buffer is then read in the read() function.

Listing 3-16. fs.open and read() inside of fs.readFile

```
fs.open(path, flag, 438 /*=0666*/, function(er, fd_) {
    if (er) return callback(er);
    fd = fd_;

    fs.fstat(fd, function(er, st) {
      if (er) return callback(er);
      size = st.size;
      if (size === 0) {
        // the kernel lies about many files.
        // Go ahead and try to read some bytes.
        buffers = [];
        return read();
      }

      buffer = new Buffer(size);
      read();
    });
});

function read() {
    if (size === 0) {
      buffer = new Buffer(8192);
      fs.read(fd, buffer, 0, 8192, -1, afterRead);
    } else {
      fs.read(fd, buffer, pos, size - pos, -1, afterRead);
    }
  }
```

You can see that the fs.readFile's internal read () function makes a call to fs.read, pointing to the file descriptor and the buffer that was created to be the size of the opened file. The result is then finally sent to the fs.readFile's callback function after executing the afterRead function and the file is closed. The close method is what actually sends the data from the buffer back to the callback.

Listing 3-17. Close Event Sending the readFile Data Back to the Caller

```
function close() {
 fs.close(fd, function(er) {
   if (size === 0) {
     // collected the data into the buffers list.
     buffer = Buffer.concat(buffers, pos);
   } else if (pos < size) {
     buffer = buffer.slice(0, pos);
   }
```

```
  if (encoding) buffer = buffer.toString(encoding);
  return callback(er, buffer);
 });
}
```

As you might imagine, the next method for reading a file, fs.readFileSync, follows a similar pattern to the fs.readFile function, but it only operates synchronously. This results not in a callback that contains the data read from the file, but the synchronous version returns the data directly, with the proper encoding applied.

```
if (encoding) buffer = buffer.toString(encoding);
return buffer;
```

Finally, in the solution for reading files with Node.js, you created a readable stream to parse the file. The readable stream is created using the fs.createReadStream function that does exactly as its name foretells: it creates a ReadStream. A ReadStream is a readable stream with an open event, which returns the file descriptor (fd) that is being used by the stream to read the file. The options passed into the readable stream is an object that has the following defaults:

```
{ flags: 'r',   encoding: null,   fd: null,   mode: 0666,   bufferSize: 64 * 1024,   autoClose: true }
```

There are two extra options that can be passed: start and end. These specify a particular slice of the file you wish to read.

The ReadStream is created with these options set, and then the stream is opened. Opening the stream makes a call to fs.open, allowing the file to be opened and read, as shown in Listing 3-18.

Listing 3-18. ReadStream Calling fs.open and Reading the File

```
ReadStream.prototype.open = function() {
  var self = this;
  fs.open(this.path, this.flags, this.mode, function(er, fd) {
    if (er) {
      if (this.autoClose) {
        self.destroy();
      }
      self.emit('error', er);
      return;
    }

    self.fd = fd;
    self.emit('open', fd);
    // start the flow of data.
    self.read();
  });
};
```

3-6. Writing Files

Problem

You want to utilize Node.js to write content or data to files in your application.

Solution

The solution for writing files from Node.js is similar to the methods addressed in Section 3-5. Just as with reading files there are several methods for writing files in Node.js. There is the typical asynchronous approach (fs.writeFile), a synchronous version of that function (fs.writeFileSync), and a stream version of writing a file (createWriteStream). There is another method, which is used to append data to a file called fs.appendFile. These functions are shown in Listing 3-19.

Listing 3-19. Writing Files

```
/**
 * Writing files
 */
var fs = require('fs');
//initial write
fs.writeFile('write.txt', 'This is the contents!', function(err) {
        if (err) throw err;
        console.log('huzzah');
});

try {
        fs.writeFileSync('./doesnotexist/newfile.txt', 'content');
} catch(err) {
        console.log('unable to create a file in a non existent sub directory');
        console.log(err);
}
//appending
fs.appendFile('write.txt', 'More content', function(err) {
        if (err) throw err;
        console.log('appended');
});

var ws = fs.createWriteStream('write.txt');
ws.write('new content\r\n', function() {
        console.log('write stream hath written.');
});
```

Listing 3-19 shows how to go about writing a file in Node.js by using three different methods. The synchronous method is purposefully targeting a file in a nonexistent subdirectory in order to demonstrate the error handling of this situation and to observe that writing a file will not create a directory. The output from executing this solution will look like the example shown in Listing 3-20.

Listing 3-20. Writing files output

```
gack~/Dropbox/book/code/Ch03: node 3-6-1.js
unable to create a file in a non existent sub directory
```

```
{ [Error: ENOENT, no such file or directory './doesnotexist/newfile.txt']
  errno: 34,
  code: 'ENOENT',
  path: './doesnotexist/newfile.txt',
  syscall: 'open' }
write stream hath written.
appended
huzzah
```

How It Works

Let's examine how files are written in Node.js by starting with the asynchronous fs.writeFile. fs.writeFile accepts up to four arguments: path, data, options, and a callback. The path points to the file you wish to write. The file does not need to exist, as it will be created if not. However, if you are targeting a directory that does not exist, the writeFile function will not automatically create the directory for you. The data argument is the data that you wish to write to the file and can be in the form of a string or a buffer. The options object contains the encoding, the mode, and the flag for the file access. Just like with the readFile method, encoding is the only configurable option as the settings for the mode and flag are set to mode: 438 /*=0666*/ and flag: 'w'. The callback will pass on any errors in order to handle them.

Once the defaults have been set within the writeFile function, fs.open is called. Since this is called with the 'w' flag set, it will either create the file or truncate the file. The data will then be written to the file as a buffer, and a string will be converted to a buffer if that is the data type provided as shown in Listing 3-21.

Listing 3-21. writeFile–Open and Write Data

```
var flag = options.flag || 'w';
 fs.open(path, options.flag || 'w', options.mode, function(openErr, fd) {
   if (openErr) {
     if (callback) callback(openErr);
   } else {
     var buffer = Buffer.isBuffer(data) ? data : new Buffer('' + data,
         options.encoding || 'utf8');
     var position = /a/.test(flag) ? null : 0;
     writeAll(fd, buffer, 0, buffer.length, position, callback);
   }
});
```

The writeAll function wraps the fs.write function and will write the buffer in its entirety to the file. Similar to the readFile and readFileSync functions, the writeFileSync functions in the same way as writeFile with the exception that all the functions are synchronous, throwing any errors that are encountered along the way. This is the reason why this code in the example was written within a try-catch block in order to gracefully catch the error thrown when the directory did not exist.

In many cases, you may not want to create or truncate a file as you are writing data to it. This is where the fs.appendFile function is useful. This function is a utility to write a file, only appending data to the file instead of writing the data fresh. It does this by simply altering the flag option for fs.writeFile and then invoking that function as shown in Listing 3-22.

Listing 3-22. Altering the flag option

```
if (!options.flag)
  options = util._extend({ flag: 'a' }, options);
fs.writeFile(path, data, options, callback);
```

As shown, this will open the file with fs.open. Setting the flag to 'a' will open the file for appending, allowing it to be created if the file does not exist.

The streaming method is fs.createWriteStream, which creates a writable stream. The createWriteStream method will take a path and options. The options that can be set are fd (a file descriptor), flags, mode, and start. The fd will point to a file handle to write data to. The flag default is w, in order to open the file for writing. The mode option defaults to 0666, or read and write permissions. The start option tells where in the file to start writing data. It should be noted that if you specify a start position that exceeds the end of a file length, you will end up with a mess of buffer output in your file, instead of the intended data or text.

A WriteStream is written by first opening the file, then calling an internal _write function. The function will ensure the data to be written are sound and that the file is indeed open. Once that is confirmed, the file will be written using the fs.write method, as shown in Listing 3-23.

Listing 3-23. WriteStream's _write Method

```
WriteStream.prototype._write = function(data, encoding, cb) {
  if (!Buffer.isBuffer(data))
    return this.emit('error', new Error('Invalid data'));

  if (typeof this.fd !== 'number')
    return this.once('open', function() {
      this._write(data, encoding, cb);
    });

  var self = this;
  fs.write(this.fd, data, 0, data.length, this.pos, function(er, bytes) {
    if (er) {
      self.destroy();
      return cb(er);
    }
    self.bytesWritten += bytes;
    cb();
  });

  if (this.pos !== undefined)
    this.pos += data.length;
};
```

3-7. Moving Files

Problem

You want to be able to move files within your directory structure from your Node.js application. You will more likely than not encounter a situation where you will need to change the location of a file for one reason or another. Perhaps you are storing a temporary cache of files in your Node.js application that you wish to move to a more permanent location. You then have a user who indicates he would like to store his favorite animated .gif file in a more permanent location.

Solution

Moving files around is important when you are building an application that accesses the file system. In the situation outlined in this problem you would move the file using Node.js, as shown in Listing 3-22.

Listing 3-24 is an example of a file, awesome.gif, that your user has cached. This file is in a temporary directory, 3-7/tmp/, in the file system and needs to be moved to a save folder, 3-7/save/. To demonstrate this you will see like many things with Node.js there are multiple methods for accomplishing this. Two of these utilize the file-system module, incorporating the rename and renameSync functions to move a file.

Listing 3-24. Moving a File: Starting from the Command Line

```
/**
 * Moving files
 */
var fs = require('fs'),
            origPath,
            newPath,
            args = process.argv;

if (args.length !== 4) {
        throw new Error('Invalid Arguments');
} else {
        origPath = args[2];
        newPath = args[3];
}
// move file asynchronously from tmp to save
fs.rename(origPath, newPath, function(err) {
        if (err) throw err;
});
```

You will start with an example using the command line, and you'll then see two other methods for accomplishing the same task of moving a file in Node.js.

This is accomplished by providing a command-line argument like the following:

```
$ node 3-7-1.js 3-7/tmp/awesome.gif 3-7/save/awesome.gif
```

Aside from setting this up through the command line, you could also implement the fs.rename function directly within your application. This could also be set up to run synchronously, as in Listing 3-25, or via a child process, as shown in Listing 3-26.

Listing 3-25. Synchronous File Move

```
//Synchronous
fs.renameSync(origPath, newPath);
```

Listing 3-26. Using a Child Process to Move a File

```
// Child process => more in Chapter 5
var child = require('child_process');
child.exec('mv 3-7/tmp/awesome.gif 3-7/save/awesome.gif', function(err, stdout, stderr) {
        console.log('out: ' + stdout);
        if (stderr) throw stderr;
        if (err) throw err;
});
```

How It Works

When you begin to examine how this works, you first look to the file-system module. The fs.rename function performs a standard POSIX rename, defined below.

> *The rename( ) function shall change the name of a file. The old argument points to the pathname of the file to be renamed. The new argument points to the new pathname of the file.*

> *If either the old or new argument names a symbolic link, rename( ) shall operate on the symbolic link itself, and it shall not resolve the last component of the argument. If the old argument and the new argument resolve to the same existing file, rename( ) shall return successfully and perform no other action.*

This means that you are leveraging the operating system's ability to change the location of a file by altering its pathname. As you look at the solution you can start to understand precisely how this works.

First, you see that for the sake of this example, the arguments passed to the Node.js process are used. You will utilize these arguments to tell your Node.js application which pathnames to use when moving files. This means that in addition to the standard first two arguments, node <app.js>, you will need to have two other parameters.

In order to validate these additional parameters, and prevent your move functions from immediately throwing an error with the wrong number of arguments, you need to ensure you have provided the proper number of arguments. This is accomplished by checking the number of arguments passed and throwing an appropriate error if an invalid number is encountered.

```
if (args.length !== 4) {
        throw new Error('Invalid Arguments');
} else {
        origPath = args[2];
        newPath = args[3];
}
```

Following this sanity check, if you have the proper number of arguments, then you assign the original path and new path variables, which will be passed to your fs.rename function. This function takes an original path and a new path argument, as well as a callback. The callback function will accept an error object only if the rename process fails for whatever reason. Examining the Node.js source for fs.rename in Listing 3-27, you will see that the module just wraps the native rename functionality of the operating system.

Listing 3-27. fs.rename Source

```
fs.rename = function(oldPath, newPath, callback) {
  callback = makeCallback(callback);
  if (!nullCheck(oldPath, callback)) return;
  if (!nullCheck(newPath, callback)) return;
  binding.rename(pathModule._makeLong(oldPath),
               pathModule._makeLong(newPath),
               callback);
};
```

You can see from the source that the original pathname and new pathname must be present or the nullCheck function will prevent a rename. You must also provide an existing path to the file. The file itself need not be present for the rename to operate, but if you provide a path that does not exist an error will be thrown (see Listing 3-28).

Listing 3-28. Path does not exist

```
$ node 3-7-1.js 3-7/tmp/awesome.gif 3-7/save/does/not/exist/awesome.gif

/Users/gack/Dropbox/book/code/Ch03/3-7-1.js:18
        if (err) throw err;
                       ^
Error: ENOENT, rename '3-7/tmp/awesome.gif'
```

The next example in the solution implemented the synchronous version of fs.rename, fs.renameSync. This is the same functionality as fs.rename, with the alteration that the function waits until the rename occurs, and then returns (see Listing 3-29).

Listing 3-29. Synchronous rename

```
fs.renameSync = function(oldPath, newPath) {
  nullCheck(oldPath);
  nullCheck(newPath);
  return binding.rename(pathModule._makeLong(oldPath),
                        pathModule._makeLong(newPath));
};
```

In the solution for moving files, these two examples are perhaps the most common methods in Node.js. You also saw in the solution a method that utilizes the standard terminal command to execute a file move:

```
'mv 3-7/tmp/awesome.gif 3-7/save/awesome.gif'
```

This is accomplished by utilizing the Node.js child process module. The details of utilizing the Node.js child process module will be discussed further in Chapter 5. You can see, however, that you can execute commands directly through this module.

3-8. Symbolically Linking Files
Problem

When building a Node.js application, you want to utilize symbolic links or links for files in your file system.

Solution

In this solution you can imagine that your Node.js application has just downloaded an executable file, which you then want to make available through the file system via the use of symbolic links. To do this there are many methods in which to build the symbolic links. Of course, you must start with the file-system module being imported via require('fs'). Then you will see that there are multiple versions of how to link to files in the file system and subsequently to read them and know to where they are linked.

Listing 3-30. Symbolically Linking Files

```
/**
* symbolic links
*/
var fs = require('fs');
```

```
fs.link('/opt/Sublime Text 2/sublime_text', '/usr/bin/sublime', function(err) {
        if (err) throw err;
});

fs.linkSync('/opt/Sublime Text 2/sublime_text', '/usr/bin/sublime');

fs.symlink('/opt/Sublime Text 2/sublime_text', '/usr/bin/sublime', function(err) {
        if (err) throw err;
});

fs.symlinkSync('/opt/Sublime Text 2/sublime_text', '/usr/bin/sublime');

fs.readlink('/usr/bin/sublime', function(err, string) {
        if (err) throw err;
        console.log(string);
});

var rls = fs.readlinkSync('/usr/bin/sublime');
console.log(rls);
```

There are four functions for creating links, with two different varieties. First are fs.link and fs.linkSync. The other two are fs.symlink and fs.symlinkSync. These are complemented with the methods for reading the links via fs.readlink and fs.readlinkSync.

How It Works

Symbolically linking files and linking files in the file system behave just like many other items in the file-system module in Node.js. That is to say, these functions are wrappers for the standard operating system commands.

First let's examine the function fs.link. This function is not a function to create a symbolic link itself; rather, it is a function that will wrap the POSIX link command. This command will create a link, or what is commonly known as a hard link, to an existing file. The link function takes three arguments: original path, new path, and a callback that will accept an error if one occurs. This function, like others in the file-system module, has a synchronous relative, fs.linkSync. linkSync, aside from being fun to say out loud, performs the same hard linking operation that fs.link does; only it returns the result instead of using a callback.

Symbolically linking files operates in the similar manner as fs.link. The function to link a file is fs.symlink. A symbolic link is a soft link, as opposed to a hard link. A symbolic link represents a link to another file or directory, just like the hard link with two distinct differences. First, a symbolic link is valid across volumes, not only to the local volume as the hard link. Second, the symbolic link can point to an arbitrary path, where the hard link must link to an existing file on the file system.

Aside from the differences in symbolic versus hard link implementation on the operating system, the Node.js implementation is very similar. The function fs.symlink accepts three arguments: the original path, a new path, and a callback that accepts any error that occurs. This is the same signature as the function fs.link. Just as fs.link had a synchronous counterpart, so does fs.symlink with fs.symlinkSync. The synchronous version returns the result directly instead of utilizing the callback.

The fs.symlink and fs.symlinkSync functions do perform a singular check before making the symbolic link on the file system. This check is a preprocess function; Listing 3-31 shows how the system makes sure that symbolic links made in a Windows environment utilize the proper protocol for resolving the file path.

Listing 3-31. Symbolic Link Preprocess

```
function preprocessSymlinkDestination(path, type) {
  if (!isWindows) {
    // No preprocessing is needed on Unix.
    return path;
  } else if (type === 'junction') {
    // Junctions paths need to be absolute and \\?\-prefixed.
    return pathModule._makeLong(path);
  } else {
    // Windows symlinks don't tolerate forward slashes.
    return ('' + path).replace(/\//g, '\\');
  }
}
```

Once a symbolic or hard link is made in the file system, you can utilize Node.js to read the link. Reading a link on the file system will resolve to where the link actually is linked. This is done with the fs.readlink function. The fs.readlink function accepts two arguments: a path for the symbolic link and a callback. The callback will contain two arguments: an error if one occurred and the string for the file path that the symbolic or hard link resolves. As with the other methods there is a synchronous version of this function that returns the error or resulting string directly, without the use of the callback function.

3-9. Altering File Permissions
Problem

Within your Node.js application, you need to control the access and permissions levels on files and directories on your file system.

Solution

In order to change the permissions for a file, you must utilize the same set of functions that your operating system uses in order to do the same. The standard sets of rules for files are determined by the access level, which is granted via the mode that the file is registered to have on the file system, and the ownership of the file. Say, for example, that you have a file that is used in your application; you may wish to make it readable by only individuals on the operating system. This can be done easily as shown in Listing 3-32. Other examples shown in this solution highlight a few of the various modes for individual access to the files. Later you will see all the various possibilities available for you to alter the modes of files.

Listing 3-32. Changing File Permissions in Node.js

```
/**
 * Altering file permissions
 */

var fs = require('fs'),
        file = '3-9/file.txt';

//CHANGING MODES chmod
//hidden file
//-rwSr-S--T 1 cgack cgack 4 May  5 11:50 file.txt
```

```
fs.chmod(file, 4000, function(err) {
        if (err) throw err;
});
//individual write
//--w------- 1 cgack cgack 4 May  5 11:50 file.txt
fs.chmod(file, 0200, function(err) {
        if (err) throw err;
});
//individual execute
//---x------ 1 cgack cgack 4 May  5 11:50 file.txt
fs.chmod(file, 0100, function(err) {
        if (err) throw err;
});
//individual write + execute
//--wx------ 1 cgack cgack 4 May  5 11:50 file.txt
fs.chmod(file, 0300, function(err) {
        if (err) throw err;
});


//CHANGING OWNERS chown
// requires root access
//--wx------ 1 root root 4 May  5 11:50 file.txt
fs.chown(file, 0 /* root */, 0, function(err) {
        if (err) throw err;
});

//--wx------ 1 cgack cgack 4 May  5 11:50 file.txt
fs.chown(file, 1000, 1000, function(err) {
        if (err) throw err;
});
```

Also shown in the listing is the ability to change the owner of the file. You can see that the ownership of the file was transferred to root, then back to my personal user easily, with the use of the fs.chown function.

How It Works

When you aim to alter permissions on a file or directory, you first might want to change ownership. In Node.js, ownership on the file system is dictated by the fs.chown function and its synchronous counterpart fs.chownSync. The fs.chown function accepts four arguments. First, you must provide the function for the file on which you wish to perform the ownership alteration. Second, you must provide the integer of the user ID on your system. Third, you add the integer of the group ID to which that user belongs. Finally, the function accepts a callback function, which will pass on any errors that occur.

The file name should be obvious to you, as you likely will know the target, or provide a file within your Node.js application that requires the ownership change. But what might not be something that you have memorized is the user ID or group IDs of all the users to which you wish to grant access. If you want to get these ID numbers, you can use the following commands in the terminal.

Listing 3-33. Determine the User and Group ID Numbers via the Terminal

```
$ id -u <username> #username user id
$ id -g <username> #username group id
```

The use of chown will directly change the owner of the file on the file system. You see that changing the owner to the root user in the file.txt as described by $ ls -l shows that the file was changed to be owned by root: //--wx------ 1 root root 4 May 5 11:50 file.txt. The same is, of course, true for the ownership change back to my user cgack. It should be noted that to change ownership of the file, you are required to operate under root access. This means that in this example you should run the application file as $ sudo node 3-9-1.js. Without this level of permission you will encounter a permissions error: Error: EPERM, chown '3-9/file.txt'.

Once you have changed ownership of a file, you still may want to explicitly set the permissions associated with the file. In the solution, you saw the file in the example was altered from a hidden file to be accessed as individual write, individual execute, and then a combined individual write + execute permissions. Setting these is quite simple, because the fs.chmod function will change the access mode of the file. This function, fs.chmod, accepts three arguments: the file name, the integer value of the octal permission code, and a callback to pass back any errors that occur.

The octal codes that determine the permissions are split into sections. The first digit represents permissions granted to the "other" set of users. The second digit represents group level access. The third and fourth represent individual user access and system level access, respectively. With the exception of the system level access, which represents whether the file is hidden, archived, or a system file, the possible values are 1 (for execute), 2 (for write), and 4 (for read). The full list is shown in Listing 3-34.

Listing 3-34. File Access Settings

```
4000        Hidden file
2000        System file
1000        Archive bit
0400        Individual read
0200        Individual write
0100        Individual execute
0040        Group read
0020        Group write
0010        Group execute
0004        Other read
0002        Other write
0001        Other execute
```

These values can all be combined together, as you saw in the solution where both individual write and execute were granted by utilizing 0300 = 0200 and 0100. As such, full access to an individual would be set at 0700 = 0400 and 0200 and 0100. You can see then that the full extent of this functionality, granting full access of read, write, and execute to all users and groups, would be 0777.

Armed with these tools, you should be able to alter access levels and file level ownership in Node.js.

3-10. Watching Files for Modifications
Problem

You want to monitor a file for all modifications within Node.js.

Solution

If you want to be able to gain as much information as possible and consider changes to files in the file system, then the file-system module of Node.js has a set of solutions that might just work. There are two approaches to this file-system monitoring. One is to use the fs.watchFile method, which will return the entire file stat object for previous and current files you are watching. The second is a newer method, mentioned briefly in Section 3-4: fs.watch. To see these two options in action, watching for changes to an arbitrary file, look no farther than Listing 3-35.

Listing 3-35. Two Methods for Watching for File Alterations

```
/**
* Watching files for modifications
*/
var fs = require('fs'),
        path = '3-10/file.txt';

fs.watchFile(path, function(current, previous) {
        for (var key in current) {
                if (current[key] !== previous[key]) {
                        console.log(key + ' altered. prev: ' + previous[key] + ' curr: ' +
current[key]);
                }
        }
});

fs.watch(path, function(event, filename) {
        if (filename) {
                console.log(filename + ' : ' + event);
        } else {
                //Macs don't pass the filename
                console.log(path + ' : ' + event);
        }
});
```

This will produce a result, if you are altering the contents of the file to some simplistic degree, that will look similar to the console output that is shown in Listing 3-36.

Listing 3-36. Watching a file

```
$ node 3-10-1.js
3-10/file.txt : change
3-10/file.txt : change
size altered. prev: 14 curr: 19
atime altered. prev: Sun May 05 2013 14:04:37 GMT-0400 (EDT) curr: Sun May 05 2013 14:07:23 GMT-0400
(EDT)
mtime altered. prev: Sun May 05 2013 14:04:37 GMT-0400 (EDT) curr: Sun May 05 2013 14:07:22 GMT-0400
(EDT)
ctime altered. prev: Sun May 05 2013 14:04:37 GMT-0400 (EDT) curr: Sun May 05 2013 14:07:22 GMT-0400
(EDT)
```

How It Works

First, you see the fs.watchFile function. This function takes a path argument and a callback that will provide the current and previous states of the file you are watching. Performing a long-polling fs.stat call on the file does this. This is configured by an optional second argument, which is an options object, defaulting to { persistent: true, interval: 5007 } and allowing for a continual or persistent interval to poll.

The fs.watchFile function creates a new StatWatcher object (Listing 3-37), which polls the stat object of the file on the set interval. These stats are returned in the listener callback if a change occurs on the StatWatcher. This will return previous and current versions of the file stat. Even if the file previously did not exist, it will show up with an add date, stat.atime, with the value: Wed Dec 31 1969 19:00:00 GMT-0500 (EST) (the beginning of the UNIX epoch).

Listing 3-37. StatWatcher EventEmitter

```
function StatWatcher() {
  EventEmitter.call(this);

  var self = this;
  this._handle = new binding.StatWatcher();

  // uv_fs_poll is a little more powerful than ev_stat but we curb it for
  // the sake of backwards compatibility
  var oldStatus = -1;

  this._handle.onchange = function(current, previous, newStatus) {
    if (oldStatus === -1 &&
        newStatus === -1 &&
        current.nlink === previous.nlink) return;

    oldStatus = newStatus;
    self.emit('change', current, previous);
  };

  this._handle.onstop = function() {
    self.emit('stop');
  };
}
util.inherits(StatWatcher, EventEmitter);

StatWatcher.prototype.start = function(filename, persistent, interval) {
  nullCheck(filename);
  this._handle.start(pathModule._makeLong(filename), persistent, interval);
};

StatWatcher.prototype.stop = function() {
  this._handle.stop();
};
```

In the solution you see that for each time the listener files, the current stat is traversed and compared against the previous. Then for each key in the current object that is different from that in the previous stat of the file (see Listing 3-38).

Listing 3-38. Traversing through the files to find altered state.

```
for (var key in current) {
        if (current[key] !== previous[key]) {
                console.log(key + ' altered. prev: ' + previous[key] + ' curr: ' + current[key]);
        }
}
```

The option to choose between this, `fs.watchFile`, and `fs.watch` is not clear-cut. Both of these solutions are still considered unstable. While `fs.watchFile` can return a full stat detail of the file being watched, it is limited to the polling functionality and thus is much slower to return that `fs.watch`, which you will see next.

The `fs.watch` function creates an FSWatcher, shown in Listing 3-39, which is a Node.js `EventEmitter`, which is similar to the `StatWatcher` `EventEmitter` in that it will produce and emit a change event when a file modification is detected.

Listing 3-39. Creating a New FSWatcher

```
watcher = new FSWatcher();
watcher.start(filename, options.persistent);

if (listener) {
  watcher.addListener('change', listener);
}
```

FSWatcher creates a new FSEvent handle on a file or directory. The FSWatcher then binds to this handle's 'change' event (see Listing 3-40).

Listing 3-40. FSWatcher

```
function FSWatcher() {
  EventEmitter.call(this);

  var self = this;
  var FSEvent = process.binding('fs_event_wrap').FSEvent;
  this._handle = new FSEvent();
  this._handle.owner = this;

  this._handle.onchange = function(status, event, filename) {
    if (status) {
      self._handle.close();
      self.emit('error', errnoException(process._errno, 'watch'));
    } else {
      self.emit('change', event, filename);
    }
  };
}
util.inherits(FSWatcher, EventEmitter);

FSWatcher.prototype.start = function(filename, persistent) {
  nullCheck(filename);
  var r = this._handle.start(pathModule._makeLong(filename), persistent);
```

```
    if (r) {
      this._handle.close();
      throw errnoException(process._errno, 'watch');
    }
};
```

The FSWatcher that is created by calling the fs.watch function on a file or directory will emit one of two events: error, or change. The change event is what your listener function is bound to in Listing 3-40. This callback provides an event and a file name (or directory), which had that event happen to it. The event can be "changed" or "renamed". This is lacking information from the fs.watchFile function that, as you saw, provides an entire stat object for the changed file.

CHAPTER 4

Building a Web Server

Web servers are the quintessential applications to be built with Node.js. This is due to Node.js's main goal. Node.js is perfect for building highly scalable, event-driven, networked applications—a web server.

In this chapter you will learn and understand how to build a web server with Node.js. You will see topics covered from simple web servers to handling static files on your server. These topics are only parts of making a web server work properly. To get a full understanding of the web server as it can be implemented via Node.js, you will also learn the following:

- Creating a Secure Sockets Layer (SSL) server with HTTPS

- Configuring headers

- Managing HTTP status codes

- Processing HTTP requests and responses

- Using HTTP events to manage your web server

4-1. Setting Up an HTTP Server
Problem

You need to create a simple web server that is to serve content over HTTP.

Solution

In Node.js, web servers are typically set up by using the HTTP module. This provides a layer in which to interact with the HTTP protocol.

Imagine that you are writing a web server that will send a status message to the client when you connect to the web server. In this solution, Listing 4-1, this has been simplified to simply write the response 'hello' and then end the response.

Listing 4-1. Simple HTTP Web Server

```
/**
* Setting up an HTTP server
*/

var http = require('http');
```

```
var server = http.createServer(function(req, res) {
        res.write('hello');
        res.end();
});

server.listen(8080);
```

How It Works

This web server is overly simplified so you can investigate how the HTTP module creates a server. In the solution you naturally start off by requiring the http module. This module exposes a function, http.createServer, which is where the server is actually created. The http.createServer method instantiates a new Server object. The Server object accepts a requestListener callback function. This will send the response and the request arguments to the callback for the web server.

The new web server is an HTTP server that derives from the net.Server object that you saw in Chapter 2. The server also provides event listeners for the events, connection, request, and clientError.

Listing 4-2. Server Source, Instantiated by createServer

```
function Server(requestListener) {
  if (!(this instanceof Server)) return new Server(requestListener);
  net.Server.call(this, { allowHalfOpen: true });

  if (requestListener) {
    this.addListener('request', requestListener);
  }

  // Similar option to this. Too lazy to write my own docs.
  // http://www.squid-cache.org/Doc/config/half_closed_clients/
  // http://wiki.squid-cache.org/SquidFaq/InnerWorkings#What_is_a_half-closed_filedescriptor.3F
  this.httpAllowHalfOpen = false;

  this.addListener('connection', connectionListener);

  this.addListener('clientError', function(err, conn) {
    conn.destroy(err);
  });

  this.timeout = 2 * 60 * 1000;
}
util.inherits(Server, net.Server);

Server.prototype.setTimeout = function(msecs, callback) {
  this.timeout = msecs;
  if (callback)
    this.on('timeout', callback);
};

exports.Server = Server;
```

You have created your web server. Next, tell the server where you want to listen for requests. This is done via `server.listen`. The `server.listen` function takes a port as well as an optional hostname, backlog, and a callback. The callback function for the `server.listen` method will listen for the 'listening' event. Providing a hostname will tell the server where you will be listening for requests to the given port.

■ **Note**   There are two other signatures for `server.listen`. One alternative is to provide only a UNIX path and a callback. This will begin a socket server on the path. The other is to provide a handle—either a socket or a server—which will then become the new server.

Once your server is listening, you can serve your response from the server. Within the request listener callback that you provided to the `http.createServer` method are two arguments. These arguments represent the HTTP request and the HTTP response that is being served. In the solution, you wanted to create a web server to send a response to the 'hello' connection . This is done by streaming a `res.write('hello')` function. This will render on the client once the `response.end()` function is called.

`Response.write` sends the chunk of the response body as the first parameter. The optional second parameter is used to set the character encoding of this chunk. You might think that a `response.write` is all that is needed for the response, but that thinking is incorrect. In fact, you need—for every response—to call the `response.end()` function.

4-2. Using SSL to Build an HTTPS Server

Problem

You created a web server, but you want to add the extra level of security by using an SSL-encrypted connection to serve your content over HTTPS.

Solution

In order to build an SSL server, you need to have a couple of items in order before you begin. First your client and server must execute a Transport Layer Security (TLS) handshake. To accomplish this you need to have a certificate and key generated in order to authenticate your HTTPS session. These keys are exchanged between the client and the server. Once the keys are exchanged, the process of authenticating and validating the session initiates. Once the keys are deemed valid, the session continues over HTTPS just as a normal HTTP connection would, only with the additional layer of security.

From there, you can use the HTTPS module in Node.js. This module will act similarly to the HTTP module, but the connection is encrypted via TLS/SSL. You then create an HTTPS server via Node.js as shown in Listing 4-3.

Listing 4-3. HTTPS Server

```
/**
* HTTPS server
*/
var https = require('https');
var fs = require('fs');

var options = {
  key: fs.readFileSync('privatekey.pem'),
  cert: fs.readFileSync('certificate.pem')
};
```

```
https.createServer(options, function (req, res) {
  res.writeHead(200);
  res.write("https!\n");
  res.end();
}).listen(8080);
```

How It Works

Creating an HTTPS connection starts with TLS/SSL. This protocol ensures a secure communication between the client and the server. This occurs because there is a handshake between client and server in which the server reveals its certificate and public key to the client. Then when the client sends a response, it is encrypted with the server's public key, which is validated. If all the data are evaluated to be valid, the session continues over HTTPS.

But how do you obtain these certificates and keys? In Node.js the SSL/TLS implementation utilizes OpenSSL. OpenSSL is an open source implementation of SSL/TLS. This is a protocol that will enable you to easily implement a key and certificate. In order to generate such a key, you will need to open your terminal and enter the commands as shown in Listing 4-4.

Listing 4-4. Creating TLS/SSL Keys and Certificates

```
$ openssl genrsa -out privatekey.pem 1024
$ openssl req -new -key privatekey.pem -out certrequest.csr
$ openssl x509 -req -in certrequest.csr -signkey privatekey.pem -out certificate.pem
```

On Windows this is slightly different, because Windows does not include an OpenSSL implementation by default. You should first download a binary distribution from http://openssl.org/related/binaries.html. By default, this will install to C:\OpenSSL-Win32 on your machine. From there you can open up PowerShell and run the following from the C:\OpenSSL-Win32\bin directory.

```
PS C:\OpenSSL-Win32\bin> .\openssl.exe genrsa -out privatekey.pem 1024
PS C:\OpenSSL-Win32\bin> .\openssl.exe req –new –key .\privatekey.pem –out certrequest.csr
PS C:\OpenSSL-Win32\bin> .\openssl.exe x509 -req -in .\certrequest.csr -signkey .\privatekey.pem
-out certificate.pem
```

Once you have created your certificate and your key, you are now able to create your secure server. This begins with the https.createServer method. This function is similar to the http.createServer method with a notable exception to create a secure connection. This is done via an options object. The options used in this example set the certificate and the key for the creation of the tls.Server. You will see more detail with respect to SSL and TLS in Chapter 6. To actually read the values of the key and certificate files you read them using the file system, as discussed in Chapter 3. Once these are read, you can create your server.

Listing 4-5. HTTPS Server Inherits tls.Server

```
function Server(opts, requestListener) {
  if (!(this instanceof Server)) return new Server(opts, requestListener);

  if (process.features.tls_npn && !opts.NPNProtocols) {
    opts.NPNProtocols = ['http/1.1', 'http/1.0'];
  }

  tls.Server.call(this, opts, http._connectionListener);

  this.httpAllowHalfOpen = false;
```

```
  if (requestListener) {
    this.addListener('request', requestListener);
  }

  this.addListener('clientError', function(err, conn) {
    conn.destroy(err);
  });

  this.timeout = 2 * 60 * 1000;
}
inherits(Server, tls.Server);
```

Once the server is created, you should be able to access it with SSL connections. To test this, simply curl the server address and you should see the response 'https!' written to your console. If, on the other hand you don't attempt to reach the HTTPS version of your server, you will not get the expected result from the server.

Listing 4-6. Use cURL to View Your Secure Connection

```
$ curl -k https://localhost:8080 # works
https!

$ curl http://localhost:8080 # nope
curl: (52) Empty response from the server
```

4-3. Processing Requests on Your Server
Problem
You have an HTTP or HTTPS server. This server will need to process incoming requests.

Solution
When you build a web server, you need to handle requests. Requests come in many forms and contain what can quickly become an overwhelming set of data. In handling requests you need to be able to sift through the incoming data efficiently in order to handle headers, methods, and URL parameters.

In this solution, you will create a web server that handles requests. It will likely look similar to many web servers that you are familiar with. This server will handle request headers and deal with them as you see fit. An example of this would be to not send a tracking cookie if the request header contains the "do not track" directive.

After properly handling the headers, you will likely want to parse the request URLs. This will help you handle 404s and general application routing by processing the incoming path. Aside from the path you may also find interest in the query string parameters that were sent along with the request.

Finally, you will want to examine the request method that initiated the request. This is the HTTP method, and it will be useful when you create any application, or a representational state transfer (REST) application programming interface (API).

Listing 4-7. Handling Requests

```
/**
* Processing Requests
*/
var http = require('http'),
                url = require('url');

var server = http.createServer(function(req, res) {
        //Handle headers
        if (req.headers.dnt == 1) {
                console.log('Do Not Track');
        }

        //Parse the URL
        var url_parsed = url.parse(req.url, true);

            //What type of request is this
    if (req.method === 'GET') {
        handleGetRequest(res, url_parsed);
    } else if (['POST', 'PUT', 'DELETE'].indexOf(req.method) > -1) {
        handleApiRequest(res, url_parsed, req.method);
    } else {
        res.end('Method not supported');
    }

});

handleGetRequest = function(res, url_parsed) {
    console.log('search: ' + url_parsed.search);
    console.log('query: ' + JSON.stringify(url_parsed.query));
    console.log('pathname: ' + url_parsed.pathname);
    console.log('path: ' + url_parsed.path);
    console.log('href: ' + url_parsed.href);
    res.end('get\n');
};

handleApiRequest = function(res, url_parsed, method) {
    if (url_parsed.path !== '/api') {
        res.statusCode = 404;
        res.end('404\n');
    }
    res.end(method);
};

server.listen(8080);
```

How It Works

The web server in this solution is built to handle requests. It does this by examining the details that surround the request received by the server. This request is in actuality an object known as the http.IncomingMessage.

The http.IncomingMessage inherits the readable stream interface. On top of this, it builds some objects that are useful in the case of HTTP messages, as shown in Listing 4-8.

Listing 4-8. http.IncomingMessage

```
function IncomingMessage(socket) {
  Stream.Readable.call(this);

  this.socket = socket;
  this.connection = socket;

  this.httpVersion = null;
  this.complete = false;
  this.headers = {};
  this.trailers = {};

  this.readable = true;

  this._pendings = [];
  this._pendingIndex = 0;

  // request (server) only
  this.url = '';
  this.method = null;

  // response (client) only
  this.statusCode = null;
  this.client = this.socket;

  this._consuming = false;

  this._dumped = false;
}
util.inherits(IncomingMessage, Stream.Readable);
```

As you can see from the source, the http.IncomingMessage brings with it several objects or settings that are important to your solution. First, it brings the headers. The request headers are objects that directly reflect the key-value pairs that were sent with the request. When I attempt to send a request to this server from my web browser, the headers look as shown in Listing 4-9.

Listing 4-9. Typical Request Headers

```
{ host: 'localhost:8080',
  'user-agent': 'Mozilla/5.0 (Macintosh; Intel Mac OS X 10.7; rv:20.0) Gecko/20100101 Firefox/20.0',
  accept: 'text/html,application/xhtml+xml,application/xml;q=0.9,*/*;q=0.8',
  'accept-language': 'en-us,en;q=0.5',
  'accept-encoding': 'gzip, deflate',
  dnt: '1',
  connection: 'keep-alive' }
```

Second, in your web server you need to handle the `request.url`. This contains all the information that is sent via the request URL. The easiest way to parse this is to utilize the URL module. You can tell the URL module to parse the request.url including the query string.

The third part of the request that can be valuable for your server is the `request.method`. `request.method` will provide you with the HTTP method that began your request. In the solution the web server was set up to imitate a web API. In a case such as this, the routing of API methods is not determined completely by the path of the URL but also by the `request.method`. These methods are simply the string names of the HTTP methods. Your solution handles these different methods in two different ways. First, you serve an HTTP GET request; using that will then log some of the details of the request and respond that the method was indeed a GET. Second, you mimic an API routing scheme with other methods. These are handled by a singular function that will check to make sure you are requesting not only the proper method but also the path. As you can see in the solution these are each handled in such a way that you could cURL each type to see a different result as you see in Listing 4-10.

Listing 4-10. Curling for different results

```
$ curl -X PUT http://localhost:8080/api
put
$ curl -X PUT http://localhost:8080/apis
404
$ curl -X DELETE http://localhost:8080/api
delete
$ curl -X TRACE http://localhost:8080/api
Method not supported
```

By understanding the information that accompanies an `http.request` in Node.js, you are able to leverage this to build your web server to handle these requests. Next, you will see how to send responses from your server.

4-4. Sending Responses from Your Server
Problem

You have your web server, but now you need to be able to send information from the server in the form of a response.

Solution

A server response is a Node.js `EventEmitter` object that is emitted as part of the request event. In this solution you will utilize the response object to directly write the content to the requester. First, you want to send an HTML document. You can do this by creating a response and sending the HTML content directly.

Listing 4-11. Response.write of HTML

```
/**
* Sending a response from your server
*/

var http = require('http');

var server = http.createServer(function(req, res) {

        res.setHeader('Content-Type', 'text/html');
        res.writeHead(200, 'woot');
        res.write('<!doctype html>');
```

```
        res.write('<html>');
        res.write('<head><meta charset="utf-8"></head>');
        res.write('<body>');
        res.write('<h2>Hello World</h2>');
        res.write('</body></html>');
        res.end();
});

server.listen(8080);
```

You are now serving HTML content directly in your response. You may need to be able to send other types of content to provide the robust solution for your application. In this case you choose to send a JavaScript Object Notation (JSON)-encoded object so the client can retrieve information from your server. This is similar in implementation with a few minor changes that you will see in detail in the How It Works section.

Listing 4-12. A JSON serverResponse

```
var http = require('http');

var server = http.createServer(function(req, res) {

        res.setHeader('Content-Type', 'application/json');
        res.writeHead(200, 'json content');
        res.write('{ "wizard": "mithrandir" }');
        res.end();
});

server.listen(8080);
```

How It Works

You now are serving content from your web server by using the serverResponse object. This object, as utilized in this solution, carries with it some valuable functions. The first line within the requestListener callback is response.setHeader. The setHeader function does exactly what the name implies; it sets the headers for the response. These are set in a name and value pairing, res.setHeader('Name', 'Value');.

In the solutions, you set the Content-Type header to define the type of content that was being sent with your request. You can also set cookies, custom header parameters, or anything that would accompany a request header from your server.

The other method that is utilized in this solution to set the response headers is the response.writeHead method. This method does not limit your header creation to a single name and value pair. This method takes up to three arguments. The first argument, which is required, sets the HTTP status code for the response. You then have the option to set a custom description, or reason phrase, that corresponds to the status code description. This can be any reason phrase you wish, departing from the HTTP standard descriptions.

Listing 4-13. HTTP Reason Phrase Override in Node.js

```
if (typeof arguments[1] == 'string') {
    reasonPhrase = arguments[1];
    headerIndex = 2;
  } else {
    reasonPhrase = STATUS_CODES[statusCode] || 'unknown';
    headerIndex = 1;
  }
```

The third parameter is actually a header object that will take the name and value pairs, not just individual name-value pairs, as an entire object. To refactor the solution for the JSON serverResponse above, you could simply make one call to response.writeHead to get the same result.

Listing 4-14. Combining HTTP Status Code, Reason Phrase, and Headers in a response.writeHead Call

```
res.writeHead(200, 'json content', {
        'Content-Type': 'application/json'});
```

You then send a body of your response to the client by using response.write. This function will take a string that represents a chunk of the response body. The second parameter of response.write is to set the encoding of the response, which defaults to utf8. The response.write does not require that you have already set the header via the previously mentioned methods. If the header is not explicitly set, the response.write method will implicitly define the header with a status code of 200. The write method then ensures that the headers have been sent. If the headers have not been sent, then they are sent along with the initial write of the data to the client.

Listing 4-15. If Headers Aren't Already Sent, Send Them with the First Chunk

```
if (!this._headerSent) {
  if (typeof data === 'string') {
    data = this._header + data;
  } else {
    this.output.unshift(this._header);
    this.outputEncodings.unshift('ascii');
  }
  this._headerSent = true;
}
return this._writeRaw(data, encoding);
```

You now have seen and executed the methods for sending a response from your web server. These options are just a subset of what is possible with HTTP responses. The full list of what is available for use is shown in Table 4-1.

Table 4-1. HTTP serverResponse Methods

Method	Description
response.addTrailers(headers)	Adds HTTP trailing headers (a header but at the end of the message) to the response. Trailers will only be emitted if chunked encoding is used for the response; if it is not (e.g., if the request was HTTP/1.0), they will be silently discarded.
response.end([data], [encoding])	Signals to the server that all of the response headers and body have been sent; the server should consider the message complete. The method, response.end(), *must* be called on each response.
response.getHeader(name)	Reads out a header that's already been queued but not sent to the client. Note that the name is case-insensitive. This can only be called before headers get implicitly flushed.

(continued)

Table 4-1. (*continued*)

Method	Description
response.headersSent	Boolean (read-only). It is true if headers were sent, but false otherwise.
response.removeHeader(name)	Removes a header that's queued for implicit sending.
response.sendDate	When true, the Date header will be automatically generated and sent in the response if it is not already present in the headers. Defaults to true.
response.setHeader(name, value)	Sets a single header value for implicit headers. If this header already exists in the to-be-sent headers, its value will be replaced. Use an array of strings here if you need to send multiple headers with the same name.
response.setTimeout(milliseconds, callback)	Sets the socket's timeout value to milliseconds. If a callback is provided, then it is added as a listener on the 'timeout' event on the response object.
response.statusCode	When using implicit headers (not calling response.writeHead() explicitly), this property controls the status code that will be sent to the client when the headers get flushed.
response.write(chunk, [encoding])	Sends a chunk of the response body. This method may be called multiple times to provide successive parts of the body.
writeContinue()	Sends an HTTP/1.1 100 Continue message to the client, indicating that the request body should be sent.
writeHead(statusCode, [reasonPhrase], [headers])	Sends the response header to the request.

4-5. Handling Headers and Status Codes

Problem

In building a Node.js web application, you will need to be able to properly deliver and handle header information and HTTP status codes.

Solution

In the scenario created for this solution, you can imagine a situation where you need to serve a particular type of file for your web application. This situation could arise when you are building a web application that you wish to publish to a hosted web application store or marketplace such as a Chrome or Firefox OS application.

In this situation you might provide an application manifest file. This is typically in the form of a JSON file that sets the details of the application in order to make it installable on the hosting platform. This requires a particular header type in order for the hosting platform to recognize this file as a manifest. So in this solution you will manipulate the headers to represent the content type appropriately as well as handle the proper status codes for your application.

Listing 4-16. Handling Headers and Status Codes

```
/**
* Headers and status codes
*/
var http = require('http');
          url = require('url');

var server = http.createServer(function(req, res) {

        if (req.headers) {
                console.log('request headers', req.headers);
        }

        var parsedUrl = url.parse(req.url);
        if (parsedUrl.path === '/manifest.webapp' && req.method === 'GET') {
                // serving an application manifest file type
                res.writeHead(200, { 'Content-Type' : 'application/x-web-app-manifest+json' });
                res.write('{ "name" : "App" }');
                res.write( '"description": "My elevator pitch goes here",');
                res.write('"launch_path": "/",');
                res.write('"icons": {');
                res.write('"128": "/img/icon-128.png" },');
                res.write('"developer": {');
                res.write(' "name": "Your name or organization",');
                res.write(' "url": "http://your-homepage-here.org" },');
                res.write('"default_locale": "en" }');
                res.end();
        } else if (parsedUrl.path !== '/') {
                res.statusCode = 404;
                res.end(http.STATUS_CODES[res.statusCode]);
        } else {
                res.writeHead(200, { 'Content-Type': 'text/html'});
                res.end('<h2>normalContent</h2>');
        }

});

server.listen(8080);
```

How It Works

This solution is designed to do two things. First, it is designed to serve static HTML from the root of the application, url path = '/'. Second, it is designed to serve a webapp.manifest file, or what you would write to package your application to be hosted on an app marketplace. To do this correctly, you need to control the headers and the status codes.

The status codes are important because they provide the information regarding the state of your response to the client. The status codes call into one of five categories segregated by each block of integers starting with 100. Status codes in the 100 range are informational codes; codes in the 200 range are the codes representing success; 300 range codes represent redirection. Errors are represented by status codes in the 400 range for client errors, and the 500 range for server errors.

In this solution your application is designed to serve only content from the root of your web app, or the manifest file itself. Other paths that your server is requested for will result in a 404 status code. This status code is a client error indicating that the path is not found.

Listing 4-17. Setting a 404 Not Found statusCode

```
if (parsedUrl.path !== '/') {
        res.statusCode = 404;
        res.end(http.STATUS_CODES[res.statusCode]);
}
```

This response is written with the data that are passed along with the `response.end` method. This utilizes the `http.STATUS_CODES` object, which will find the corresponding status code reason description for the passed `response.statusCode`.

The URLs that you are targeting will both return a 200 or "OK" status code. The first of these is for the root of your web application. Along with the status code, you want to serve this root as an HTML document. This is controlled not only by the content that you serve, but also the headers.

Controlling the headers is important when serving content from any type of web server because the headers direct the client how to handle content, or what to do with the content once it is handled. Examples of this are the Content-Type header, directing the request how to serve the content; Cache-Control header, which tells the client how to handle caching the content; and Content-Length, which indicates the length of the request. These are just three of the standard and nonstandard header names that can be set in the request in Node.js.

In this solution, when you were sending the application manifest file, you sent a custom nonstandardized header: { 'Content-Type' : 'application/x-web-app-manifest+json' }. This header indicated that the content was of application manifest type and expects to be a JSON file. If you are in the root of your application, the response serves a Content-Type header of 'text/html', which as you can probably assume, is meant to be an HTML document. Of course, you could add any additional headers you need to these responses, but it is important to know that the Content-Type of certain responses—such as the manifest file—are required to be precise.

4-6. Creating an HTTP Client
Problem

You want to create a Node.js application that will act as an HTTP client.

Solution

Creating an HTTP client out of a Node.js application is as straightforward as creating an HTTP server. In this solution you will begin by setting the options for your client. These options tell your application where to send the request and by what means to fetch it. You do this so that you can communicate with the REST API you created for your application in Section 4-3. This will parse a set of arguments, determine which method and path to send to the API, then process the `http.request`.

Listing 4-18. HTTP Client

```
/*
 * Creating an HTTP client
 */

var http = require('http'),
            args = process.argv.slice(2);
```

```
//Set defaults
var clientOptions = {
       host: 'localhost',
       // hostname:'nodejs.org',
       port: '8080',
       path: '/',
       method: 'GET'
};

args.forEach(function(arg) {
       switch(arg) {
              case 'GET':
                     clientOptions.method = 'GET';
                     break;
              case 'SUBMIT':
              case 'POST':
                     clientOptions.method = 'POST';
                     clientOptions.path = '/api';
                     break;
              case 'UPDATE':
              case 'PUT':
                     clientOptions.path = '/api';
                     clientOptions.method = 'PUT';
                     break;
              case 'REMOVE':
              case 'DELETE':
                     clientOptions.method = 'DELETE';
                     clientOptions.path = '/api';
                     break;
              default:
                     clientOptions.method = 'GET';
                     clientOptions.path = '/';
       }

       var clientReq = http.request(clientOptions, function(res) {
              console.log('status code', res.statusCode);
              switch(res.statusCode) {
                     case 200:
                            res.setEncoding('utf8');
                            res.on('data', function(data) {
                                   console.log('data', data);
                            });
                            break;
                     case 404:
                            console.log('404 error');
                            break;
              }
       });
```

```
        clientReq.on('error', function(error) {
                throw error;
        });

        clientReq.end();
});
```

How It Works

This works by leveraging the Node.js HTTP module. This module provides an interface to easily create a client request, http.request. In the solution, you first utilize the process.argv to strip out any relevant command-line arguments that initiated your application. For this example you simply instantiate the application passing the HTTP method you wish to provide and the application will loop through these, creating a request for each.

```
$ node 4-6-1.js GET POST PUT DELETE NOTHING
```

If you are targeting the server that you created in Section 4-3, you can see a similar result to the following, showing that you successfully hit the API endpoint that your client requested.

```
status code 200
data get

status code 200
data get

status code 200
data post

status code 200
data put

status code 200
data delete
```

That covers how the implementation works, but now you will see how Node.js processes an http.request. The http.request takes two arguments, an options object, and a callback function that will receive the response.

When you invoke http.request, you initialize a ClientRequest object. The ClientRequest object inherits from the Node.js OutgoingMessage object. The ClientRequest object has a full set of defaults that are processed based on what you pass into the options parameter. As you walk through the ClientResponse object, you will see these defaults becoming configured.

Table 4-2. *ClientRequest Object Options*

Option	Function
agent	Controls agent behavior. When an agent is used, the request will default to Connection: keep-alive.
auth	Basic authentication (i.e., 'user:password').
headers	An object containing request headers.
host	A domain name or IP address of the server to issue the request to (defaults to 'localhost').
hostname	To support url.parse(), a hostname is preferred over a host.
localAddress	Local interface to bind for network connections.
method	A string specifying the HTTP request method (defaults to GET).
path	Request path (defaults to '/'). Should include a query string if any.
port	Port of remote server (defaults to 80).
socketPath	Unix domain socket (use one of host:port or socketPath).

The callback function that is passed to the `http.request` function will be called from within the `ClientRequest` object, only when the response is returned. You also set up an event listener for the error event in order to capture any errors that may occur during the request. Once the response is returned, you handle the response. In the case of this example, you check the `statusCodes` and log accordingly. You will see more on handling the responses in the next section.

It is important to note that for a `clientResponse` to work you must call the `request.end()` function. This is necessary regardless of the amount of data that are sent via the request body because you must signify the end of the request.

4-7. Processing Client Responses
Problem

You have created an HTTP client; you now need to understand how to handle the client responses.

Solution

Properly handling the response that you have received on your HTTP client is important. You need to respond to things like status codes, or particular headers upon which your application depends.

For this solution you can imagine a scenario in which your HTTP client needs to look for a custom header set by the server, `x-ample`, which, if set to the proper value, will alert the client to perform a special action. You then will check the status codes to ensure you have a good response before performing your action.

Listing 4-19. Processing Responses

```
/**
* Processing client responses
*/

var http = require('http');
```

```
var clientOptions = {
        host: 'localhost',
        port: '8080',
        path: '/',
        method: 'GET'
};

var clientReq = http.request(clientOptions, function(res) {
        //Handle custom header for something special
        if (res.headers['x-ample'] === 'trigger') {
                console.log('x-ample header trigger');

                //work with status codes
                switch(res.statusCode) {
                      case 200:
                                res.setEncoding('utf8'); // unless you can read buffer chunks
                                res.on('data', function(data) {
                                        console.log('data', data);
                                });
                                break;
                      case 404:
                                console.log('404 error');
                                break;
                      default:
                                console.log(res.statusCode + ': ' + http.STATUS_CODES[res.statusCode]);
                                break;
                }
        } else {
                console.log('required header not present');
        }
});

clientReq.on('error', function(error) {
        throw error;
});

clientReq.setHeader('Cache-Control', 'no-cache');
clientReq.end();
```

How It Works

The callback function on the http.request function is an event handler for the 'response' event. This event listener is the only way to receive data from the server response. If you omit the 'response' listener or callback, your client request will never receive any data from the server.

Once you have set up a client request with the proper listener to the 'response' event, you then are able to get the data from the response. The response is a readable stream, so you are able to process the data either by adding a listener for the 'data' event or by calling response.read() once the stream becomes "readable."

In this example, you avoid reading the data from the response directly until you have examined a certain value from the response. One of these values is to inspect the headers that are sent from the response. Because the response is a readable stream that contains the headers object, you simply check for the header wish to parse; compare its value against the value required in your application.

Listing 4-20. Response Headers

```
if (res.headers['x-ample'] === 'trigger') {
        console.log('x-ample header trigger');
        /* . . . */
}
```

You then continue on with the processing of the response. In this solution the next step is to check the response status code. If the status code is anything besides a 200 OK, you will not read the data from the response. Of course, if everything checks out, you will read the response body.

Listing 4-21. Response Status Codes

```
switch(res.statusCode) {
        case 200:
                res.setEncoding('utf8');
                res.on('data', function(data) {
                        console.log('data', data);
                });
                break;
        case 404:
                console.log('404 error');
                break;
        default:
                console.log(res.statusCode + ': ' + http.STATUS_CODES[res.statusCode]);
                break;
}
```

Reading the response is done in two steps. First, for the purpose of making the response readable, set the encoding to UTF-8.

Listing 4-22. Response Default Encoding

```
data <Buffer 67 65 74 0a>
```

Listing 4-23. Response UTF-8 Encoded

```
data get
```

By strategically reviewing the response object that is returned to your HTTP request callback, you can handle a variety of parameters and tasks that are specific to your Node.js solution.

4-8. Processing Client Requests

Problem

You have created an HTTP client, and you have learned how to handle responses from it. Now you need to control your client requests in greater detail.

Solution

You start off by building an HTTP GET request. A GET request can be formed in two ways. First, if you do not need to control custom headers or when to send the `request.end()` event, you can swiftly implement an HTTP GET request with Node.js by using `http.get()`.

Listing 4-24. Using http.get()

```
var http = require('http');

var getReq = http.get('http://localhost:8080', function(res) {
  console.log('status code', res.statusCode, ': ', http.STATUS_CODES[res.statusCode]);
});

getReq.on('error', function(err) {
        console.log(err);
});
```

Alternatively, if you need to be able to control certain aspects of your headers, but you still just need to process an HTTP GET request, you will want to use the full `http.request` method instead.

Listing 4-25. HTTP GET Using http.request

```
var http = require('http');

var clientOptions = {
  host: 'localhost',
  port: '8080',
  path: '/',
  method: 'GET',
  headers: { 'Connection': 'keep-alive',
             'Content-Length': 0 }
};

var clientReq = http.request(clientOptions, function(res) {
  console.log('status code', res.statusCode, ': ', http.STATUS_CODES[res.statusCode]);
});

clientReq.on('continue', function(res) {
        console.log('continue event due to 100-continue');
});
```

```
clientReq.on('error', function(error) {
  throw error;
});

clientReq.end();
```

As you build a Node.js application you may encounter the situation at some point where you need to process a data upload. In Node.js you would process this http.request with the POST method. This request then writes the upload with the request.write function.

Listing 4-26. Uploading with an HTTP POST

```
var http = require('http');

var opt = {
        host : 'localhost',
        port : 8080,
        path : '/upload',
        method : 'POST'
};

var upload = http.request(opt, function(res) {
        console.log('status code', res.statusCode, ': ', http.STATUS_CODES[res.statusCode]);
});

upload.on('error', function(err) {
        console.log(err);
});

upload.write('my upload stuff');
upload.end();
```

How It Works

The first solution for retrieving content via a client request is using http.get(). The HTTP GET is an abstraction of the http.request. In fact the http.get() function calls the default http.request, allowing all the default options to be set; it then immediately calls the request.end() method and completes the request.

Listing 4-27. Node.js http Module, GET Method

```
exports.get = function(options, cb) {
  var req = exports.request(options, cb);
  req.end();
  return req;
};
```

Next, you retrieve content via the http.request method with the method option set to 'GET'. This is a standard GET request but you also pass along two specific headers with it. The Connection header with the value set to 'keep-alive' will tell Node.js to keep the connection to the server open until the next request. The other header set in this solution is the Content-Length header. This header, once set, will prevent Node.js from using the default chunked encoding. In the http.request options, there are two other noteworthy headers that are not used in this solution.

One of these headers is the Expect Header. Setting this header will immediately send the request headers in order to account for the potential Expect: 100-continue header, which we will see in more detail when handling events in Section 4-9.

The final noteworthy header for http.request is when you send an authorization header. This header will replace the need for utilizing the auth option when configuring the settings for your http.request.

The last part of your solution for working with HTTP client requests is to demonstrate how to handle a file upload request. To do this, a few things must happen. First, as you might expect, do not utilize the HTTP GET method. Instead, set the method option to HTTP POST for the upload. You then process the upload by sending the data through the http.request's write method.

You now have seen how to handle requests using an HTTP client request on your web server. Next, you will see various events emitted and consumed on your web server.

4-9. Responding to Events
Problem

You have a web server that you have built in Node.js. You now need to handle and properly respond to events that are emitted or listened for on your server.

Solution

To properly represent this solution, you need to understand both sides of the event. To do this you will build both an HTTP web server and an HTTP client.

The server (see Listing 4-28) is built to handle different methods of requests and events. First, your web server will listen for incoming requests. In the event of these requests, you will want to welcome the requester with a plaintext response.

Second, you will want to monitor connections to this server by listening for the connection event. This will then increment the total number of connections that have been made to your server.

You want your server to handle a few special events as well. One of these events is the event that listens for incoming requests that have sent the 'Expect: 100-continue' header. This is for client connections that wish to determine if your server is capable of receiving the message before actually sending the body of the request. The event you need to listen for in this case is the 'checkContinue' event. You will also want to allow for the 'Request: Upgrade' header in order for the request to be upgraded by listening for the 'upgrade' event on your server. The upgrade header can then be sent to upgrade the transport to TLS or, in this case, WebSockets.

Listing 4-28. Web Server Events

```
/**
 * Responding to events
 */

var http = require('http'),
            server = http.createServer(),
            connections = 0;

// request event
server.on('request', function(req, res) {
        console.log('request');//, req);
        res.writeHead(200, { 'Content-Type': 'text/plain'});
        res.end('heyo');
});
```

```
server.on('connection', function(socket) {
        connections++;
        console.log('connection count: ', connections);
});

server.on('checkContinue', function(req, res) {
        console.log('checkContinue');
        res.writeContinue();
});

server.on('upgrade', function(req, socket, head) {
        console.log('upgrade');
        socket.write('HTTP/1.1 101 Web Socket Protocol Handshake\r\n' +
                'Upgrade: WebSocket\r\n' +
                'Connection: Upgrade\r\n' +
                'Sec-WebSocket-Accept: s3pPLMBiTxaQ9kYGzzhZRbK+xOo=\r\n' +
                'Sec-WebSocket-Protocol: chat\r\n' +
                '\r\n');
        socket.pipe(socket);
});

server.listen(8080);
```

In order to properly experience these events you need to have two sets of clients that connect to this server. The first client you will build, Listing 4-22, is one in which you need to provide the events necessary in order to provide both the Expect header, 'Expect: 100-continue', and to properly respond to the continue event emitted from the server.

Listing 4-29. Client Events for Handling Expect: 100-continue

```
/*
* client events
*/

var http = require('http');

var clientOptions = {
        host: 'localhost',
        // hostname:'nodejs.org',
        port: '8080',
        path: '/',
        method: 'GET',
        headers: { 'Expect': '100-continue' }
};

var clientReq = http.request(clientOptions, function(res) {
        console.log('status code', res.statusCode);
        switch(res.statusCode) {
                case 200:
                        res.setEncoding('utf8'); // unless you can read buffer chunks
```

```
                    res.on('data', function(data) {
                            console.log('data', data);
                    });
                    break;
              case 404:
                    console.log('404 error');
                    break;
        }
});

clientReq.on('continue', function() {
        console.log('client continue');
});

clientReq.on('error', function(error) {
        throw error;
});

clientReq.end();
```

The second client you will create to demonstrate the events emitted and consumed by your web server is to create one that will handle the upgrade to a WebSocket server. This happens in the client that you create in Listing 4-30, which is similar in design to Listing 4-29. However, it handles different events to provide a different implementation.

Listing 4-30. Upgrade Client

```
/*
* client events
*/

var http = require('http');

var clientOptions = {
        host: 'localhost',
        // hostname:'nodejs.org',
        port: '8080',
        path: '/',
        method: 'GET',
        headers: { 'Connection': 'Upgrade',
        'Upgrade': 'websocket',
        'Sec-WebSocket-Key': 'dGhlIHNhbXBsZSBub25jZQ==',
        'Origin' :'localhost',
        'Sec-WebSocket-Protocol': 'chat',
        'Sec-WebSocket-Version': 13 }
};

var clientReq = http.request(clientOptions, function(res) {
        console.log('status code', res.statusCode);
        switch(res.statusCode) {
                case 200:
                        res.setEncoding('utf8'); // unless you can read buffer chunks
```

```
                        res.on('data', function(data) {
                                console.log('data', data);
                        });
                        break;
                case 404:
                        console.log('404 error');
                        break;
        }
});

clientReq.on('upgrade', function(res, socket, head) {
        console.log('client upgrade');
});

clientReq.on('error', function(error) {
        throw error;
});

clientReq.end();
```

How It Works

Events are a critical part of building a successful Node.js application. To that point, building a successful web server in Node.js must incorporate a proper handling of events that are emitted between the client and server. In the solution in this section you created a web server that solves multiple problems all at the same time.

This server starts off listening for the request event. This request event is emitted each time there is a request to the server. Once the request is received, you send a response to the requester, in this case a simple greeting. The callback to the request event is one that provides both the request and the response object; in fact, this event is the same as adding the callback to the http.createServer function directly.

Your next listener on this is used to track connections to the server by listening to when the connection event is emitted. This happens each time there is a connection to the server. This occurs when you increment a counter each time there is a connection. The connection event sends the connected socket object along in the callback function, allowing you access to the net.Socket if you desire.

Handling the 'Expect: 100-continue' header happens in the next event listener. This listener is bound to the 'checkContinue' event. This event is emitted only when the request sends an expect header. If you are not listening for this event, the server will send the appropriate continue response itself.

Listing 4-31. Node.js Emitting checkContinue When the Expect Header Is Present

```
if (req.headers.expect !== undefined &&
        (req.httpVersionMajor == 1 && req.httpVersionMinor == 1) &&
        continueExpression.test(req.headers['expect'])) {
    res._expect_continue = true;
    if (EventEmitter.listenerCount(self, 'checkContinue') > 0) {
        self.emit('checkContinue', req, res);
    } else {
        res.writeContinue();
        self.emit('request', req, res);
    }
}
```

If you are handling this event appropriately, you need to signify to the request that it is allowable to continue sending the body of the request. This is done by calling the response.writeContinue() function. This function writes the appropriate HTTP 100 response to the requester.

Listing 4-32. response.writeContinue Sending the HTTP 100 Continue Response

```
ServerResponse.prototype.writeContinue = function() {
  this._writeRaw('HTTP/1.1 100 Continue' + CRLF + CRLF, 'ascii');
  this._sent100 = true;
};
```

This continue event only works if you send the appropriate header, as in the client request from Listing 4-22: headers: { 'expect' : '100-continue' }. You then listen for the connect event from your client request application, signifying when the response.writeContinue() function has been called and the HTTP 100 response has been sent.

Finally, your server is set up to handle an upgrade to the WebSocket protocol. This protocol is initiated through a handshake process handled by events emitted from both your client request and your web server. This process starts when the client sends an upgrade header: headers: { 'Connection': 'Upgrade', 'Upgrade': 'websocket'}. Along with these header fields a WebSocket key is sent that the server will then utilize to validate that the request handshake was received. When this header is present, an 'upgrade' event will be emitted, and you will listen for this upgrade event on your server.

The 'upgrade' event on your server has a callback function with three arguments: the request, the socket, and the header. In order to complete the requesting WebSocket handshake, you must send the appropriate HTTP response. In this case that is a HTTP 101 Web Socket Protocol Handshake with the same upgrade and connection headers. Also sent back is the websocket-accept header, which is a validation of receipt of the key from the request. Once the headers have been sent, then your client can receive an upgrade event as well as complete the WebSocket upgrade handshake.

This upgrade event also introduces the .pipe method on the socket stream. Streams are an integral part to building many Node.js applications. This is a way of managing in a concise and uniform manner the input and the output of a stream. This can occur by taking a source stream that is readable and piping it to a destination stream that is writable. This results in the return of the destination stream. In this upgrade event callback, you write socket.pipe(socket);. This takes the source (or socket) that you have just called socket.write() on in order to add the WebSocket upgrade headers. It then pipes that out to .pipe(socket), which represents the destination stream.

4-10. Serving a Static Page via the File System
Problem

You are building a web server. Serving HTML directly from your Node.js code is not maintainable or desirable. You need to be able to serve your content from files that reside on the file system itself.

Solution

To build a web server that serves content, you need to leverage both the HTTP module and the file system module that are part of the Node.js core. You will build your server to handle errors on the server, and you can then respond with the proper status codes. You will also be sure to send the appropriate response headers with your files you are serving. This means you need to be mindful of the mime type of the content you are serving. To do this, use a simple URL structure to know what routes in your application will request which types of files from your web server.

Listing 4-33. A Static File Web Server

```
/**
* serving static HTML with the file system
*/

var http = require('http'),
    fs = require('fs'),
    path = require('path');

//Content types map
var contentTypes = {
    '.htm'  : 'text/html',
    '.html' : 'text/html',
    '.js'   : 'text/javascript',
    '.json' : 'application/json',
    '.css'  : 'text/css'
};

var server = http.createServer(function(req, res) {

    var fileStream = fs.createReadStream(req.url.split('/')[1]);

    fileStream.on('error', function(error) {
        if (error.code === 'ENOENT') {
            res.statusCode = 404;
            res.end(http.STATUS_CODES[404]);
        } else {
            res.statusCode = 500;
            res.end(http.STATUS_CODES[500]);
        }
    });
    //Get the extension
    var extension = path.extname(req.url);

    //read the extension against the content type map - default to plain text
    var contentType = contentTypes[extension] || 'text/plain';

    // add the content type header
    res.writeHead(200, { 'Content-Type' : contentType });

    // pipe the stream to the response stream
    fileStream.pipe(res);

});

server.listen(8080);
```

You now have a web server from which to serve static files from the file system. To test this functionality, you need to build two test files as well. One will be the base HTML file. The second is a JSON file. This file is to represent the response of a hypothetical API you may build to be accessed from your application. These files are shown in Listings 4-34 and 4-35.

Listing 4-34. Base HTML File to Serve

```
<!doctype html>
<html>
<head>
<title>Static HTML</title>
</head>
<body>
        <h2>Node.js Recipes</h2>
        <p> Tasty </p>
        <button id='getJSON'>Get JSON file</button>
        <script type='text/javascript'>
                // bind to click
                var btn = document.getElementById('getJSON');
                btn.addEventListener('click', getJSONContent, false);
                // Send a request to the server for the JSON file
                function getJSONContent() {
                        var xhr = new XMLHttpRequest();
                        xhr.onload = jsonRetrieved;
                        xhr.open('GET', '/4-10-1.json', true);
                        xhr.send();
                }
                // Log to the console
                function jsonRetrieved() {
                        console.log(this.responseText);
                }
        </script>
</body>
</html>
```

Listing 4-35. Sample JSON File to Be Served

```
{
    'Test': 'if',
    'this':'sends'
}
```

How It Works

Let us investigate how your fully functional web server works. First, you utilize the HTTP module for this server. You also augment that module with the file system and the URL modules. This will allow you to fetch and read files from your web server's file system, and the URL module allows for parsing of the URLs in order to properly route your content.

Now you create a web server by calling `http.createServer` and having that server listen to your specified port. The real meat of this solution lies in the `requestListener` callback. Within this callback you can handle both the incoming request and the outgoing response.

When you receive a request, the first thing your server does is read the incoming request URL into a stream by using fs.createReadStream. You then immediately bind to the error event of the file stream. This will allow you to create the appropriate error response code to send to the client. In your case you send a 404 not found if the error code is ENOENT (no such file or directory) and fall back to a general 500 server error for other errors.

You then parse the extension from the request URL. This is done by using the Node.js path module, which has a method 'extname' that will return the extension of a given path. This is then used against a content-type object that you have created to map a given extension to the appropriate content type you wish to serve from your server. Once you have mapped the extension to a content type you are able to write that content-type header to the response. This is followed by piping the file stream to the response.

Next you examine the case of the mocked-up JSON API you have built into your web server. This route is on the URL /*.json. This represents what would possibly be a call to a database to retrieve information, but in our case it retrieves a JSON file that will be sent with "Content-Type: application/json" in the header.

You can now generically serve any type of content that is requested of your web server. You can test this by running your server and then navigating to various URLs. If you navigate to //localhost:8080/4-10-1.html, you will then be presented with an HTML page. This page has a button you can press that will submit an XMLHttpRequest to your JSON API, logging the content to the console. You can, of course, navigate to the /4-10-1.json route directly, where you will receive the JSON as well. Testing for a 404, you can simply attempt to curl http://localhost:8080/404 and you will receive the 404 as expected:

```
> GET /404 HTTP/1.1
> User-Agent: curl/7.21.4 (universal-apple-darwin11.0) libcurl/7.21.4 OpenSSL/0.9.8r zlib/1.2.5
> Host: localhost:8080
> Accept: */*
>
< HTTP/1.1 404 Not Found
< Date: Sat, 18 May 2013 19:17:55 GMT
< Connection: keep-alive
< Transfer-Encoding: chunked
```

CHAPTER 5

Using Events and Child Processes

As you have already seen in this book, Node.js has a robust framework for handling many routines and important tasks. In this chapter you will get a full understanding of a few concepts that you saw in earlier chapters. You will first take an in-depth look at a cornerstone of Node.js, EventEmitters. Regarding these you will see recipes on how to create custom events and add listeners for them, as well as how to create single events. All of this will come together to demonstrate how you can reduce an unending callback nightmare by strategically implementing events in Node.js.

Next, you will unravel the mysteries that are involved with extending a Node.js process with a child process. You will see how to spawn a child process and how to execute shell commands and files. You will then learn how to fork a process, which will lead us into the ability to cluster processes in Node.js.

5-1. Creating a Custom Event

Problem

You have created a Node.js application, but you need to communicate within it by emitting a custom event.

Solution

In this solution you will create a Node.js application that will demonstrate how to create and listen for custom events. You will create an event that executes after a timeout period has expired. This represents a situation in your application that will occur when an operation completes. This then will call a function, doATask, which will return a status of whether the operation was successful or failed. There are two approaches to accomplish this.

First, you will create events that are specific to the status. This requires checking the status and creating an event specifically for that status, as well as binding to those specific events to handle the special cases. This is demonstrated in Listing 5-1.

Listing 5-1. Custom Events for Individual Statuses

```
/**
 * Custom Events
 */

var events = require('events'),
        emitter = new events.EventEmitter();
```

```
function doATask(status) {
        if (status === 'success') {
                emitter.emit('taskSuccess'); // Specific event
        } else if (status === 'fail') {
                emitter.emit('taskFail');
        }
}

emitter.on('taskSuccess', function() {
        console.log('task success!');
});

emitter.on('taskFail', function() {
        console.log('task fail');
});

// call task with success status
setTimeout(doATask, 500, 'success');

// set task to fail
setTimeout(doATask, 1000, 'fail');
```

While you see that this effectively gets the events to propagate appropriately, this still causes you to create two individual events to emit. This can easily be modified to be more streamlined and efficient, as you will see in Listing 5-2.

Listing 5-2. One Emitter to Rule Them All

```
/**
 * Custom Events
 */

var events = require('events'),
        emitter = new events.EventEmitter();

function doATask(status) {
        // This event passes arguments to detail status
        emitter.emit('taskComplete', 'complete', status);
}

// register listener for task complete
emitter.on('taskComplete', function(type, status) {
        console.log('the task is ', type, ' with status ', status);
});

// call task with success status
setTimeout(doATask, 500, 'success');

// set task to fail
setTimeout(doATask, 1000, 'fail');
```

This is a much leaner and more efficient implementation. You can emit a single event that will work for multiple states in your application. In these examples you have seen an implementation in which the events are all handled and emitted from the same source file. In Listing 5-3 you see an example of sharing an event emitter to emit an event that will be received in a module outside of the current module.

Listing 5-3. Emitting Module

```
/**
* Custom Events
*/

var events = require('events'),
        emitter = new events.EventEmitter(),
        myModule = require('./5-1-3.js')(emitter);

emitter.on('custom', function() {
        console.log('custom event received');
});

emitter.emit('custom');
```

One other way in which you are able to create custom events for your application is to utilize the global process object. This Node.js object is an EventEmitter, and it will allow you to register events that will be shared within the process. This type of event is emitted from the code from Listing 5-4.

Listing 5-4. Emitting an Event on the Node.js Process

```
/* Module.js file */
var myMod = module.exports = {
        emitEvent: function() {
                process.emit('globalEvent');
        }
};
```

How It Works

In this example you saw multiple ways in which you are able to create custom events. These events can be emitted anywhere there is a Node.js EventEmitter. The Node.js EventEmitter class is one of the cornerstones of communication between and within the modules that make up your application.

The first thing that you encounter when you build an event is the EventEmitter class. This class consists of an object collection of events that refer to the different types of events that are registered. The concept of type is simply the name that you give your event such as taskComplete or taskFail. This is important when you actually emit the event using the EventEmitter's emit method.

Listing 5-5. EventEmitter's Emit Method

```
EventEmitter.prototype.emit = function(type) {
  var er, handler, len, args, i, listeners;

  if (!this._events)
    this._events = {};
```

```
      // If there is no 'error' event listener then throw.
      if (type === 'error') {
        if (!this._events.error ||
            (typeof this._events.error === 'object' &&
             !this._events.error.length)) {
          er = arguments[1];
          if (this.domain) {
            if (!er) er = new TypeError('Uncaught, unspecified "error" event.');
            er.domainEmitter = this;
            er.domain = this.domain;
            er.domainThrown = false;
            this.domain.emit('error', er);
          } else if (er instanceof Error) {
            throw er; // Unhandled 'error' event
          } else {
            throw TypeError('Uncaught, unspecified "error" event.');
          }
          return false;
        }
      }

      handler = this._events[type];

      if (typeof handler === 'undefined')
        return false;

      if (this.domain && this !== process)
        this.domain.enter();

      if (typeof handler === 'function') {
        switch (arguments.length) {
          // fast cases
          case 1:
            handler.call(this);
            break;
          case 2:
            handler.call(this, arguments[1]);
            break;
          case 3:
            handler.call(this, arguments[1], arguments[2]);
            break;
          // slower
          default:
            len = arguments.length;
            args = new Array(len - 1);
            for (i = 1; i < len; i++)
              args[i - 1] = arguments[i];
            handler.apply(this, args);
        }
      } else if (typeof handler === 'object') {
        len = arguments.length;
```

```
    args = new Array(len - 1);
    for (i = 1; i < len; i++)
      args[i - 1] = arguments[i];

    listeners = handler.slice();
    len = listeners.length;
    for (i = 0; i < len; i++)
      listeners[i].apply(this, args);
  }

  if (this.domain && this !== process)
    this.domain.exit();

  return true;
};
```

This method consists of two main parts. First, there is the special handling of "error" events. This will emit the error event as you expect, unless there is not a listener for the error event. In this case then Node.js will throw the error and the method will return false. The second part of this method is the portion where nonerror events are handled.

After checking to make sure that there is a handler for the given event of the specified type, Node.js then checks to see if the event handler is a function. If it is a function, Node.js will parse the arguments from the emit method and apply those to the handler. This is how Listing 5-2 is able to pass the parameters to the taskComplete event. The extra arguments supplied are applied when the emit method invokes the handler.

The other solutions all utilize the same emit method, but they get the result of emitting events in different ways. Listing 5-4 represents a Node.js module that is shared throughout an application. This module contains a function that will emit an event to the rest of the app. The way this is accomplished in this solution is to leverage the knowledge that the main Node.js process is an EventEmitter. This means you simply emit the event by invoking process.emit('globalEvent'), and a portion of the application that is sharing that process will receive the event.

5-2. Adding a Listener for Custom Events
Problem

You have emitted custom events in the previous section, but without an appropriate way to bind to these events you are unable to use them. For this you need to add listeners to those events.

Solution

This solution is the counterpart to Section 5-1. In the previous section you implemented EventEmitters and emitted the events. Now you need to add listeners for those events so you can handle them in your application. The process is just as simple as emitting events, as shown in Listing 5-6.

Listing 5-6. Adding Event Listeners to Custom Events and System Events

```
/**
 * Custom Events
 */

var events = require('events'),
      emitter = new events.EventEmitter();
```

```
function doATask(status) {
        if (status === 'success') {
                emitter.emit('taskSuccess'); // Specific event
        } else if (status === 'fail') {
                emitter.emit('taskFail');
        }
        // This event passes arguments to detail status
        emitter.emit('taskComplete', 'complete', status);
}
emitter.on('newListener', function(){
        console.log('a new listener was added');
});
emitter.on('taskSuccess', function() {
        console.log('task success!');
});

emitter.on('taskFail', function() {
        console.log('task fail');
});

// register listener for task complete
emitter.on('taskComplete', function(type, status) {
        console.log('the task is ', type, ' with status ', status);
});

// call task with success status
setTimeout(doATask, 2e3, 'success');

// set task to fail
setTimeout(doATask, 4e3, 'fail');
```

You can also pass your EventEmitter to an external module and then listen for events from within that separate section of code.

Listing 5-7. Event Listening from an External Module

```
/**
* External Module
*/
module.exports = function(emitter) {
        emitter.on('custom', function() {
                console.log('bazinga');
        });
};
```

Just as you had emitted the event by using the Node.js process EventEmitter, you are able to bind listeners to that process and receive the events.

Listing 5-8. Node.js Processwide Listener

```
/**
* Global event
*/
var ext = require('./5-1-5.js');

process.on('globalEvent', function() {
        console.log('global event');
});

ext.emitEvent();
```

How It Works

As you examine the solution in Listing 5-6 you should quickly notice how to go about adding a listener to an event. This is as simple as calling the EventEmitter.on() method. The .on method of the EventEmitter accepts two arguments: first, the event type name; second, the listener callback, which will accept any of the arguments that were passed to the emit() event. The .on method is really just a wrapper to the EventEmitter addListener function, which takes the same two arguments. You could call this method directly in place of calling the .on function as they are the same.

Listing 5-9. EventEmitter addListener

```
EventEmitter.prototype.addListener = function(type, listener) {
  var m;

  if (typeof listener !== 'function')
    throw TypeError('listener must be a function');

  if (!this._events)
    this._events = {};

  // To avoid recursion in the case that type === "newListener"! Before
  // adding it to the listeners, first emit "newListener".
  if (this._events.newListener)
    this.emit('newListener', type, typeof listener.listener === 'function' ?
            listener.listener : listener);

  if (!this._events[type])
    // Optimize the case of one listener. Don't need the extra array object.
    this._events[type] = listener;
  else if (typeof this._events[type] === 'object')
    // If we've already got an array, just append.
    this._events[type].push(listener);
  else
    // Adding the second element, need to change to array.
    this._events[type] = [this._events[type], listener];

  // Check for listener leak
  if (typeof this._events[type] === 'object' && !this._events[type].warned) {
    var m;
```

```
    if (this._maxListeners !== undefined) {
      m = this._maxListeners;
    } else {
      m = EventEmitter.defaultMaxListeners;
    }

    if (m && m > 0 && this._events[type].length > m) {
      this._events[type].warned = true;
      console.error('(node) warning: possible EventEmitter memory ' +
                    'leak detected. %d listeners added. ' +
                    'Use emitter.setMaxListeners() to increase limit.',
                    this._events[type].length);
      console.trace();
    }
  }

  return this;
};
```

```
EventEmitter.prototype.on = EventEmitter.prototype.addListener;
```

The addListener method, as you can see from the source snippet, accomplishes several tasks. First, after verifying that the listener callback is a function, the addListener method emits its own event 'newListener' in order to signify that a new listener of a given type has been added.

The second thing that happens is the addListener function will push the listener function to the event to which it is bound. In the previous section, this function is what became the handler function for each event type. The emit() function will then either .call() or .apply() to that function, depending on the number of arguments that are provided by the emitter itself.

Lastly in the addListener function, you will find that Node.js is very kind and attempts to protect you from potential memory leaks. It does this by checking to see if the number of listeners exceeds a predefined limit that defaults to 10. You can, of course, configure this to be a higher number by using the setMaxListeners() method as instructed by the helpful warning that appears once you exceed this number of listeners.

5-3. Implementing a One-time Event
Problem

You need to implement an event in your Node.js application that you only wish to execute one time.

Solution

Imagine that you have an application that has an important task to accomplish. This task needs to be accomplished, but only one time. Imagine that you have an event that listens for a member of a chat room who will either exit the application or disconnect. This event only needs to be handled once. It wouldn't make sense for this event to be broadcast to other users of the application twice, so you limit the number of times you handle the event.

There are two ways to do this. One is to manually handle registering the event and then remove the event listener once the event has been received once.

Listing 5-10. Registering an Event Listener Once, Manually

```
/**
* Implementing a One time event
*/

var events = require('events'),
            emitter = new events.EventEmitter();

function listener() {
        console.log('one Timer');
        emitter.removeListener('oneTimer', listener);
}
emitter.on('oneTimer', listener);

emitter.emit('oneTimer');
emitter.emit('oneTimer');
```

This requires a secondary call within the listener function in order to be able to remove the listener from the event. This can become unwieldy as the project grows, so Node.js has a native implementation for the same effect.

Listing 5-11. emtter.once()

```
/**
* Implementing a One-time event
*/

var events = require('events'),
            emitter = new events.EventEmitter();

/* EASIER */

emitter.once('onceOnly', function() {
        console.log('one Only');
});

emitter.emit('onceOnly');
emitter.emit('onceOnly');
```

How It Works

The first example of registering an event listener to bind only once to the emitted event is quite clear to see and understand. You first bind to the event with a function callback for the listener. You then handle that callback within the listener and remove that listener from the event. This prevents any further handlings of the event from the same emitter.

This works because of the removeListener method, which accepts an event type and a specific listener function.

Listing 5-12. EventEmitter removeListener method

```javascript
EventEmitter.prototype.removeListener = function(type, listener) {
  var list, position, length, i;

  if (typeof listener !== 'function')
    throw TypeError('listener must be a function');

  if (!this._events || !this._events[type])
    return this;

  list = this._events[type];
  length = list.length;
  position = -1;

  if (list === listener ||
      (typeof list.listener === 'function' && list.listener === listener)) {
    this._events[type] = undefined;
    if (this._events.removeListener)
      this.emit('removeListener', type, listener);

  } else if (typeof list === 'object') {
    for (i = length; i-- > 0;) {
      if (list[i] === listener ||
          (list[i].listener && list[i].listener === listener)) {
        position = i;
        break;
      }
    }

    if (position < 0)
      return this;

    if (list.length === 1) {
      list.length = 0;
      this._events[type] = undefined;
    } else {
      list.splice(position, 1);
    }

    if (this._events.removeListener)
      this.emit('removeListener', type, listener);
  }

  return this;
};
```

The removeListener function will target the specific event that you need to remove by recursively searching through the events object in order to find the type and function combination that you are searching for. It will then remove the event binding so that the listener will no longer be registered on subsequent events.

A similar method to your handmade emit once function is the EventEmitter.once method.

Listing 5-13. EventEmitter once method

```
EventEmitter.prototype.once = function(type, listener) {
  if (typeof listener !== 'function')
    throw TypeError('listener must be a function');

  function g() {
    this.removeListener(type, g);
    listener.apply(this, arguments);
  }

  g.listener = listener;
  this.on(type, g);

  return this;
};
```

This method accepts the listener and the event type that you wish to bind to one time. It then creates an internal function that will then apply the listener. Before this listener is called in the internal function, the actual listener is removed from the event. This works just as your custom one-time method works, because it removes the listener the first time that the event executes.

In the next section we will investigate how to incorporate using these events and custom events in general to reduce the amount of callbacks in your Node.js application.

5-4. Reducing Callbacks Using Events
Problem

You have a Node.js application that has multiple callback functions. This code has become a little unwieldy so you would like to reduce the callbacks by utilizing EventEmitter.

Solution

Imagine a shopping application that has to access data from a database, manipulate that data, then refresh the database and send the status back to the client. This could be fetching a shopping cart, adding an item, and letting the customer know that the cart has been updated. The first example of this is written using callbacks.

Listing 5-14. Shopping Cart Using Callbacks

```
var initialize = function() {
      retrieveCart(function(err, data) {
            if (err) console.log(err);

            data['new'] = 'other thing';

            updateCart(data, function(err, result) {
                  if (err) console.log(err);
```

```
                    sendResults(result, function(err, status) {
                            if (err) console.log(err);
                            console.log(status);
                    });
            });
        });
};

// simulated call to a database
var retrieveCart = function(callback) {
        var data = { item: 'thing' };
        return callback(null, data );
};
// simulated call to a database
var updateCart = function(data, callback) {
        return callback(null, data);
};

var sendResults = function(data, callback) {
        console.log(data);
        return callback(null, 'Cart Updated');
};

initialize();
```

First, understand that there is nothing wrong with using callbacks in Node.js. In fact, it is probably the most popular way to handle asynchronous programming in Node.js. However, you can also see that, in the case where you have a nontrivial amount of callbacks that must happen in succession such as in Listing 5-14, the code can become less easy to follow. To rectify this you can incorporate events to manage the application flow in an arguably more concise way.

Listing 5-15. Using Events Instead of Callbacks

```
/**
 * Reducing callbacks
 */

var events = require('events');

var MyCart = function() {
        this.data = { item: 'thing' };
};
MyCart.prototype = new events.EventEmitter();

MyCart.prototype.retrieveCart = function() {
        //Fetch Data then emit
        this.emit('data', this.data);
};

MyCart.prototype.updateCart = function() {
        // Update data then emit
        this.emit('result', this.data);
};
```

```
MyCart.prototype.sendResults = function() {
        console.log(this.data);
        this.emit('complete');
};

var cart = new MyCart();

cart.on('data', function(data) {
        cart.data['new'] = 'other thing';
        cart.updateCart();
});

cart.on('result', function(data) {
        cart.sendResults(data);
});

cart.on('complete', function() {
        console.log('Cart Updated');
});

cart.retrieveCart();
```

With the different solutions to the same task, both utilize a similar amount of code, but the amount of callback has been reduced considerably by moving to an event-driven module instead of the callback flow.

How It Works

Using callback exclusively can become a burden when you want to examine the code that is critical to your application. This can also cause a headache to developers who are contributing to your project, because they might not be as familiar with the project to know where the given callback function is nested. This can also become a problem when you wish to refactor your application to add another method to execute during a callback. These are all reasons that you might choose to move to the event-driven model.

In the event-driven solution from Listing 5-11, you start off by creating a new object called MyCart. You can assume MyCart initializes with an item stored in it, MyCart.data. Your MyCart object then inherits the events.EventEmitter object. This now means that MyCart can send and receive data through the Node.js event module.

Now that your object can emit and listen for events, you augment your object by making methods that utilize the EventEmitter. For example, you created a retrieveCart method, which would fetch data from a data store; once completed, the 'data' event is emitted, passing along any data retrieved from the cart. Similarly you create an updateCart method and a sendResults method that will alert the client of the result of the update.

You then instantiate a new instance of MyCart. This new cart can now bind to the events that will be sent from the MyCart object. You have a separate function to handle each of the events. This makes the code much more maintainable and in many cases more extensible. For example, say you need to add another logging function to MyCart. You can now bind that to each event and log the interactions without rewriting the entire callback flow.

5-5. Spawning a Child with .spawn

Problem

You need to create a child process to execute an auxiliary action in your Node.js application.

Solution

There are many reasons why you would want to spawn a child process from your Node.js application. Several of these could simply be to execute a command-line task without the need to require or build an entire module for the application. In this solution you will highlight two command-line applications and a third solution that will execute another Node.js process from the spawn method.

Listing 5-16. Spawning Children

```
/**
 * .spawn
 */

var spawn = require('child_process').spawn,
                pwd = spawn('pwd'),
                ls = spawn('ls', ['-G']),
                nd = spawn('node', ['5-4-1.js']);

pwd.stdout.setEncoding('utf8');

pwd.stdout.on('data', function(data) {
        console.log(data);
});

pwd.stderr.on('data', function(data) {
        console.log(data);
});

pwd.on('close', function(){
        console.log('closed');
});

ls.stdout.setEncoding('utf8');

ls.stdout.on('data', function(data) {
                    console.log(data);
});

nd.stdout.setEncoding('utf8');

nd.stdout.on('data', function(data) {
        console.log(data);
});
```

The first spawn is to just run the 'pwd' command in the current directory; the second is to list all the files in that directory. These are just command-line utilities built into the operating system. However, the third example in this solution executes the command to run a Node.js file; then, like the previous examples, you log the output to the console.

How It Works

Spawning is one method for invoking a child process in Node.js and is a method of the child_process module. The child_process module creates a way to stream data through stdout, stdin, and stderr. Because of the nature of this module this can be done in a nonblocking way, fitting nicely into the Node.js model.

The child_process spawn method will instantiate a ChildProcess object, which is a Node.js EventEmitter. The events that are associated with the ChildProcess object are shown in Table 5-1.

Table 5-1. *ChildProcess Events*

Event	Detail
'message'	Transfers a message object, which is JSON, or a value. This can also transfer a socket or server object as an optional second parameter.
'error'	Transmits the error to the callback. This can happen when the child process fails to spawn, is unable to be killed, or the message transfer fails.
'close'	Happens when all of the stdio streams of the child process are completed. This will transmit the exit code and the signal that was sent with it.
'disconnect'	Emits when you terminate a connection by utilizing the .disconnect() method on the child (or parent).
'exit'	Emits after the child process ends. If the process terminated normally, code is the final exit code of the process, otherwise null. If the process terminated due to receipt of a signal, signal is the string name of the signal, otherwise null.

Aside from these ChildProcess events, the spawned child is also a stream, as you saw above. The stream contains the data from the standard I/O of the child processes. The methods that are associated with these streams are outlined in Table 5-2 along with other methods on the child.

Table 5-2. *Stream Events of the Child Process and Other Methods*

Method	Description
.stdin	A writable stream that is representative of the child process stdin.
.stdout	A readable stream representing the stdout of the child process.
.stderr	A readable stream of the stderr of the child process.
.pid	The child process process identifier (PID).
.kill	Kills a process, optionally sends the termination signal.
.disconnect	Disconnects from the parent.
.send	Sends a message to a .fork'd process. (There is more detail on this in Section 5-8.)

Now that you have a little more understanding of what the ChildProcess is and how that fits into the child_process module, you can see that your solution of spawning a child process invokes the process directly. You create three spawned processes. Each of these begins with a command argument. This argument, 'pwd,' 'ls,' 'node' is the command that will be executed as if you were running it on the command line in your terminal application. The next argument in the child_process.spawn method is an optional array of arguments to pass to the command argument.

You see then that the spawned processes from this example are the same as running the following in the command line of your terminal:

```
$ pwd &
$ ls -G &
$ node 5-4-1.js &
```

You can read the output of these commands from your spawned process as well. This happens by listening to the child_process.stdout stream. If you bind to the data event you see the standard output of these commands just as if you were running the command in the terminal. In the case of the third spawn, you see the output from the entire module from the previous section of this chapter.

There is also an optional third argument that can be present in the child_process.spawn method. This argument represents the set of options to help set up the spawned process. These options can have the values shown in Table 5-3.

Table 5-3. Spawn Options

Option	Type	Description
cwd	String	Current working directory of the child process.
stdio	Array or string	The stdio configuration of the child process.
customFds	Array	Deprecated functionality.
env	Object	Environment key-value pairs.
detached	Boolean	This child process will become a group leader.
uid	Number	Sets the user identity of the process.
gid	Number	Sets the group identity of the process.

5-6. Running Shell Commands with .exec
Problem

You want to directly execute a shell command as a child process from your Node.js application.

Solution

In the previous section, you saw how you could easily spawn a child process by using the child_process module. This could be a long-running process where you then wish to access the stdio streams that are available on the process. Similar to this is the child_process.exec method. The difference between these two methods is that the .spawn method will return all the data as a stream, whereas the .exec method returns data as a buffer. With this method you can execute a shell command, cmd.exe in Windows or /bin/sh elsewhere, directly from your Node.js application. With the solution in this section, you will list a set of files and log the result of that operation to the console. You will then search your system for all running processes that contain the word node, again logging the output to your console.

Listing 5-17. .exec

```
/**
* Running Shell commands with .exec
*/

var exec = require('child_process').exec;

exec('ls -g', function(error, stdout, stderr) {
        if (error) console.log(error);

        console.log(stdout);
});

exec('ps ax | grep node', function(error, stdout, stderr) {
        if (error) console.log(error);

        console.log(stdout);
});
```

How It Works

This solution works by leveraging the aspects of both the child_process.spawn method and the child_process.execFile method that you will examine in the next section. Essentially, when you tell the child_process to use the exec method, you are telling it to run a process with the /bin/sh file (cmd.exe on Windows) as the executable.

Listing 5-18. Child Process .exec Function

```
exports.exec = function(command /*, options, callback */) {
  var file, args, options, callback;

  if (typeof arguments[1] === 'function') {
    options = undefined;
    callback = arguments[1];
  } else {
    options = arguments[1];
    callback = arguments[2];
  }

  if (process.platform === 'win32') {
    file = 'cmd.exe';
    args = ['/s', '/c', '"' + command + '"'];
    // Make a shallow copy before patching so we don't clobber the user's
    // options object.
    options = util._extend({}, options);
    options.windowsVerbatimArguments = true;
  } else {
    file = '/bin/sh';
    args = ['-c', command];
  }
  return exports.execFile(file, args, options, callback);
};
```

This function does, in fact, call the execFile method. You will see in the next section that this means the process spawns based on the file parameter passed to the function.

```
var child = spawn(file, args, {
  cwd: options.cwd,
  env: options.env,
  windowsVerbatimArguments: !!options.windowsVerbatimArguments
});
```

This means that anything you want to run in the command line, you can run via exec. That is why when you attempt to run the exec function as ps ax | grep node to identify all running processes that contain the word node in them, you see the stdout results just as you would if you had run it in the shell.

```
17774 s001  S+      0:00.06 node 5-6-1.js
17776 s001  S+      0:00.00 /bin/sh -c ps ax | grep node
17778 s001  S+      0:00.00 grep node
11503 s002  S+      0:00.07 node
```

5-7. Executing Shell Files with .execFile
Problem

Within your application, you need to execute a file as a child process to your Node.js process.

Solution

You are already somewhat familiar with this method of the child_process module. In this solution, you have a shell script that contains several steps that you wish to execute from your Node.js application. These could be done in Node.js directly either by spawning them or calling the .exec method. However, by calling them once as a file you can group them together and still get the benefit of having their combined output buffered to the callback function of execFile. You can see in the next two listings the example Node.js application and the file that is to be executed.

Listing 5-19. Using .execFile

```
/**
 * execFile
 */

var execFile = require('child_process').execFile;

execFile('./5-7-1.sh', function(error, stdout, stderr) {
        console.log(stdout);
        console.log(stderr);
        console.log(error);
});
```

Listing 5-20. Shell File to Execute

```
#!/bin/sh
echo "running this shell script from child_process.execFile"
# run another node process
```

```
node 5-6-1.js
# and another
node 5-5-1.js

ps ax | grep node
```

How It Works

As you begin to examine how the execFile method works, you quickly realize it is a derivative of the .spawn method. This method is quite intricate and does a lot of things in order to execute a file. First, the execFile function will accept four arguments. The first is the file and is required to find the file and path to execute.

The second is the args array, which will pass the arguments to the file to be executed; the third consists of the particular options to set on the spawned process; and the fourth is a callback. The options, as you can see, are defaulted to common settings such as utf8 encoding, timeout set to zero, and the others as shown in Listing 5-21. This callback is just like the callback available from child_process.exec in that it passes a buffered set of error, stdout, and stderr to the function and you are able to consume those streams directly from the callback.

Listing 5-21. Setting File, Args, and Options of execFile

```
exports.execFile = function(file /* args, options, callback */) {
  var args, optionArg, callback;
  var options = {
    encoding: 'utf8',
    timeout: 0,
    maxBuffer: 200 * 1024,
    killSignal: 'SIGTERM',
    cwd: null,
    env: null
  };

  // Parse the parameters.

  if (typeof arguments[arguments.length - 1] === 'function') {
    callback = arguments[arguments.length - 1];
  }

  if (Array.isArray(arguments[1])) {
    args = arguments[1];
    options = util._extend(options, arguments[2]);
  } else {
    args = [];
    options = util._extend(options, arguments[1]);
  }
```

Node.js now spawns the child process by passing in the options object. The child that is spawned is then passed along through various event listeners and callbacks in order to get the stdio streams aggregated into the callback function that is provided to the execFile method before returning the child itself, as shown in Listing 5-22. This is a difference from the .spawn method that would return the stdout and stderr streams directly. Here, using the .exec method you are returning a buffer that is created from the stdout and stderr streams.

Listing 5-22. Spawning execFile

```
var child = spawn(file, args, {
  cwd: options.cwd,
  env: options.env,
  windowsVerbatimArguments: !!options.windowsVerbatimArguments
});

var stdout = '';
var stderr = '';
var killed = false;
var exited = false;
var timeoutId;

var err;

function exithandler(code, signal) {
  if (exited) return;
  exited = true;

  if (timeoutId) {
    clearTimeout(timeoutId);
    timeoutId = null;
  }

  if (!callback) return;

  if (err) {
    callback(err, stdout, stderr);
  } else if (code === 0 && signal === null) {
    callback(null, stdout, stderr);
  } else {
    var e = new Error('Command failed: ' + stderr);
    e.killed = child.killed || killed;
    e.code = code;
    e.signal = signal;
    callback(e, stdout, stderr);
  }
}

function errorhandler(e) {
  err = e;
  child.stdout.destroy();
  child.stderr.destroy();
  exithandler();
}

function kill() {
  child.stdout.destroy();
  child.stderr.destroy();
```

```
    killed = true;
    try {
      child.kill(options.killSignal);
    } catch (e) {
      err = e;
      exithandler();
    }
  }
}

if (options.timeout > 0) {
  timeoutId = setTimeout(function() {
    kill();
    timeoutId = null;
  }, options.timeout);
}

child.stdout.setEncoding(options.encoding);
child.stderr.setEncoding(options.encoding);

child.stdout.addListener('data', function(chunk) {
  stdout += chunk;
  if (stdout.length > options.maxBuffer) {
    err = new Error('stdout maxBuffer exceeded.');
    kill();
  }
});

child.stderr.addListener('data', function(chunk) {
  stderr += chunk;
  if (stderr.length > options.maxBuffer) {
    err = new Error('stderr maxBuffer exceeded.');
    kill();
  }
});

child.addListener('close', exithandler);
child.addListener('error', errorhandler);

  return child;
};
```

5-8. Using .fork for Interprocess Communication

Problem

You need to create a child process in Node.js but you also need to be able to easily communicate between these child processes.

Solution

The solution to using the fork method to communicate between processes is straightforward. You will build a main process that will create an HTTP server. This process will also fork a child process and pass the server object to that child. The child will then be able to process requests from that server even though the server was not created on the child process. The server object and all messages are sent to the child process via the .send() method.

Listing 5-23. Parent Process

```
/**
 * .fork main
 */

var cp = require('child_process');
            http = require('http');

var child = cp.fork('5-8-2.js');

var server = http.createServer(function(req, res) {
        res.end('hello');
}).listen(8080);

child.send('hello');
child.send('server', server);
```

Listing 5-24. Forked Process

```
/**
 * forked process
 */

process.on('message', function(msg, hndl) {
        console.log(msg);

        if (msg === 'server') {
                hndl.on('connection', function() {
                console.log('connected on the child');
        });
        }

});
```

How It Works

Creating a forked process is nearly identical to that of making a spawned process, as you saw in Section 5-5. The main difference is the cross-process communication that is made available by the child.send method.

This send event sends a message string and an optional handle. The handle can be one of five types: net.Socket, net.Server, net.Native, dgram.Socket, or dgram.Native. At first glance this could be daunting to have to accommodate these different types of methods. Fortunately, Node.js converts the handle types for you. This handling also applies to the response from the spawned processes.

The event that occurs when a message is sent to the child process is the 'message' event. In this solution you saw that the 'message' event contained the named type of the message. First you sent a greeting message. Next you sent a server object. This object was then bound to the 'connection' event once the event was determined to be a server. You then handled the connection just as you would in a single process module.

Summary

In this chapter you investigated and implemented solutions for two important modules that are native to Node.js: events and child processes.

In the events module you first created a custom event, then you solved how to bind to that event with a listener. After that you examined the special case of adding a one-time event listener when you only want one binding. Finally, you were able to see how, utilizing the Node.js event module, you can very clearly reduce the amount of callbacks by using events to drive functionality.

In the second part of this chapter you examined the child process module. You first saw how to spawn a child process to run a command outside of the main process. Then you saw how to directly run shell commands and files by using the exec and execFile methods. These both derived from the spawn process, as did the .fork() process, which is a special case of spawn that allows for simple interprocess communication, providing limitless possibilities for multiprocess Node.js applications.

CHAPTER 6

■ ■ ■

Implementing Security and Cryptography

In this chapter you will investigate a critical part to any application, regardless of the framework you choose to use to develop it: security. However, not only will you investigate how to incorporate security features into your application, you will also get a unique perspective on how Node.js handles security and cryptography within its core and through third-party implementations.

You will examine various types of hashing algorithms that are available in Node.js, analyzing how they work and also for which applications they might be better suited than others. You will see solutions to verifying file integrity with hash algorithms. Hash algorithms are common when you build applications as they are designed to take an arbitrary amount of data and convert it into a manageable fixed-length representation of that data, like a signature for the original data. These are common in applications and used for scenarios such as password storage where you should store a reference that can be utilized to verify the text, not the actual text of the password. Hash algorithms are also integral to building. You will utilize hash-based message authentication code (HMAC) to verify and authenticate messages for your application. Aside from hash algorithms are encryption algorithms, which are used to actually retrieve the original data after it has been encrypted. This difference with hashing algorithms is that hash algorithms are limited to one-way hashing, meaning that you do not plan to unhash a hashed message.

Next you will also examine the OpenSSL cyphers that are available to encrypt your data and keep it secure. You will then build on that to examine how to use the Node.js Transport Layer Security (TLS) module to secure your servers. Finally, an examination of encrypting credentials with the crypto module as well as using a third-party authentication module will complete your journey through the Node.js security landscape.

6-1. Analyzing Types of Hash Algorithms
Problem

You have a command-line interface for which you have access to all of the hash algorithms available to a Node.js user to create a hash of their data. Before you distribute this application, you want a better understanding of each of the algorithms.

Solution

The solution for this is actually quite simple. You are going to build a list of the available hash algorithms that are currently present in Node.js. You will then see a breakdown of how many of these hashes are designed and what their common uses are in the How It Works section. First, you will build a list of the hashes, as shown in Listing 6-1.

Listing 6-1. Building a List of Hashes Available in Node.js

```
/**
 * Hashes
 */

var crypto = require('crypto'),
    hashes = crypto.getHashes();

console.log(hashes.join(', '));
```

You now run this code to get the full list of available hashes for Node.js.

Listing 6-2. Available Hashes in Node.js

```
$ node 6-1-1.js
DSA-SHA1-old, dsa, dsa-sha, dsa-sha1, dsaEncryption, dsaWithSHA, dsaWithSHA1, dss1, ecdsa-with-SHA1,
md4, md4WithRSAEncryption, md5, md5WithRSAEncryption, mdc2, mdc2WithRSA, ripemd, ripemd160,
ripemd160WithRSA, rmd160, rsa-md4, rsa-md5, rsa-mdc2, rsa-ripemd160, rsa-sha, rsa-sha1, rsa-sha1-2,
rsa-sha224, rsa-sha256, rsa-sha384, rsa-sha512, sha, sha1, sha1WithRSAEncryption, sha224,
sha224WithRSAEncryption, sha256, sha256WithRSAEncryption, sha384, sha384WithRSAEncryption, sha512,
sha512WithRSAEncryption, shaWithRSAEncryption, ssl2-md5, ssl3-md5, ssl3-sha1, whirlpool
```

Some of these are deprecated (for example 'DSA-SHA1-old') or are not truly cryptographic hash functions but rather other cryptographically useful implementations. That is to say, an RSA encryption is not truly a hash function, but it can be utilized in a way that leverages a hash. In this section you will focus on the Digital Signature Algorithm (DSA), Message Digest (MD4, MD5, etc.), Secure Hash Algorithm (SHA), and WHIRLPOOL hash functions, their uses, and potential vulnerabilities.

How It Works

This works by utilizing the Node.js crypto module. This module is built to provide a robust implementation of many of the cryptographic needs you might encounter when building your Node.js application. The getHashes method is a shortcut to list all the available hashes, which is a list of the OpenSSL hashes that are available on the platform that is running Node.js.

Before you begin using these hashes in your application, it is important to note how they work and what they are good for; the following subsections will break down the most common algorithms and their features. In general a cryptographic hash is a way to encrypt data, or a message, into a fixed-length digest, known as the hash. This fixed-length digest will serve as a signature or fingerprint representing the original data that hashed, without divulging the contents of the original data. What follows is a listing of the common algorithms and their functions.

DSA

This type of encryption can encode data that were originally proposed by the National Institute for Standards and Technology for the DSS (Digital Signature Standard). Because of this, these two abbreviations are sometimes used interchangeably. It should be noted that the DSA is not directly a hash but utilizes a hash function to generate the encrypted value. This hash function was originally designed to utilize SHA-1, but SHA-2 has also been used; you will read more about these hash functions later.

MD4

The MD4 hash is still used, but in many cases it has been supplanted by MD5 and other more advanced hashing algorithms. It has been designated as obsolete. MD4 was designed to execute fast. What it does is to accept a message and encrypt it into a 128-bit digest.

The MD4 is not strong on security. Shortly after its creation, it was found to be highly probable that there would be hash collision. This means that even though slight variances in the original messages usually create a unique hash, there are several proofs and methods in which creating the same hash from multiple messages can occur. Because of this, the algorithm was improved in the MD5 specification.

MD5

The MD5 is the progression of MD4, in order to improve the security of the hash. It again produces a 128-bit hash, but it sacrifices the speed of the algorithm, albeit slightly. The main difference you will see from MD4 is that MD5 introduces a fourth auxiliary function that is used to process the intermediate steps of the hashing. These functions also contain some additional constants and slight variances from MD4 in order to make the hash more secure.

All of that said, the MD5 hash is still not secure because it is still prone to collision and thus collision attacks. However, it is still very popular for validating file integrity, or checking for changes in files. There are various other uses for MD5, including the universally unique identifier (UUID version 3) and CRAM-MD5 (a challenge-response authentication), among others. As stated, it is still a sound hashing algorithm but because of its security vulnerabilities it should be avoided for hardened security applications, or actions like securing an SSL connection.

RIPEMD

There are several variants of the RIPEMD message digest that are based on the MD4 algorithm in its initial design. The most common RIPEMD implementation is RIPEMD-160. A later generation variant of the original 128-bit hash, it creates a 160-bit hash just like SHA-1. RIPEMD-160 does not currently have any cases of collision vulnerability as it is also expected to remain secure for perhaps another decade. RIPEMD-160 is slightly slower than SHA-1, which may be one reason why it is not as widely utilized. It is however used in Pretty Good Privacy (PGP) encryption. Another reason why RIPEMD is not widely used is that it is not marketed as the de facto standard like SHA-1 is by the National Institute for Standards and Technology.

SHA

SHA is available in several variants, most of which are available in Node.js.

The original SHA algorithm, now known as SHA-0 and available as sha in the Node.js getHashes function, is a 160-bit hash that is known to have collisions possible. For this reason it has fallen out of popularity to be replaced by the later versions of the algorithm.

After SHA-0 came SHA-1, which is still one of the most widely utilized cryptographic hash functions in computing today. Like SHA-0 before it, SHA-1 also creates a 160-bit digest. SHA-1 is used in nearly all of the most popular secure software protocols today. It is used in Secure Sockets Layer (SSL), Secure Shell (SSH), TLS, and IP Security (IPsec) protocols, among thousands of other implementations that include hashing files in the Git version control systems. However, it has been theoretically shown that SHA-1 has collision vulnerabilities, so there have been efforts to create an even more secure hashing algorithm based on SHA-1.

SHA-2 is an envelope name for SHA-256 (256-bit digest), SHA-224 (224-bit digest), SHA-384 (384-bit digest), and SHA-512 (512-bit digest) all of which are available for use in Node.js. These represent evolutions from the SHA-1 algorithm. The 224-bit variety is a truncation of the 256; likewise, the 384 is a truncation of the 512.

The SHA-2 hash is already implemented in many of the same places that SHA-1 is, including SSL, TLS, PGP, and SSH. It is also a part of the bitcoin hashing methods as well as next-generation password hashing on many platforms.

WHIRLPOOL

The WHIRLPOOL algorithm is another hashing algorithm available to you in Node.js. This algorithm produces a 512-bit hash and is not known to have collision vulnerabilities at this time. It has been adopted by the International Organization for Standards as a standard, but it does not have as much support as the MD5 and SHA families.

There are various hashing algorithms available to you when you are writing your Node.js application, each with its own cryptographic algorithm and potential vulnerabilities. You should consider each of these hashes carefully when securing your application, and be sure to scrutinize everything when it comes to evaluating cryptographic hashes.

6-2. Hashing Data with createHash
Problem

You have examined the different types of hashes that are available in Node.js. You now want to implement a hash in order to secure a message.

Solution

In this solution you will examine the cryptographic hash functions that are available to Node.js by seeing how they hash two different forms of input: an empty string and a nonempty string (see Listing 6-3). Listing 6-4 shows an example of the SHA-1 and MD5 hashing algorithms with their different encodings.

Listing 6-3. Using Various Hashing Algorithms

```
/**
 * Analyzing types of data
 */

var crypto = require('crypto'),
    hashes = crypto.getHashes();

hashes.forEach(function(hash) {

    ['', 'The quick brown fox jumped over the lazy dog.'].forEach(function(txt) {
        var hashed;
        try {
            hashed =crypto.createHash(hash).update(txt).digest('hex');
        } catch (ex) {
            if (ex.message === 'Digest method not supported') {
                // not supported for this algo
            } else {
                console.log(ex, hash);
            }
        }

        console.log(hash, hashed);
    });
});
```

Listing 6-4. Hashing with Different Digest Encoding

```
/**
 * Different Encodings
 */

var crypto = require('crypto'),
        message = 'this is a message';

console.log('sha1');
console.log(crypto.createHash('sha1').update(message).digest('hex'));
console.log(crypto.createHash('sha1').update(message).digest('base64'));
console.log(crypto.createHash('sha1').update(message).digest('binary'));

console.log('md5');
console.log(crypto.createHash('md5').update(message).digest('hex'));
console.log(crypto.createHash('md5').update(message).digest('base64'));
console.log(crypto.createHash('md5').update(message).digest('binary'));
```

The hashing varies greatly between algorithms. For example, the hash of the empty string with MD5 looks like d41d8cd98f00b204e9800998ecf8427e whereas the same string hashed with SHA-1 is da39a3ee5e6b4b0d3255bfef95601890afd80709. These, of course, have different appearances when utilizing different encodings, but the hashing is the same.

How It Works

To understand the hashing of these functions in Node.js, you must first examine the process of generating a hashed digest, and then you can look at the source code for the createHash method of the crypto module.

In the solutions above, you first saw how to implement the createHash method across a variety of hash algorithms available to you in Node.js. The createHash function accepts an algorithm, which must be an acceptable algorithm to create a hash. If, for example, you were to use the algorithm 'cheese', which does not exist, you will get the error "Digest method not supported".

After you pass the algorithm to the createHash method, you now have an instance of the Node.js Hash class. This class is a stream that is readable and writable. Now you need to send a message that you want to have hashed to the update() method of the Hash class. The update function receives a message and (optionally) the encoding for that message. If not, input encoding is defined, which could be 'utf8', 'ascii', or 'binary'; then the input is assumed to be a buffer. This means that as new data are read into the stream, this method could be called multiple times.

After you have called the update method on the hash stream you are now ready to create the digest, or the actual output of the hash. This function will accept an output encoding, again defaulting to a buffer if none is provided. The types of encoding that are available are 'hex', 'binary', and 'base64'. Typically in hashing algorithms, like checking the shasum (SHA-1 hash), as you will see in the next section, it is more typical to utilize 'hex', but in Listing 6-4, you saw an example of using multiple types of encoding for the output.

Now you can examine the source for the createHash method and the hash object in the Node.js source, shown in Listing 6-5.

Listing 6-5. createHash Source

```
exports.createHash = exports.Hash = Hash;
function Hash(algorithm, options) {
  if (!(this instanceof Hash))
    return new Hash(algorithm, options);
  this._binding = new binding.Hash(algorithm);
  LazyTransform.call(this, options);
}

util.inherits(Hash, LazyTransform);

Hash.prototype._transform = function(chunk, encoding, callback) {
  this._binding.update(chunk, encoding);
  callback();
};

Hash.prototype._flush = function(callback) {
  var encoding = this._readableState.encoding || 'buffer';
  this.push(this._binding.digest(encoding), encoding);
  callback();
};

Hash.prototype.update = function(data, encoding) {
  encoding = encoding || exports.DEFAULT_ENCODING;
  if (encoding === 'buffer' && typeof data === 'string')
    encoding = 'binary';
  this._binding.update(data, encoding);
  return this;
};

Hash.prototype.digest = function(outputEncoding) {
  outputEncoding = outputEncoding || exports.DEFAULT_ENCODING;
  return this._binding.digest(outputEncoding);
};
```

You can note the createHash, update, and digest functions that were discussed above, but note especially the binding.Hash(algorithm) method. This is where the Node.js binds to the C++ that powers the Node.js core. This is actually where the OpenSSL hashes are processed and where things like the error that is thrown if your algorithm does not exist occurs. Aside from that, you see the hash stream checks the optional encoding values, sets them appropriately, then sends the request on the C++ binding methods respective to the caller.

You have now seen how to hash a message in Node.js, by selecting an algorithm, updating the hash with a message, and then creating the digest in the encoding of your choice. In the next section you will examine how to verify a file's integrity by using common hashing functions.

6-3. Verifying File Integrity with Hashes

Problem

You need to utilize a cryptographic hash algorithm to validate the integrity of files utilized in your Node.js application.

Solution

You may often encounter a situation where you need to check whether the content of your file or files that you access in your Node.js application has changed from a previous version. You can do this with the Node.js crypto module by generating a hash of the file's content.

In this solution you will create an application that demonstrates the abilities of four hashing algorithms to handle the task of reading the content of a file. In Listing 6-6, you will pass in the file you wish to hash, and then your application will read the file stream, updating the message as the stream is read, then log the resultant hash for each algorithm.

Listing 6-6. Checking File Integrity

```
/**
 * Checking File Integrity
 */

var fs = require('fs'),
    args = process.argv.splice('2'),
    crypto = require('crypto');
var algorithm = ['md5', 'sha1', 'sha256', 'sha512'];

algorithm.forEach(function(algo) {
    var hash = crypto.createHash(algo);

    var fileStream = fs.ReadStream(args[0]);

    fileStream.on('data', function(data) {
        hash.update(data);
    });

    fileStream.on('end', function() {
        console.log(algo);
        console.log(hash.digest('hex'));
    });
});
```

You can imagine building a deploy process in Node.js where you are sending or retrieving files from a remote server and you want to ensure that these files match the expected hash of the content from where they came.

You might also need to download a file. Once you download the file, you might need to check the integrity of this file to verify it against the value that you know to be accurate. In Listing 6-7 you download the node executable for version 0.10.10 for Windows and check the shasum against the known value of this hash.

Listing 6-7. Downloading a File and Checking shasum

```
/**
 * Verifying file integrity
 */

var http = require('http'),
        fs = require('fs'),
        crypto = require('crypto');

var node_exe = fs.createWriteStream('node.exe');

var req = http.get('http://nodejs.org/dist/v0.10.10/node.exe', function(res) {
        res.pipe(node_exe);
        res.on('end', function() {
                var hash = crypto.createHash('sha1');

                readr = fs.ReadStream('node.exe');

                readr.on('data', function(data) {
                        hash.update(data);
                });

                readr.on('end', function() {
                        // Should match 419fc85e5e16139260f7b2080ffbb66550fbe93f  node.exe
                        // from http://nodejs.org/dist/v0.10.10/SHASUMS.txt
                        var dig = hash.digest('hex');
                        if (dig === '419fc85e5e16139260f7b2080ffbb66550fbe93f') {
                                console.log('match');
                        } else {
                                console.log('no match');
                        }
                        console.log(dig);
                });
        });
});
```

How It Works

The solution in Listing 6-6 begins by requiring the crypto and the file-system modules, both needed for this implementation. You then create an array of different algorithms to use for your hashing. As you saw in the previous sections, the two most commonly used are MD5 and SHA-1, but the variants of SHA-2 are gaining popularity as well.

As you loop through each of the algorithms, you then create a new hash by using `crypto.getHash`, passing the algorithm to use. You then create a file stream using `fs.ReadStream`, passing in a file name you provided as an argument on the command line. You could just as easily pass any file name to be read from your application. As the file is read by Node.js, the data event is emitted.

Within the callback to the data event listener, you begin to process the message portion of your hash. This is done by passing the data directly to the hash's `update()` function. After the file is finished reading, the 'end' event is emitted. Within this callback you will actually generate the hash digest and log the result to the console.

When you are hashing files, it is easy to see how slight variations in content will result in a different hash. For example, a file that contains only the string 'This is text.' will generate an shasum, which is drastically independent from the shasum of a similar file containing the string 'This is test.'

In the second example, Listing 6-7, you created a very practical solution that checks for the integrity of a file once it has been downloaded to your server using an shasum. To do this you need to import the http, file system, and crypto modules. This implementation begins by creating a file on your file system that is writable via fs.createWriteStream. Next you make an HTTP GET request to the file source; in this case you retrieve the Node.js executable for Windows, version 0.10.10. You know the correct shasum that the file should match because it is freely available from the download page for this version.

The response from this GET request is then piped into the file you created using response.pipe(file). Once the response is complete, signified by the 'end' event, you are able to read the file from your file system. Just as in the previous example you create a hash with the given algorithm, which in this case is SHA-1, and update the message on the 'data' event of the file reader stream. Once the read is completed, you are able to generate the hash by calling the digest('hex') method on the hash. You now have the shasum of the file you downloaded and you can compare this to the expected value to ensure that the download is complete and not corrupted.

Checking the integrity of the file on your system is critical, but if you just want to get the hash of a remote file, you are able to generate the shasum of the file by hashing the response stream directly, as shown in Listing 6-8.

Listing 6-8. Hashing the HTTP Response Stream

```
/**
 * Verifying file integrity
 */

var http = require('http'),
        fs = require('fs'),
        crypto = require('crypto');

var req = http.get('http://nodejs.org/dist/v0.10.10/node.exe', function(res) {
        var hash = crypto.createHash('sha1');

        res.on('data', function(data) {
                hash.update(data);
        });

        res.on('end', function() {
                console.log(hash.digest('hex'));
        });
});
```

This eliminates the file writing and simply updates the hash when the response stream emits the 'data' event, finally generating the digest when the response ends.

6-4. Using an HMAC to Verify and Authenticate Messages
Problem

You need to authenticate a message in your Node.js application by using HMAC.

Solution

To generate an HMAC, you need to have a basic understanding of the cryptographic hash functions outlined in the earlier sections of this chapter. Node.js provides a method, similar to the createHash function, that will allow you to easily secure your messages with HMAC. Listing 6-9 shows how to implement an SHA-1-based HMAC in Node.js and also compares that to the SHA-1 hashing method directly.

Listing 6-9. Using HMAC

```
/**
 * Using Hash-Based Message Authentication
 */

var crypto = require('crypto')
        secret = 'not gonna tell you';

var hash = crypto.createHash('sha1').update('text to keep safe').digest('hex');
var hmac = crypto.createHmac('sha1', secret).update('text to keep safe').digest('hex');

console.log(hash);
console.log(hmac);
```

This will generate an output of two 160-bit encoded hashes, but even though they are encoding the same text, they are quite different because the HMAC utilizes the secret key to authenticate the hash.

SHA-1 Hash versus SHA-1 HMAC

```
f59de5dd5f2d5c49e45e1317448031baa38ab7e9
c6b314dbebdd4ff17d0fc84e9ee0d5ab5821df5f
```

How It Works

HMAC creates a way to validate the integrity of a message, like any cryptographic hash could, and it also, because of the integration of a secret key, allows you to validate the authenticity of a message. This may not be the Holy Grail of cryptographic functions, but it surpasses the security of simply hashing a message because it does provide an extra method for validation. This will help you to assert that your message has not been altered in transit, providing a level of assurance more than a higher level of cryptography.

You could theoretically produce a valid message with a key attached by concatenating a secret with a message when you are creating an SHA-1 hash of a message, but there still remains vulnerability in this structure. This is due to the fact that if an attacker is able to determine the message, he or she could programmatically extract the secret key and gain access to protected information on messages that he or she has yet to encounter. This is dangerous.

Basically an SHA-1 based HMAC is essentially running SHA-1 on the message twice. This automatically means that your hash is better but still is not authenticated. However, in HMAC the secret key is added to the message so that the HMAC then becomes an authenticable digest. You know that the sender of your HMAC is the actual sender because the secret key that is passed is automatically verified as authentic when you compare the digest of the HMAC. This is structured independently so that regardless of the messages you've encountered, and the secret keys that are passed, you will not be able to determine information for the secrets that are yet to come. This provides the extra level of assurance, as mentioned above, that your message has not been altered.

In your solution you create the HMAC by calling the createHmac function. This function accepts the type of hashing algorithm that you are going to use in your HMAC, and it also will take the secret key in the constructor arguments. After instantiation, the crypto.Hmac is created and processes with the same methods are attached to the prototype as the hash object. The difference is that the C++ binding is directed to the HMAC binding and not the hash, meaning that the processing implements the correct HMAC algorithms instead. The C++ then parses the arguments for the HMAC and then processes the HMAC by utilizing the OpenSSL HMAC implementation to generate the final result.

Node.js HMAC implementation

```
//hmac in crypto.js
exports.createHmac = exports.Hmac = Hmac;

function Hmac(hmac, key, options) {
  if (!(this instanceof Hmac))
    return new Hmac(hmac, key, options);
  this._binding = new binding.Hmac();
  this._binding.init(hmac, toBuf(key));
  LazyTransform.call(this, options);
}

util.inherits(Hmac, LazyTransform);

Hmac.prototype.update = Hash.prototype.update;
Hmac.prototype.digest = Hash.prototype.digest;
Hmac.prototype._flush = Hash.prototype._flush;
Hmac.prototype._transform = Hash.prototype._transform;

//hmac in node_crypto.cc
void Hmac::Initialize(v8::Handle<v8::Object> target) {
  HandleScope scope(node_isolate);

  Local<FunctionTemplate> t = FunctionTemplate::New(New);

  t->InstanceTemplate()->SetInternalFieldCount(1);

  NODE_SET_PROTOTYPE_METHOD(t, "init", HmacInit);
  NODE_SET_PROTOTYPE_METHOD(t, "update", HmacUpdate);
  NODE_SET_PROTOTYPE_METHOD(t, "digest", HmacDigest);

  target->Set(FIXED_ONE_BYTE_STRING(node_isolate, "Hmac"), t->GetFunction());
}

void Hmac::New(const FunctionCallbackInfo<Value>& args) {
  HandleScope scope(node_isolate);
  Hmac* hmac = new Hmac();
  hmac->Wrap(args.This());
}

void Hmac::HmacInit(const char* hash_type, const char* key, int key_len) {
  HandleScope scope(node_isolate);
```

```
  assert(md_ == NULL);
  md_ = EVP_get_digestbyname(hash_type);
  if (md_ == NULL) {
    return ThrowError("Unknown message digest");
  }
  HMAC_CTX_init(&ctx_);
  if (key_len == 0) {
    HMAC_Init(&ctx_, "", 0, md_);
  } else {
    HMAC_Init(&ctx_, key, key_len, md_);
  }
  initialised_ = true;
}

void Hmac::HmacInit(const FunctionCallbackInfo<Value>& args) {
  HandleScope scope(node_isolate);

  Hmac* hmac = ObjectWrap::Unwrap<Hmac>(args.This());

  if (args.Length() < 2 || !args[0]->IsString()) {
    return ThrowError("Must give hashtype string, key as arguments");
  }

  ASSERT_IS_BUFFER(args[1]);

  const String::Utf8Value hash_type(args[0]);
  const char* buffer_data = Buffer::Data(args[1]);
  size_t buffer_length = Buffer::Length(args[1]);
  hmac->HmacInit(*hash_type, buffer_data, buffer_length);
}

bool Hmac::HmacUpdate(const char* data, int len) {
  if (!initialised_) return false;
  HMAC_Update(&ctx_, reinterpret_cast<const unsigned char*>(data), len);
  return true;
}

void Hmac::HmacUpdate(const FunctionCallbackInfo<Value>& args) {
  HandleScope scope(node_isolate);

  Hmac* hmac = ObjectWrap::Unwrap<Hmac>(args.This());

  ASSERT_IS_STRING_OR_BUFFER(args[0]);

  // Only copy the data if we have to, because it's a string
  bool r;
  if (args[0]->IsString()) {
    Local<String> string = args[0].As<String>();
    enum encoding encoding = ParseEncoding(args[1], BINARY);
    if (!StringBytes::IsValidString(string, encoding))
      return ThrowTypeError("Bad input string");
```

```cpp
  size_t buflen = StringBytes::StorageSize(string, encoding);
  char* buf = new char[buflen];
  size_t written = StringBytes::Write(buf, buflen, string, encoding);
  r = hmac->HmacUpdate(buf, written);
  delete[] buf;
} else {
  char* buf = Buffer::Data(args[0]);
  size_t buflen = Buffer::Length(args[0]);
  r = hmac->HmacUpdate(buf, buflen);
}

if (!r) {
  return ThrowTypeError("HmacUpdate fail");
}
}

bool Hmac::HmacDigest(unsigned char** md_value, unsigned int* md_len) {
  if (!initialised_) return false;
  *md_value = new unsigned char[EVP_MAX_MD_SIZE];
  HMAC_Final(&ctx_, *md_value, md_len);
  HMAC_CTX_cleanup(&ctx_);
  initialised_ = false;
  return true;
}

void Hmac::HmacDigest(const FunctionCallbackInfo<Value>& args) {
  HandleScope scope(node_isolate);

  Hmac* hmac = ObjectWrap::Unwrap<Hmac>(args.This());

  enum encoding encoding = BUFFER;
  if (args.Length() >= 1) {
    encoding = ParseEncoding(args[0]->ToString(), BUFFER);
  }

  unsigned char* md_value = NULL;
  unsigned int md_len = 0;

  bool r = hmac->HmacDigest(&md_value, &md_len);
  if (!r) {
    md_value = NULL;
    md_len = 0;
  }

  Local<Value> rc = StringBytes::Encode(
        reinterpret_cast<const char*>(md_value), md_len, encoding);
  delete[] md_value;
  args.GetReturnValue().Set(rc);
}
```

6-5. Reviewing OpenSSL Ciphers and Security

Problem

You need a high-level understanding of the OpenSSL ciphers that are available to you as a Node.js developer.

Solution

Node.js provides a wrapper for the OpenSSL ciphers. Because of this, the ciphers that are available to you are those that are available via OpenSSL. To view these available ciphers, you can run a simple program (see Listing 6-10) that will output the various ciphers that are available in Node.js.

Listing 6-10. Ciphers Available to Node.js

```
/**
 * Reviewing ciphers
 */

var crypto = require('crypto');

var ciphers = crypto.getCiphers();
console.log(ciphers.join(', '));
```

In Listing 6-11, you see the output of the getCiphers() function. These are all of the ciphers available, of which several will be discussed in the How It Works section.

Listing 6-11. crypto.getCiphers()

```
[ 'CAST-cbc', 'aes-128-cbc', 'aes-128-cbc-hmac-sha1', 'aes-128-cfb', 'aes-128-cfb1', 'aes-128-cfb8',
'aes-128-ctr', 'aes-128-ecb', 'aes-128-gcm', 'aes-128-ofb', 'aes-128-xts', 'aes-192-cbc', 'aes-192-cfb',
'aes-192-cfb1', 'aes-192-cfb8', 'aes-192-ctr', 'aes-192-ecb', 'aes-192-gcm', 'aes-192-ofb', 'aes-256-
cbc', 'aes-256-cbc-hmac-sha1', 'aes-256-cfb', 'aes-256-cfb1', 'aes-256-cfb8', 'aes-256-ctr', 'aes-256-
ecb', 'aes-256-gcm', 'aes-256-ofb', 'aes-256-xts', 'aes128', 'aes192', 'aes256', 'bf', 'bf-cbc', 'bf-
cfb', 'bf-ecb', 'bf-ofb', 'blowfish', 'camellia-128-cbc', 'camellia-128-cfb', 'camellia-128-cfb1',
'camellia-128-cfb8', 'camellia-128-ecb', 'camellia-128-ofb', 'camellia-192-cbc', 'camellia-192-cfb',
'camellia-192-cfb1', 'camellia-192-cfb8', 'camellia-192-ecb', 'camellia-192-ofb', 'camellia-256-cbc',
'camellia-256-cfb', 'camellia-256-cfb1', 'camellia-256-cfb8', 'camellia-256-ecb', 'camellia-256-ofb',
'camellia128', 'camellia192', 'camellia256', 'cast', 'cast-cbc', 'cast5-cbc', 'cast5-cfb', 'cast5-ecb',
'cast5-ofb', 'des', 'des-cbc', 'des-cfb', 'des-cfb1', 'des-cfb8', 'des-ecb', 'des-ede', 'des-ede-cbc',
'des-ede-cfb', 'des-ede-ofb', 'des-ede3', 'des-ede3-cbc', 'des-ede3-cfb', 'des-ede3-cfb1', 'des-ede3-
cfb8', 'des-ede3-ofb', 'des-ofb', 'des3', 'desx', 'desx-cbc', 'id-aes128-GCM', 'id-aes192-GCM', 'id-
aes256-GCM', 'idea', 'idea-cbc', 'idea-cfb', 'idea-ecb', 'idea-ofb', 'rc2', 'rc2-40-cbc', 'rc2-64-cbc',
'rc2-cbc', 'rc2-cfb', 'rc2-ecb', 'rc2-ofb', 'rc4', 'rc4-40', 'rc4-hmac-md5', 'seed', 'seed-cbc', 'seed-
cfb', 'seed-ecb', 'seed-ofb' ]
```

How It Works

Ciphers are a way to encrypt and decrypt data by using a set algorithm. There are many algorithms available to you as you saw in the solution to this section. Many of these are block ciphers, or ciphers that act on a fixed block of data, as opposed to a cipher that would act on a stream of data and turn the plaintext into an encrypted form, or ciphertext. Each cipher has its own implementation, which I will discuss in detail.

■ **Note**   This section discusses some relatively complex material concerning algorithms and implementations for various ciphers. Some terminology that is common when referring to cryptographic ciphers is defined here for your reference.

attack vector: A set of malicious code that can target a security vulnerability.

block: A group of bits of a specified size that is commonly used in a block cipher.

block cipher: A type of cipher that operates within individual blocks, performing permutations on separate blocks until the final ciphertext is obtained.

ciphertext: The end result of encrypting plaintext by using a cipher.

permutation: A round of processing, or transformation, of the data.

related-key attack: An attack vector that targets a cipher using multiple and mathematically related keys. The results of these ciphers can then be used to extrapolate the cipher and compromise encrypted values.

DES

DES stands for Data Encryption Standard, and it is a block cipher originally designed at IBM in the 1970s. DES utilizes a cipher block size of 64 bits, and also the key size is 64 bits. The algorithm will take a 64-bit block of plaintext, operate an initial permutation on the block, split the block into two 32-bit halves, and then process them in an alternating fashion by XORing them against a portion of the key. This process repeats for 16 rounds until a final permutation occurs. The result is the DES ciphertext.

DES is vulnerable to a brute-force attack, like other ciphers, where an attacker will be able to perform a check against all possible keys. Because the key length in DES is 56 bits (64 minus the last 8 bits for parity check), the key is relatively short and thus makes a brute-force attack feasible. Still, even though DES is vulnerable it was not until it had been present in the market for more than 20 years before an attack was successfully demonstrated.

Because of its vulnerabilities, DES is not favored for many applications; however, there is a superseding implementation that is still widely utilized: Triple DES.

Triple DES is a way to increase the key size of the DES algorithm by essentially running the process three times. The overall design is the same but chooses three keys. The first key is used to encrypt the plaintext. The second key is then used to decrypt the first encryption. Finally, a third key runs DES again in order to generate the ciphertext. These keys can be either all the same, one different, or all three different, and they vary in strength according to the differences in keys, because essentially you are determining the key length of the cipher. While there are still known attacks against Triple DES, it is a more secure option than DES by itself.

RC2

RC2 (or Rivest Cipher 2), also a block cipher, was created by Ron Rivest of RSA fame in the late 1980s. The RC2 cipher is composed of 64-bit blocks, like DES, and it incorporates 18 rounds in the algorithm. There are 16 rounds of "mixing" and 2 rounds of "mashing." The key size for the RC2 algorithm is variable from 8 to 128 bits, defaulting to 64. There is a known vulnerability for this cipher by a related-key attack.

RC4

RC4 is a stream cipher also designed by Ron Rivest in the late 1980s. It is well known for its speed and simplicity. This cipher works by generating a stream of near random bits, which are used for the encryption. This happens in two steps: first, there is an array generation step, then a pseudo-random generation step. The output is generated by looping through the semirandom bytes of the array two at a time, swapping values of each in the array, then processing those modulo 256. The result is used to look up the sum of this operation in the bytes array.

RC4 has been widely used in many applications, such as TLS, Wired Equivalent Privacy (WEP), and Wi-Fi Protected Access (WPA). However, it is not impenetrable to attack vectors partially due to the pseudo-random values. Because of this, in 2001, WEP encryption of wireless networks was attacked, and this prompted a subsequent implementation for wireless encryption.

CAST

CAST is a block cipher. It is widely used in versions of PGP and GNU Privacy Guard (GPG) encryption. The algorithm itself utilizes key sizes from 40 to 128 bits and will run either 12 rounds or 16, though 12 only occurs if the key size is fewer than 80 bits. The underlying function consists of eight 32-bit substitution boxes that are based on other various algorithms, such as XOR, modular addition, bent functions, and rotations. There are three different round functions that are used in the CAST cipher. The first version of the round function is used in rounds 1, 4, 7, 10, 13, 16; the second on rounds 2, 5, 8, 11, 14; and the third with rounds 3, 6, 9, 12 and 15.

CAMELLIA

The Camellia cipher is another 128-bit block cipher, and its block size is 16 bytes. The key size is variable between 128, 192, and 256 bits. Camellia is another Feistel cipher that will use 18 rounds if using 128-bit keys or 24 rounds when using the larger key sizes. Like CAST, Camellia uses substitution boxes. For Camellia these boxes are 8-bit by 8-bit boxes and four of them are utilized. There is a special transform applied to this cipher every six rounds.

BLOWFISH

The Blowfish cipher is a block cipher designed by Bruce Scheiner. It is highly regarded, even though it is vulnerable to vectors, including a differential attack. The block size is 64 bits and the key can be anywhere from 32 to 448 bits. It utilizes 16 rounds and large S-boxes. The speed of this algorithm is 8.3 MB/s on a Pentium at 150 Hz.

There are several well-known password management products that utilize Blowfish. These include 1Password, Password Safe, and Password Wallet, among others. It is also utilized in GPG and many file and disk encryption softwares.

AES

AES (aka Rijndael), or Advanced Encryption Standard, is an encryption algorithm designed to supersede DES. AES has a block size of 128 bits, and key sizes can be 128, 192, or 256 bits. AES will operate in 10 rounds for the 128-bit keys, 12 rounds for 192-bit keys, or 14 rounds for 256-bit keys. The process of the AES cipher operations on a 4-byte by 4-byte matrix is called the "state." The process first expands the key by using a Rijndael key schedule and then the rounds can begin.

The first round is known as "AddRoundKey," which extracts a subkey, and a byte from the state is combined by using XOR.

This begins the remaining rounds with exclusion of a final round. The rounds start by executing a "SubBytes" step that replaces each byte in the "state" by way of an 8-bit substitution box. This is followed by a "ShiftRows" step, which will shift all the values of the rows by a set amount. This amount varies per row. The next step is the "MixColumns" step. In this step a column in the "state" is combined by using an invertible linear transform. Through this step, each column is essentially transposed by multiplication with a known polynomial or matrix to get the resultant mixed columns. Then there is another "AddRoundKey" step.

After the rounds complete, there is a final round that operates in the same way as the previous rounds except the "MixColumns" step is omitted. The result is the AES ciphertext.

AES is vulnerable to a related-key attack, distinguishing attack, and key-recovery attack. However, the complexity of these attacks is nontrivial and AES is still fundamentally secure. In fact it is arguably the most widely used encryption cipher in practice today.

It is used to encrypt file archives in instances of 7Zip, RAR, and WinZip. Other places where AES is used is a disk encryption technology like BitLocker. Also using forms of AES are GPG, IPsec, IronKey, OpenSSL (the wrapper from which Node.js's crypto derives), Pidgin, and the Linux Kernel Crypto API. There are, of course, many more places where AES is being used today but these are just a handful.

There are various ciphers at your disposal when you build your Node.js application. You should choose the implementation that suits the particular needs of your solution and keep up to date on changing standards and new implementations.

6-6. Using OpenSSL Ciphers to Encrypt Data
Problem

You have gained some understanding of OpenSSL ciphers that are available in Node.js. Now you need to encrypt data by utilizing these ciphers.

Solution

It is important to understand how to implement a cipher in your code. To do this, you will build a solution that will take a key and a string of text and then utilize an AES-256 algorithm to create a ciphertext from your plaintext and decrypt it again, as shown in Listing 6-12.

Listing 6-12. Creating Ciphertext from Plaintext

```
/**
 * encrypting data
 */

var crypto = require('crypto'),
        algo = 'aes256',
        key = 'cheese',
        text = 'the itsy bitsy spider went up the water spout';

var cipher = crypto.createCipher(algo, key);
var encrypted = cipher.update(text, 'utf8', 'hex') + cipher.final('hex');

console.log(encrypted);

var decipher = crypto.createDecipher(algo, key);
var decrypted = decipher.update(encrypted, 'hex', 'utf8') + decipher.final('utf8');

if (decrypted === text) {
        console.log('success!');
}
```

Encrypting plaintext in your application is important, but there may be situations where you wish to encrypt the content of an entire file and then decipher that text later on. This solution requires the use of the file-system module so that you are capable of reading the file's contents.

Listing 6-13. Encrypting the Contents of a File

```
/**
 * using ciphers on files
 */

var crypto = require('crypto'),
      fs = require('fs'),
      algo = 'aes256',
      key = 'cheese';

var text = fs.readFileSync('6-6-1.txt', { encoding: 'utf8' });

var cipher = crypto.createCipher(algo, key);
var encrypted = cipher.update(text, 'utf8', 'hex') + cipher.final('hex');

console.log(encrypted);

var decipher = crypto.createDecipher(algo, key);
var decrypted = decipher.update(encrypted, 'hex', 'utf8') + decipher.final('utf8');

if (decrypted === text) {
      console.log('success!');
      console.log(text);
}
```

How It Works

The `createCipher` function is essential when you use the crypto module in Node.js. The `createCipher` method will accept an algorithm and a password or key. The result of this method is to create a cipher object. The cipher object is a stream and has three methods.

Node.jscrypto.createCipher object

```
exports.createCipher = exports.Cipher = Cipher;
function Cipher(cipher, password, options) {
  if (!(this instanceof Cipher))
    return new Cipher(cipher, password, options);
  this._binding = new binding.CipherBase(true);

  this._binding.init(cipher, toBuf(password));
  this._decoder = null;

  LazyTransform.call(this, options);
}

util.inherits(Cipher, LazyTransform);
```

```
Cipher.prototype._transform = function(chunk, encoding, callback) {
  this.push(this._binding.update(chunk, encoding));
  callback();
};

Cipher.prototype._flush = function(callback) {

  this.push(this._binding.final());

  callback();
};
```

To encrypt a data, or a string of data as in the solutions in this section, you use the update function. The update method accepts the data you wish to encrypt, an input encoding, and an output encoding. The result of this method is the enciphered data, and, like the crypto hashes, it can be called multiple times on a cipher. Once you have completed the cipher you will then call the `cipher.final` function that accepts an output encoding, leaving you with the result of your cipher.

Cipher Update and Final Output

```
Cipher.prototype.update = function(data, inputEncoding, outputEncoding) {
  inputEncoding = inputEncoding || exports.DEFAULT_ENCODING;
  outputEncoding = outputEncoding || exports.DEFAULT_ENCODING;

  var ret = this._binding.update(data, inputEncoding);

  if (outputEncoding && outputEncoding !== 'buffer') {
    this._decoder = getDecoder(this._decoder, outputEncoding);
    ret = this._decoder.write(ret);
  }

  return ret;
};

Cipher.prototype.final = function(outputEncoding) {
  outputEncoding = outputEncoding || exports.DEFAULT_ENCODING;
  var ret = this._binding.final();

  if (outputEncoding && outputEncoding !== 'buffer') {
    this._decoder = getDecoder(this._decoder, outputEncoding);
    ret = this._decoder.end(ret);
  }

  return ret;
};
```

Lastly, you are able to override the padding on the cipher's input data into block size by using the setAutoPadding(false) function. This needs to be called before .final().

```
Cipher.prototype.setAutoPadding = function(ap) {
  this._binding.setAutoPadding(ap);
  return this;
};
```

As you may already suspect, the `crypto.createDecipher` function, used to reverse the process of encryption, functions in a similar way to the `createCipher` function. It does indeed, as it creates a Decipher object during instantiation. Once it is created, you are given access to the same API that the cipher object has.

Node.js crypto.createDecipher

```
exports.createDecipher = exports.Decipher = Decipher;
function Decipher(cipher, password, options) {
  if (!(this instanceof Decipher))
    return new Decipher(cipher, password, options);

  this._binding = new binding.CipherBase(false);
  this._binding.init(cipher, toBuf(password));
  this._decoder = null;

  LazyTransform.call(this, options);
}

util.inherits(Decipher, LazyTransform);

Decipher.prototype._transform = Cipher.prototype._transform;
Decipher.prototype._flush = Cipher.prototype._flush;
Decipher.prototype.update = Cipher.prototype.update;
Decipher.prototype.final = Cipher.prototype.final;
Decipher.prototype.finaltol = Cipher.prototype.final;
Decipher.prototype.setAutoPadding = Cipher.prototype.setAutoPadding;
```

In your solution, you created two examples of a ciphertext and deciphered that text within the same application. For the case of the plaintext string in the file, this works by using the password key 'cheese' and using that in the `createCipher` method. This essentially is no different than the second example where you used the file system to read the contents of a file, encoded to UTF-8, and deciphered the resultant ciphertext to find the expected result. In this example you utilized the AES-256 cipher algorithm, but any of the acceptable OpenSSL algorithms would work. For example, you could easily replace aes256 with 'cast' or 'camellia256', provided that you are consistent between enciphering and deciphering the data.

6-7. Using Node.js's TLS Module for Securing Your Server
Problem

You have a Node.js server that is transmitting information and you want to ensure the security of that transmission by utilizing Node.js's TLS module.

Solution

Building a TLS server in Node.js will look familiar. It is similar to the HTTPS server that you created in Chapter 4. This is because the underlying architecture of the HTTP server object is inherited from the TLS module.

To create a TLS server you need to start with the TLS module itself. Then you will build a reference to your server key and certificate files and pass them as options, as shown in Listing 6-14.

Listing 6-14. Create a TLS Server

```
/**
 * using TLS
 */

var tls = require('tls'),
        fs = require('fs');

var options = {
        key: fs.readFileSync('srv-key.pem'),
        cert: fs.readFileSync('srv-cert.pem')
};

tls.createServer(options, function(s) {
        s.write('yo');
        s.pipe(s);
}).listen(8888);
```

Once you have created your secure TLS server with a valid key and certificate, you need to create a client that is capable of connecting to it. This is a capability of Node.js as well. In fact, as Listing 6-15 shows, it is nearly identical to the net module's ability to create a connection; however, you need to be mindful to point to the certificate authority and credentialing for the secure transport to be authenticated.

Listing 6-15. TLS Connection

```
/**
 * tls connection
 */

var tls = require('tls'),
        fs = require('fs');

var options = {
        key: fs.readFileSync('privatekey.pem'),
        cert: fs.readFileSync('certificate.pem'),
        ca: fs.readFileSync('srv-cert.pem')
};

var connection = tls.connect(8888, options, function() {
        if (connection.authorized) {
                console.log('authorized');
        } else {
                console.log(':( not authorized');
        }
});

connection.on('data', function(data) {
        console.log(data);
});
```

How It Works

TLS is a way to encrypt data that are sent to and from a server. In this solution you created a server that utilized a key and certification, generated via OpenSSL commands in the terminal just as you saw in Chapter 4.

Listing 6-16. Generating OpenSSL Keys

```
$ openssl genrsa -out srv-key.pem 1024
$ openssl req -new -key srv-key.pem -out src-crt-request.csr
$ openssl x509 -req -in srv-crt-request.csr -signkey srv-key.pem -out srv-cert.pem
```

Once you have the key and the certificate, you pass these into the options object when you call tls.createServer and tell it to listen on port 8888. The createServer function takes not only the options argument but also a callback. This callback is emitted on a connection to the server and passes along the secure stream with the function. In your solution, you write a string to the stream and then pipe that out.

There are many more options that are available when you create a server, such as setting a timeout for the handshake or rejecting unauthorized connections. All of these are taken into account to secure your server.

- ca: An array of strings or buffers of trusted certificates.

- cert: A string or buffer containing the certificate key of the server in Privacy Enhanced Mail (PEM) format. (Required)

- ciphers: A string describing the ciphers to use or exclude.

- crl: A string or list of strings of PEM-encoded certificate revocation lists (CRLs)

- handshakeTimeout: Aborts the connection if the SSL/TLS handshake does not finish in a certain number of milliseconds. The default is 120 seconds.

- honorCipherOrder: When choosing a cipher, uses the server's preferences instead of the client preferences.

- key: A string or buffer containing the private key of the server in PEM format. (Required)

- NPNProtocols: An array or buffer of possible Next Protocol Negotiation (NPN) protocols. (Protocols should be ordered by their priority.)

- passphrase: A string or passphrase for the private key (or pfx).

- pfx: A string or buffer containing the private key, certificate, and certificate authority (CA) certificates of the server in PFX (or PKCS #12) format. (This is mutually exclusive with the key, cert, and ca options.)

- rejectUnauthorized: If true, the server will reject any connection that is not authorized with the list of supplied CAs. (This option only has an effect if the requestCert is true; the default is false.)

- requestCert: If true, the server will request a certificate from clients that connect and will attempt to verify that certificate. (The default is false.)

- sessionIdContext: A string containing an opaque identifier for session resumption.

- SNICallback: A function that will be called if the client supports the Server Name Identification (SNI) TLS extension.

It is interesting to note that these values become part of the credentials that are created to identify your server. This is done by passing the relevant parameters into the crypto.createCredentials function.

Listing 6-17. createServer Methos Credentials

```
var sharedCreds = crypto.createCredentials({
    pfx: self.pfx,
    key: self.key,
    passphrase: self.passphrase,
    cert: self.cert,
    ca: self.ca,
    ciphers: self.ciphers || DEFAULT_CIPHERS,
    secureProtocol: self.secureProtocol,
    secureOptions: self.secureOptions,
    crl: self.crl,
    sessionIdContext: self.sessionIdContext
});
```

Now you have a secure TLS server. You need to connect to it. To test the connection, simply open a terminal window and connect.

■ **Note**   On Windows, OpenSSL is not included by default. You can easily add it to your machine by downloading a binary at `http://openssl.org/related/binaries.html`. This will install to C:\OpenSSL-Win32 on your machine. You can then run OpenSSL from PowerShell from within the C:\OpenSSL-Win32\bin directory.

Listing 6-18. Connecting to a Secure Server

```
$ openssl s_client –connect localhost:8888
```

However, a more robust client, such as one built with Node.js, is possible. To build your client connection in your solution, you first create a connection with `tls.connect`. To this you pass the port (and optionally a URL). Then there is the options object, which you will notice looks quite similar to the options of the server, with the exception of the 'ca' option. This is the value of the CA of your server. Because the credentials for your server were self-signed, the only way to identify it is through itself. Once you have connected, you have access to the connection stream. This stream has a property that will tell you if you are actually authenticated to the server or not. From there, once you are authorized, you can perform the client-server interactions that you normally might in a networked application, but you now have the added security of TLS.

6-8. Encrypting User Credentials with the Crypto Module
Problem

You have a Node.js application that requires authentication to a server, which you need to ensure is encrypted.

Solution

If you are going to build any sort of secure application with Node.js, you are likely going to want a way to authenticate a user to your database. For example, imagine you have an online shopping cart for which you would like to have your users register an account for to make checkouts swifter, and also to send them promotions. You could easily implement a users table, or document, in your data store that will hold a username and a password, but storing a plaintext password is not a good idea. It is also completely unnecessary because, as you will see, it is easy to have added security when using the Node.js crypto module.

To build this solution, imagine that your user has just submitted a password to your site and now you want to store that as a hash. This is great because you don't have to store the plaintext password at all, and with the use of a salt, you are able to verify subsequent logins with ease. Listing 6-19 shows how you would go about creating a version of this implementation to store credentials.

Listing 6-19. Creating Secure Credentials

```
/**
 * user credentials
 */

var crypto = require('crypto'),
        password = 'MySuperSecretPassword';

function getHmac(password, salt) {
        var out = crypto.createHmac('sha256', salt).update(password).digest('hex');
        return out;
}
function getHash(password, salt) {
        var out = crypto.createHash('sha256').update(salt + password).digest('hex');
        return out;
}

function getSalt() {
        return crypto.randomBytes(32).toString('hex');
}
var salt = getSalt();
var hmac = getHmac(password, salt);
var hash = getHash(password, salt);
console.log('my pwd: ', password, ' salted: ', salt, ' and hashed: ', hash);
console.log('hmac: ' , hmac);
```

How It Works

As you take a look at how this is working, you will notice there are basically only two parts to this solution. First, you generate a random salt that will be the key when you hash your password with createHash or createHmac; second, you hash your password.

There are differing opinions about the proper way to secure your passwords. Some people argue that something like SHA-256 (SHA256[password]) is secure enough. However, most others will argue that you need to salt your hashes, as shown in this solution. Then the debate arises as to how large your hash should be, and whether it is necessary for it to be a cryptographically secure pseudo-random number or whether any collection of random bytes will work. For this solution, your code grabs a random set of 32 bytes.

You see this in the getSalt function. Here you access the crypto module and the randomBytes function, which is indeed a cryptographically secure pseudo-random collection of bytes. The randomBytes call in the Node.js source is a direct binding from the JavaScript to the C++ implementation.

Now that you have the salt, you can use that to securely hash your password. This is demonstrated in two ways in this solution. One is by the getHmac function. This function will use the salt that you generated to create your SHA-256-based HMAC. You then update the password with that HMAC, and generate the digest as Hex encoded.

The alternative to using the Hmac method is to append the salt to the password, and then SHA-256 has that result, as shown in the getHash function.

The important thing for both of these methods is to not use the same salt for each user. If you were to utilize the same salt, you would be vulnerable to a dictionary reverse-lookup attack. This means that if you and your friend use the same password, their hashes would be identical because the salt remains the same. A crafty malevolent source would be able to determine these patterns and eventually extract the secure data. However, using different salts, you will not run into this case; because the salts generated are cryptographically sound, the likelihood that they will ever collide on the same salt and password hash is minimized to a near insignificant degree.

6-9. Using a Third-Party Authentication Module
Problem

You need to authenticate your users in Node.js. To do this you want to utilize an appropriate third-party module for authentication.

Solution

You can imagine that you have the Node.js-based shopping cart that was discussed in the previous section. You know that you need a secure way to store user login and authentication data, but you may not be willing to roll your own authentication module. To mitigate this, you do a lot of research on the subject and find a couple of solutions. One is similar in approach to rolling your own, but it comes packaged in the npm as a module called 'bcrypt'. This module will allow for random salt generation, hashing of your passwords, and access to those values so you are able to store them securely on your data store. This implementation is shown in Listing 6-20. This implementation is a snippet from what you can imagine is a larger-scale application. This snippet is an example of a registration route in an application that will fetch user data, and if no users are found, it will utilize bcrypt to generate a salt and hash for a user, saving that to the data store.

Listing 6-20. Using bcrypt to Hash Passwords

```
app.post("/register", function(req, res) {
  var usrnm = req.body.name;
  User.findOne({username: usrnm}, function(err, usrData) {
      if (usrData === null) {
        //create
        bcrypt.genSalt(10, function(err, salt) {

          bcrypt.hash(req.body.pwd, salt, function(err, hash) {

            var newUser = new User({ username: usrnm, email: req.body.email, pwHash: hash });
              newUser.save(function(err) {
                if (err) {
                    res.send({name: usrnm, message: "failure", error: err});
                    return;
                }
                res.send({name: usrnm, message: "success"});
              });
          });
      });
      });
```

```
        } else {
        //emit to client
        res.send({name: usrnm, message: "failure", error: "User already exists"});
        }
    });
});
```

An alternative that you then are able to uncover is one that is built on the express.js framework. But this is an extension of the Mozilla Persona identity provider.

■ **Note** Express.js is a highly popular framework for building web applications, which you will read about in more detail later in the book. Mozilla Persona is a way to utilize your e-mail address as your identity provider, eliminating the need for your users to have specific passwords for your site.

You do this by installing a module that works with Express.js, 'express-persona', and you implement it as shown in Listing 6-21.

Listing 6-21. Using Persona for Authentication

```
require('express-persona')(app, {
        audience: 'http://localhost:3000', // Must match your browser's address bar
        verifyResponse: function(error, req, res, email) {
                var out;
                if (error) {
                        out = { status: 'failure', reason: error };
                        res.json(out);
                } else {
                        models.user.findOrCreate(email, function(result) {
                                if (result.status === 'okay' ) {
                                        out = { status: 'okay', user: result.user };
                                } else {
                                        out = { status: 'failure', reason: 'mongodb failed to find or
create user' };
                                }
                                res.json(out);
                        });
                }
        }
});
```

You have seen two possible implementations of third-party authentication modules, but there is a seemingly limitless supply if you examine the npm registry. It is important to scrutinize all security implementations that you will utilize on your server or in your Node.js application.

How It Works

You first implemented a solution that utilized the bcrypt module. This is installed by using the command npm install bcrypt, and then requiring the module within your code. bcrypt sets out to solve any underlying vulnerabilities in hashing passwords that are vulnerable to dictionary attacks.

The bcrypt solution is derived from Blowfish. It implements the key schedule from that particular cipher. It goes beyond normal salting and hashing after that by creating an adaptive hashing algorithm that is slow. It is good to be slow, because it causes an attacker to be unable to perform as many operations, increasing the time it takes to subsequently crack a password by orders of magnitude.

The essential implementation in this Node.js module requires only creating a salt, and then passing that to a hashing function, giving you a hashed password.

Listing 6-22. Generating a Salt and Hash with bcrypt

```
bcrypt.genSalt(10, function(err, salt) {
    bcrypt.hash(req.body.pwd, salt, function(err, hash) {
        //store password
    });
});
```

The genSalt function accepts a number of rounds (which defaults to 10), a seed length (defaults to 20), and a callback, which is required. The callback will provide an error if one occurs, as well as the salt value. From this salt you should create the hash, using the bcrypt.hash function. This takes the plaintext password you wish to encrypt, the salt, and a callback. The callback will produce the hash of the password, which you can then store in your data store.

To decrypt a password at login and compare it to the values in your data store, you can call the bcrypt.compare method. This accepts the password to validate as a first argument, then the hashed value from your database. This will return a result which is a boolean value—true if it matches, false if not.

In the second part of the solution you saw how to implement Mozilla Persona for user authentication. This was by using 'express-persona', which fits into an Express.js application. There are other implementations of Mozilla Persona, including persona-id, which is not tied to a particular framework, or you could roll your own implementation.

You see that in your solution, you require the module and then pass to it your express.js application and an object. This object contains the target audience, which is the URL of your application. It also contains a verifyResponse function that will generate a route on success or failure of verification, allowing you the opportunity to store the user information in your database. The complement to this Node.js implementation is the client side.

For the client to communicate with the server, you need to include the login.persona.org/include.js script in your source. You then need to register events for navigator.id.login() and logout() events.

Listing 6-23. Binding to a Persona Login and Logout

```
document.querySelector("#login").addEventListener("click", function() {
  navigator.id.request();
}, false);

document.querySelector("#logout").addEventListener("click", function() {
  navigator.id.logout();
}, false);
```

Persona also needs you to implement a watch function that will listen for these events. When one is detected, it will send an XMLHttpRequest to the /persona/verify or /persona/logout routes in your Express.js application.

Listing 6-24. Persona Navigator watch Method

```
navigator.id.watch({
  onlogin: function(assertion) {
    var xhr = new XMLHttpRequest();
    xhr.open("POST", "/persona/verify", true);
    xhr.setRequestHeader("Content-Type", "application/json");
    xhr.addEventListener("loadend", function(e) {
      var data = JSON.parse(this.responseText);
      if (data && data.status === "okay") {
        console.log("You have been logged in as: " + data.email);
      }
    }, false);

    xhr.send(JSON.stringify({
      assertion: assertion
    }));
  },
  onlogout: function() {
    var xhr = new XMLHttpRequest();
    xhr.open("POST", "/persona/logout", true);
    xhr.addEventListener("loadend", function(e) {
      console.log("You have been logged out");
    });
    xhr.send();
  }
});
```

As mentioned above, there are many third-party modules for user identification. These should all be implemented with scrutiny to ensure that you are properly securing your user's login credentials. You can, of course, roll your own implementation of the security principles involved in any of these modules.

Summary

Node.js is fully capable of creating applications that are just as secure as any other framework. The crypto module, which is a wrapping of the OpenSSL hashes, ciphers, and encryption capabilities, provides top-tier support for generating secure hashes and ciphertexts and for keeping your data safe.

Node.js also presents a framework for keeping server communication secure with the TLS module. This allows you to create safe connections between a client and server, as well as encrypting your HTTP traffic over HTTPS.

You also saw how it is possible to build a user authentication module to store user credentials in a more secure way. And, lastly, you saw how to build on existing frameworks to create a secure method for authentication via third-party modules.

Securing applications is not a trivial task, and it takes time and research to get the right solution and implementation. You also need to remain current and mindful of changes to best practices, how they affect your application, and how you can strengthen your security mechanisms through Node.js crypto modules.

CHAPTER 7

■ ■ ■

Discovering Other Node.js Modules

You have seen many different Node.js modules that you are able to utilize in the Node.js applications you wish to build. There are, however, many other modules and portions of the Node.js core that you can use when building a Node.js application. This chapter will touch on some of these native Node.js modules and expand on their implementations, giving you a better understanding of these modules. It is important to understand that these modules play a critical role in building a Node.js application.

In this chapter you will use the Domain Name System (DNS) module to resolve hostnames and IP addresses for remote servers. You will get a better handling of streams by using buffers, and you will look at clustering your applications. You will use the global process object, utilize timers, and work with query strings on server requests. You will also get a look at what is exposed in the Node.js console and get a look at the debugger URLs that are available in Node.js.

7-1. Creating a Simple DNS Server with DNS
Problem

You want to be able to gain information from remote servers in your Node.js application. This information can be IP addresses or domain names.

Solution

Node.js provides a means for you to access the domain names and IP addresses and domain names of remote servers. This is possible by creating a simple Node.js command-line application (shown in Listing 7-1) that will accept a domain name. The result is a listing of all IP addresses associated with that domain name.

Listing 7-1. DNS Lookup Command-Line Tool

```
/**
* DNS
*/
var dns = require('dns'),
        args = process.argv.splice(2),
        domain = args[0];

dns.resolve(domain, function (err, addresses) {
  if (err) throw err;
```

```
    addresses.forEach(function (address) {
        getDomainsReverse('resolve', address);
    });
});

dns.lookup(domain, function(err, address, family) {
        if (err) console.log(err);
        getDomainsReverse('lookup', address);
});

function getDomainsReverse(type, ipaddress) {
        dns.reverse(ipaddress, function(err, domains) {
                if (err)  {
                    console.log(err);
                } else if (domains.length > 1) {
                        console.log(type + ' domain names for '  + ipaddress + ' ' + domain);
                } else {
                        console.log(type + ' domain name for '   + ipaddress + ' ' + domain);
                }
        });
}
```

Utilizing this command-line tool will result in an output similar to what is in Listing 7-2, showing you the result of your query and which type of Node.js DNS tool was used to gather the result.

Listing 7-2. Using the Node.js DNS Lookup Command-Line Tool

```
$ node 7-1-1.js g.co
resolve domain name for 173.194.46.37 g.co
resolve domain name for 173.194.46.38 g.co
resolve domain name for 173.194.46.39 g.co
resolve domain name for 173.194.46.40 g.co
resolve domain name for 173.194.46.46 g.co
resolve domain name for 173.194.46.32 g.co
resolve domain name for 173.194.46.33 g.co
resolve domain name for 173.194.46.34 g.co
resolve domain name for 173.194.46.36 g.co
lookup domain name for 74.125.225.78 g.co
resolve domain name for 173.194.46.41 g.co
resolve domain name for 173.194.46.35 g.co
```

How It Works

Node.js implements a version of DNS that is a wrapped version of 'C-ares'. This is a C library that is built for asynchronous DNS requests. This module is the Node.js 'dns' module and it is required for the above solution.

The above solution allows you to run a Node.js command and by passing in the domain name you wish to resolve, or lookup. This will then be parsed from the Node.js process's arguments, passing into two methods of querying for this domain name. These two methods on the DNS object are dns.resolve() and dns.lookup(). Each of these performs a similar task in that they each will fetch from the DNS server the IP address that is associated with the domain name that is passed to the function. However, the implementation is quite different.

The dns.lookup() function will accept a domain name and a callback. There is an optional second parameter into which you can pass a family parameter. The family parameter will be either a 4 or a 6 and represents which

IP family you wish to query for the address. The callback for the dns.lookup() function will provide an error, address, and family parameter if they are available. As you can see from the source of the lookup function below, once the initial arguments are configured, Node.js calls the native wrapper for the C-ares DNS module cares.getaddrinfo and returns the wrapped results.

Listing 7-3. Dns.lookup Method from the Node.js dns.js Source

```
exports.lookup = function(domain, family, callback) {
  // parse arguments
  if (arguments.length === 2) {
    callback = family;
    family = 0;
  } else if (!family) {
    family = 0;
  } else {
    family = +family;
    if (family !== 4 && family !== 6) {
      throw new Error('invalid argument: `family` must be 4 or 6');
    }
  }
  callback = makeAsync(callback);

  if (!domain) {
    callback(null, null, family === 6 ? 6 : 4);
    return {};
  }

  if (process.platform == 'win32' && domain == 'localhost') {
    callback(null, '127.0.0.1', 4);
    return {};
  }

  var matchedFamily = net.isIP(domain);
  if (matchedFamily) {
    callback(null, domain, matchedFamily);
    return {};
  }

  function onanswer(addresses) {
    if (addresses) {
      if (family) {
        callback(null, addresses[0], family);
      } else {
        callback(null, addresses[0], addresses[0].indexOf(':') >= 0 ? 6 : 4);
      }
    } else {
      callback(errnoException(process._errno, 'getaddrinfo'));
    }
  }

  var wrap = cares.getaddrinfo(domain, family);
```

```
  if (!wrap) {
    throw errnoException(process._errno, 'getaddrinfo');
  }

  wrap.oncomplete = onanswer;

  callback.immediately = true;
  return wrap;
};
```

The second function utilized in this solution was the dns.resolve() function, utilized to resolve a domain. This function also accepts a domain and a callback, with an optional second parameter. The callback function provides an error and an array of addresses that have been resolved. If the method results in an error, it will be one of the codes shown in Table 7-1.

Table 7-1. *DNS Error codes*

Error (of the Form dns.ERROR)	Description
ADDRGETNETWORKPARAMS	Could not find GetNetworkParams function
BADFAMILY	Unsupported address family
BADFLAGS	Illegal flags specified
BADHINTS	Illegal hints flags specified
BADNAME	Malformed domain name
BADQUERY	Malformed DNS query
BADRESP	Malformed DNS reply
BADSTR	Misformatted string
CANCELLED	Cancels DNS query
CONNREFUSED	Could not contact DNS servers
DESTRUCTION	Channel is being destroyed
EOF	End of file
FILE	Error reading file
FORMERR	DNS server claims query was malformed
LOADIPHLPAPI	Error loading iphlpapi.dll
NODATA	DNS server returned an answer with no data
NOMEM	Out of memory
NONAME	Given hostname is not numeric
NOTFOUND	Domain name not found
NOTIMP	DNS server does not implement requested operation
NOTINITIALIZED	c-ares not initialized
REFUSED	DNS server refused query
SERVFAIL	DNS server returned general failure
TIMEOUT	Timeout while contacting DNS servers

Differing from the dns.lookup() method, this method's optional second parameter is a record type, indicating the type of DNS record you are attempting to resolve. Record types are of the following: 'A', 'AAAA', 'MX', 'TXT', 'SRV', 'PTR', 'NS', and 'CNAME'. The dns.resolve() method can take any of these seven record types as the parameter; however, if none are provided it defaults to the 'A' type, or IPv4.

Related to this method, and not shown in the solution, are wrappers for each of the seven record types. These are shorthand methods to get the exact resolution you desire without the need to pass the optional parameter. These include dns.resolve4, dns.resolve6, dns.resolveMx, dns.resolveTxt, dns.resolveSrv, dns.resolvePtr, dns.resolveNs, and dns.resolveCname.

Listing 7-4. Dns.resolve and Relatives from dns.js

```
var resolveMap = {};
exports.resolve4 = resolveMap.A = resolver('queryA');
exports.resolve6 = resolveMap.AAAA = resolver('queryAaaa');
exports.resolveCname = resolveMap.CNAME = resolver('queryCname');
exports.resolveMx = resolveMap.MX = resolver('queryMx');
exports.resolveNs = resolveMap.NS = resolver('queryNs');
exports.resolveTxt = resolveMap.TXT = resolver('queryTxt');
exports.resolveSrv = resolveMap.SRV = resolver('querySrv');
exports.resolveNaptr = resolveMap.NAPTR = resolver('queryNaptr');
exports.reverse = resolveMap.PTR = resolver('getHostByAddr');

exports.resolve = function(domain, type_, callback_) {
  var resolver, callback;
  if (typeof type_ == 'string') {
    resolver = resolveMap[type_];
    callback = callback_;
  } else {
    resolver = exports.resolve4;
    callback = type_;
  }

  if (typeof resolver === 'function') {
    return resolver(domain, callback);
  } else {
    throw new Error('Unknown type "' + type_ + '"');
  }
};
```

For the final part of your solution, you built a getDomainsReverse function. This was a wrapper for the dns.reverse function that is designed to accept an IP address and find all the domains that match the IP address provided. In your solution you abstract this away so that both the dns.lookup() and the dns.resolve() methods can reuse the function. The results of this retrieval are then logged to the console.

You can see that the DNS module affords you many opportunities to gather information about domains and servers that are remote to your location. In your solution to the problem of resolving a host, you were able to utilize the dns.lookup, dns.resolve, and dns.reverse methods to accomplish this task.

7-2. Handling Streams with the Buffer
Problem
You need to use the Buffer object to better handle streams.

Solution

Buffers are data that are in the form of binary data similar to an array and not just a string. Buffer is a Node.js global object that is used to handle buffers. This means that you will likely not ever need require('buffer'), though that is possible, because of the global nature of the object. To examine the capabilities of the Buffer object, you will create a Node.js file, as in Listing 7-5, that will execute most of the functionality available to buffers. This will allow you to understand better how you can handle buffers that become available in many parts of the Node.js ecosystem.

Listing 7-5. Buffers in Node.js

```
/**
* Buffer
*/

var buffer = new Buffer(16);
console.log('size init', buffer.toString());

buffer = new Buffer([42, 41, 41, 41, 41, 41, 41, 42, 42,4, 41, 41, 0, 0, 7, 77], 'utf-8');
console.log('array init', buffer.toString());

buffer = new Buffer('hello buffer', 'ascii');
console.log(buffer.toString());

buffer = new Buffer('hello buffer', 'ucs2');
console.log(buffer.toString());

buffer = new Buffer('hello buffer', 'base64');
console.log(buffer.toString());

buffer = new Buffer('hello buffer', 'binary');
console.log(buffer.toString());

console.log(JSON.stringify(buffer));
console.log(buffer[1]);
console.log(Buffer.isBuffer('not a buffer'));
console.log(Buffer.isBuffer(buffer));
// allocate size
var buffer = new Buffer(16);
// write to a buffer
console.log(buffer.write('hello again', 'utf-8'));
// append more starting with an offset
console.log(buffer.write(' wut', 11, 'utf8'));
console.log(buffer.toString());
// slice [start, end]
buf = buffer.slice(11, 15);
```

```
console.log(buf.toString());
console.log(buffer.length);

console.log(buffer.readUInt8(0));
console.log(buffer.readUInt16LE(0));
console.log(buffer.readUInt16BE(0));
console.log(buffer.readUInt32LE(0));
console.log(buffer.readUInt32BE(0));
console.log(buffer.readInt16LE(0));
console.log(buffer.readInt16BE(0));
console.log(buffer.readInt32LE(0));
console.log(buffer.readInt32BE(0));
console.log(buffer.readFloatLE(0));
console.log(buffer.readFloatBE(0));
console.log(buffer.readDoubleLE(0));
console.log(buffer.readDoubleBE(0));

buffer.fill('4');

console.log(buffer.toString());

var b1 = new Buffer(4);
var b2 = new Buffer(4);
b1.fill('1');
b2.fill('2');

console.log(b1.toString());
console.log(b2.toString());

b2.copy(b1, 2, 2, 4);

console.log(b1.toString());
```

The solution in Listing 7-5 highlights many of the capabilities that are available to you when you are utilizing a buffer in Node.js. Next you will see an example using the 'net' module and how when you communicate between client and server you are sending the data in the form of a buffer.

Listing 7-6. Using Buffers

```
var net = require('net');

var PORT = 8181;

var server = net.Server(connectionListener);

function connectionListener(conn) {
    conn.on('readable', function() {
        //buffer
        var buf = conn.read();
```

```
        if (Buffer.isBuffer(buf)) {
            console.log('readable buffer: ' , buf);
            conn.write('from server');
        }
    });

    conn.on('end', function() {
    });
}

server.listen(PORT);

//Connect a socket
var socket = net.createConnection(PORT);

socket.on('data', function(data) {
    console.log('data recieved: ',  data.toString());
});

socket.on('connect', function() {
    socket.end('My Precious');
});

for (var i = 0; i < 2000; i++) {
    socket.write('buffer');
}

socket.on('end', function() {
});

socket.on('close', function() {
    server.close();
});
```

How It Works

Buffers are the best ways to handle octet streams in Node.js. They represent raw data being transferred from within your Node.js application, and they are found in multiple places in Node.js. Buffers are very versatile. As you saw in Listing 7-5, they have many methods available to provide you with the best solution for a given job.

There are several methods that you can use when you wish to create a buffer. In the solution, you first created a buffer by allocating a size to the buffer, var buffer = new Buffer(16);. You then were able to generate a new buffer by passing an array directly into the constructor of the Buffer, var buffer = new Buffer([42, 42]...);. The third way in which you can create a new buffer is to directly pass a string to the constructor function, var buffer = new Buffer('hello world');. The constructor function also accepts a type of encoding, set as a string. If no encoding is passed, then the encoding will default to utf8.

Once you have created your buffer, you can now manipulate the buffer. There are methods that are directly available on the Buffer object itself. These methods include Buffer.isEncoding(encoding), Buffer.isBuffer(object), and Buffer.byteLength(buffer), which, respectively, evaluate if the encoding is set as expected, sees whether the given object is a buffer, and returns the byte length of the buffer.

In addition to these Buffer methods that are on the class itself, there are several methods, outlined in Table 7-2, that you can utilize when working with a Buffer.

Table 7-2. *Buffer Methods and Events*

Method (buffer.<method>)	Description
write(string, [offset], [length], [encoding])	Writes the string to the buffer at the given offset and encoding.
toString([encoding], [start], [end])	Converts the buffer to a stfing with a given encoding within a given range, start to end.
toJSON()	Returns a JSON-ized version of the buffer.
Length	Returns the size of the buffer in bytes.

copy([targetBuffer], [targetStart], [sourceStart], [sourceEnd])	Copies buffer data from the source to the target:
	
	```var b1 = new Buffer('1111');```
	```var b2 = new Buffer('2222');```
	```b2.copy(b1, 2, 2, 4);```
	```//b2 == 1121```

slice([start],[end])	Slices a buffer between the start and the end parameters. Results in a new buffer.
readUInt8(offset, [noassert])	Reads the buffer, starting at the offset, as an unsigned 8-bit integer.
readUInt16LE(offset, [noassert])	Reads the buffer, starting at the offset, as an unsigned 16-bit integer little endian.
readUInt16BE(offset[noassert])	Reads the buffer, starting at the offset, as an unsigned 16-bit integer big endian.
readUInt32LE(offset, [noassert])	Reads the buffer, starting at the offset, as an unsigned 32-bit integer, little endian format.
readUInt32BE(offset, [noassert])	Reads the buffer, starting at the offset as an unsigned 32-bit integer, big endian format.
readInt8(offset,[noassert])	Reads the buffer, starting at the offset, as an 8-bit integer.
readInt16LE(offset, [noassert])	Reads the buffer, starting at the offset, as a 16-bit little endian.
readInt16BE(offset, [noassert])	Reads the buffer, starting at the offset, as a 16-bit big endian.
readInt32LE(offset, [noassert])	Reads the buffer, starting at the offset, as a 32-bit little endian.
readInt32BE(offset, [noassert])	Reads the buffer, starting at the offset, as a 32-bit big endian.
readFloatLE(offset, [noassert])	Reads the buffer, starting at the offset, as a float, little endian.
readFloatBE(offset, [noassert])	Reads the buffer, starting at the offset, as a float, big endian.
readDoubleLE(offset, [noassert])	Reads the buffer, starting at the offset, as a double, little endian.
readDoubleBE(offset, [noassert])	Reads the buffer, starting at the offset, as a double, big endian.
writeUInt8(value, offset, [noassert]	Writes an unsigned 8-bit integer to the buffer, starting at the offset.
writeUInt16LE(value, offset, [noassert])	Writes an unsigned 16-bit integer to the buffer, starting at the offset, little endian.
writeUInt16BE(value, offset, [noassert])	Writes an unsigned 16-bit integer to the buffer, starting at the offset, big endian.
writeUInt32LE(value, offset, [noassert])	Writes an unsigned 32-bit integer to the buffer, starting at the offset, little endian.

(continued)

Table 7-2. (*continued*)

Method (buffer.<method>)	Description
writeUInt32BE(value, offset, [noassert])	Writes an unsigned 32-bit integer to the buffer, starting at the offset, big endian.
writeInt8(value, offset, [noassert])	Writes an 8-bit integer to the buffer, starting at the offset.
writeInt16LE(value, offset, [noassert])	Writes a 16-bit integer to the buffer, starting at the offset, little endian.
writeInt16BE(value, offset, [noassert])	Writes a 16-bit integer to the buffer, starting at the offset, big endian.
writeInt32LE(value, offset, [noassert])	Writes a 32-bit integer to the buffer, starting at the offset, little endian.
writeInt32BE(value, offset, [noassert])	Writes a 32-bit integer to the buffer, starting at the offset, big endian.
writeFloatLE(value, offset, [noassert])	Writes a float value to the buffer, starting at the offset, little endian.
siwriteFloatBE(value, offset, [noassert])	Writes a float value to the buffer, starting at the offset, big endian.
writeDoubleLE(value, offset, [noassert])	Writes a double value to the buffer, starting at the offset, little endian.
writeDoubleBE(value, offset, [noassert])	Writes a double value to the buffer, starting at the offset, big endian.
fill(value, [offset], [end])	Fills the buffer with the value specified from the offset to end range.

There are many methods available on a buffer that can be utilized for very specific purposes. For example, if you need to read and write unsigned 32-bit integers in little endian format, buffers can do that. While these methods are very flexible, in most cases, you will utilize buffers as shown in Listing 7-4. This is an example of a 'net' server and client that send data between each other. The data become a readable stream, which is a buffer. You will be able to perform the methods described in the section on any buffers, allowing you to manipulate data and streams that are used in your application.

7-3. Clustering with Node.js
Problem

You want to build a cluster of processes to run your application more efficiently.

Solution

Node.js provides a solution for clustering. This feature is still experimental at the time of this writing but it is capable of turning your single threaded Node.js application into one that utilizes multiple cores on your machine. In this way you are able to delegate Node.js tasks to separate threads, allowing for greater scalability. In this solution you will generate a Node.js application that will use the cluster module. The first example is a self-contained solution that will split a simple HTTP server and log the results of various cluster methods to your console.

Listing 7-7. Clustering

```
/**
* Clustering
*/

var cluster = require('cluster'),
    http = require('http'),
    cpuCount = require('os').cpus().length;
```

```javascript
if (cluster.isMaster) {
    for (var i = 0; i < cpuCount; i++) {
        cluster.fork();
    }
cluster.on('fork', function(worker) {
    console.log(worker + ' worker is forked');
});
cluster.on('listening', function(worker, address) {
    console.log(worker + ' is listening on ' + address);
});
cluster.on('online', function(worker) {
    console.log(worker + ' is online');
});
cluster.on('disconnect', function(worker) {
    console.log(worker + ' disconnected');
});
cluster.on('exit', function(worker, code, signal) {
    console.log('worker ' + worker.process.pid + ' died');
  });
} else {
  // Workers can share any TCP connection
  // In this case it is an HTTP server
  http.createServer(function(req, res) {
    res.writeHead(200);
    res.end("hello world\n");
  }).listen(8000);
}
```

Now you will configure the cluster to execute a second Node.js file, once for each core on your machine.

Listing 7-8. Clustering a Node.js Process

```javascript
/**
* Clustering
*/

var cluster = require('cluster'),
            cpuCount = require('os').cpus().length;

cluster.setupMaster({
        exec: '7-3-3.js'
});
if (cluster.isMaster) {
        for (var i = 0; i < cpuCount; i++) {
                cluster.fork();
        }
        cluster.on('fork', function(worker) {
                console.log(worker + ' worker is forked');
        });
```

```
        cluster.on('listening', function(worker, address) {
                console.log(worker + ' is listening on ' + address);
        });
        cluster.on('online', function(worker) {
                console.log(worker + ' is online');
        });
        cluster.on('disconnect', function(worker) {
                console.log(worker + ' disconnected');
        });
        cluster.on('exit', function(worker, code, signal) {
    console.log('worker ' + worker.process.pid + ' died');
  });
}
```

Listing 7-9, the worker process, is shown here.

Listing 7-9. The Worker Process

```
var http = require('http');

http.createServer(function(req, res) {
        console.log(req.url);
  res.writeHead(200);
  res.end("hello world\n");
}).listen(8000);
```

How It Works

Clustering in Node.js is essentially a solution to utilize one Node.js module and to split worker processes, utilizing the child_process.fork() function, all while maintaining reference and communication between the master and worker processes. The workers can be TCP or HTTP servers, and the requests are handled by the master process. This master process then utilizes round-robin load balancing to distribute the load through the server. It does this by listening for a connection, then calling a distribute method and handing off the processing to the worker process.

Listing 7-10. Master Listening, Then Distributing Load

```
this.server.once('listening', function() {
    self.handle = self.server._handle;
    self.handle.onconnection = self.distribute.bind(self);
    self.server._handle = null;
    self.server = null;
  });
RoundRobinHandle.prototype.distribute = function(handle) {
  this.handles.push(handle);
  var worker = this.free.shift();
  if (worker) this.handoff(worker);
};
```

```
RoundRobinHandle.prototype.handoff = function(worker) {
  if (worker.id in this.all === false) {
    return;                     // Worker is closing (or has closed) the server.
  }
  var handle = this.handles.shift();
  if (typeof handle === 'undefined') {
    this.free.push(worker);     // Add to ready queue again.
    return;
  }
  var message = { act: 'newconn', key: this.key };
  var self = this;
  sendHelper(worker.process, message, handle, function(reply) {
    if (reply.accepted)
      handle.close();
    else
      self.distribute(handle);  // Worker is shutting down. Send to another.
    self.handoff(worker);
  });
};
```

In your solutions you are working with the master process primarily. In both cases you have a simple HTTP server that will respond with a 'hello world' when a request is made to the server address. After importing the cluster module, you then check to see if the process is the cluster's master process by using cluster.isMaster. You now check to see how many clusters you should make on your machine by checking the number of cores that your machine has using the 'os' module. For each CPU, you fork a new worker process calling cluster.fork(). Since the underlying framework still generates a new child process, which is still a new instance of v8, you can assume that the startup time for each worker will be greater than 0 and less than 100 ms in most cases. It will also generate approximately 10 MB of memory consumption per process at startup.

You now know that this is the master process, so you are able to bind to events that will be communicated to the master process. The events of interest are 'fork', 'listening', 'exit', 'online', and 'setup'. The 'fork' event is emitted when a worker process is successfully forked and provides the worker object for the process that was forked. The 'online' event happens as soon as the forked process is created and running. The 'listening' event is sent once the worker has started listening. The 'exit' event is emitted when the worker process dies. If this happens you may want to call the .fork() method again to replace the downed worker.

Cluster is a powerful module that will allow you to distribute the load of your servers between multiple processes on your machine. As your Node.js application grows, this functionality can quickly become important in creating a scalable application.

7-4. Working with Query Strings
Problem

You built a web server with Node.js. You would like to smartly handle various differences with the query strings that are passed to your application with the HTTP requests.

Solution

Node.js has a query string module that will allow you to properly parse and encode query string parameters for your Node.js application.

Listing 7-11. Using the Query String Module

```
/**
 * querystrings
 */

var qs = require('querystring');

var incomingQS = [ 'foo=bar&foo=baz',
                   'trademark=%E2%84%A2',
                   '%7BLOTR%7D=frodo%20baggins'];

incomingQS.forEach(function(q) {
        console.log(qs.parse(q));
});

var outgoingQS = { good: 'night', v: '0.10.12', trademark: '™'};
console.log(qs.stringify(outgoingQS));

var newQS = qs.stringify(outgoingQS, '|', '~');
console.log(newQS);

console.log(qs.parse(newQS));
```

You are able to take an arbitrary query string as input and then parse it to an object. You are also capable of taking an arbitrary object and parsing it to a URL safe query string.

How It Works

While the query string module is not a huge module, it only exports four methods. It provides a very useful solution for dealing with query strings. In this solution, you began by requiring the 'querystring' module. This module provides several methods to help deal with query strings in your application.

First, the querystring.parse function accepts a string and optionally overrides for the separators, which default to ampersand and equals. There is also an options object that will allow you to override the default of 1000 maximum keys (maxKeys) that are to be processed. For each of the keys within the query string, the 'querystring' module will attempt to parse the value by first using the decodeURIComponent() function that is native to JavaScript. If this produces an error, then the module will move on to its own implementation that is called querystring.unescape.

Second, the querystring.stringify function will accept an object that you wish to encode into a querystring. Optionally, this method will also allow you to override the default ampersand and equals separators. The querystring.stringify method will parse the object, turning it into a string, then it will call the module's QueryString.escape method. This method is simply a wrapper for JavaScript's encodeURIComponent().

7-5. Processing Events with 'Process'

Problem

You want to be able to handle events globally in your Node.js application.

Solution

The Node.js Process module is a global object that is accessible anywhere within your Node.js application. In this solution, you can imagine a situation where you have a module and an auxiliary module. The main module has bindings to the events of initialization, and it begins a call to certain methods of the auxiliary module. The main module will look like the one shown in Listing 7-12 and the auxiliary module will look like the one shown in Listing 7-13.

Listing 7-12. Main Module, Dealing with Process

```
/**
* using the process
*/

function log(msg) {
        if (typeof msg === 'object') {
                msg = JSON.stringify(msg);
        }
        process.stdout.write(msg + '\n');
}
//add listeners
process.on('power::init', function() {
        log('power initialized');
});

process.on('power::begin', function() {
        log('power calc beginning');
});

process.on('exit', function() {
        log(process.uptime());
        log('process exiting...');
});

process.on('uncaughtException', function(err) {
        log('error in process ' + err.message + '\n');
});
log(process.cwd());
process.chdir('..');
log(process.cwd());
log(process.execPath);
log(process.env.HOME);
```

```
log(process.version);
log(process.versions);
log(process.config);
log(process.pid);
log(process.platform);
log(process.memoryUsage());
log(process.arch);

var pow = new require('./power');

var out = pow.power(42, 42);
log(out);

// throws
setTimeout(pow.error, 1e3);
```

Listing 7-13. Auxiliary Module

```
/**
 * power module
 */
process.emit('power::init');

exports.power = function(base, exponent) {
  var result = 1;
  process.emit('power::begin');
  for (var count = 0; count < exponent; count++)
    result *= base;
  return result;
};
```

How It Works

The Node.js process object can gain you valuable information and utility for your application. The Process object is global and is an EventEmitter. This is why in the example above you are able to emit 'power::init' from the power.js file. You also bind to this by calling process.on('power::init', callback). You then bind to other events. First you bind to another custom event that you emit when you begin to execute the power.js module's power function.

The two other events are built-in events to the Node.js process. First, you bind to the 'exit' event. This will be triggered when the process is ready to exit, giving you one last chance to log errors or notify users of an imminent end of process. The other built-in event that you listen for is the 'uncaughtException' event. This event is triggered by any exception that would otherwise bubble up to the console and crash your application. In the solution, you were able to trigger this event by attempting to call a method that did not exist on the power.js module.

The process module does more than just handle events. In fact, it can provide a large amount of information relevant to your current Node.js process, many of which you were able to utilize when creating your solution. Table 7-3 details these other methods and attributes on the process object.

Table 7-3. *Process Object Methods and Attributes*

Method	Description
abort()	This method will abort the process.
arch	Architecture of your system.
argv	This is the argument that instantiates your Node.js process. You have seen this before to parse parameters that are passed to your application.
chdir(director)	Changes the directory that your process is currently working from.
config	Lists the configuration of the Node.js application.
cwd()	Prints the current working directory for your process.
env	Lists the environmental variables on your system as an object.
execPath	This is the path to the Node.js executable on your system.
exit([code])	Emits the exit event with the specified code.
getgid()	Gets the group ID of the process. Not available on Windows.
getgroups()	Gets the group ID array of the processes' supplementary groups. Not available on Windows.
getuid()	Gets the user ID of the process. Not available on Windows.
hrtime([hrtime])	High-resolution time array (seconds, nanoseconds) since an arbitrary epoch in the past. This can be used with a previous hrtime reading to get the difference.
initgroups	Reads /etc/groups. Not available on Windows.
kill(process_id, [signal])	Sends a signal to the process ID.
maxTickDepth	You can use this to set the number of ticks to go before allowing the event loop to process. This prevents using .nextTick from locking I/O.
memoryUsage()	Bytes of memory usage in your process.
nextTick(callback)	Next time around the event loop, the callback will be executed. This can be done in this fashion: ```\nfunction definitelyAsync(arg, cb) {\n if (arg) {\n process.nextTick(cb);\n return;\n }\n\n fs.stat('file', cb);\n}\n```
pid	Process identifier.
platform	Lists the platform on which the process is running.
setgid()	Sets the group ID of the process. Not available on Windows.
setgroups	Sets the group array for the process. Not available on Windows.
setuid()	Sets the user ID of the process. Not available on Windows.
stderr	Standard error; this is a writeable stream.

(continued)

Table 7-3. (*continued*)

Method	Description
stdin	Readable stream that represents stdin.
| | ```
function log(msg) {
  if (typeof msg === 'object') {
    msg = JSON.stringify(msg);
  }
  process.stdout.write(msg + '\n');
}
``` |
| stdout | This is the standard output for your process and is a writeable stream. You were able to recreate console logging by creating your log() function: |
| | ```
function log(msg) {
  if (typeof msg === 'object') {
    msg = JSON.stringify(msg);
  }
  process.stdout.write(msg + '\n');
}
``` |
title	Title of the process.
umask([mask])	Setter and getter for the process's file mode creation mask.
uptime()	Number of seconds (not milliseconds) that Node has been running.
version	Prints the version of Node.js that the process is using.
versions	Lists an object containing the version of Node.js and its dependencies.

7-6. Using Timers

Problem

You want to be able to utilize timers in your Node.js application to control the flow.

Solution

Controlling the timing of particular processes in any application, including those built with Node.js, can be critical. Using timers in Node.js should be familiar to you if you have utilized timers in a web application, as some of the methods are available in browsers as well.

In this solution you will create an application that will utilize timers to poll a fictionally remote resource. This solution will represent a scenario where you need to fetch data from a remote queue. There are several solutions for polling on an interval, or simply utilizing timers to invoke a method efficiently on the event loop.

Listing 7-14. Using Timers

```
/**
* Using Timers
*/

var count = 0;
var getMockData = function(callback) {
```

```
        var obj = {
                status: 'lookin good',
                        data: [
                          "item0",
                          "item1"
                        ],
                        numberOfCalls: count++
                };
        return callback(null, obj);
};

var onDataSuccess = function(err, data) {
        if (err) console.log(err);
        if (data.numberOfCalls > 15) clearInterval(intrvl);
        console.log(data);
};

// getMockData(onDataSuccess);
setImmediate(getMockData, onDataSuccess);

var tmr = setTimeout(getMockData, 2e3, onDataSuccess);
tmr.unref();
var intrvl = setInterval(getMockData, 50, onDataSuccess);
```

How It Works

There are several timers that you can use in Node.js. First, there is the set of timers that you would find in a web browser. These are setTimeout and setInterval with their corresponding clearTimeout and clearInterval functions.

setTimeout is a way that you can schedule a one-time event after a given time delay. The structure of a setTimeout call takes at least two arguments. The first argument is the callback that you want to have executed when the timer fires. The second is a number of milliseconds to wait until that callback is executed. Optionally, you may add additional arguments to the function, which will be applied to the callback when the timer executes. setTimeout can be canceled by calling clearTimeout and passing a reference to the initial timeout timer.

■ **Note** Because of the JavaScript Node.js event loop, you are unable to rely directly on the timings of the callback execution. Node.js will attempt to execute the callback as close to the timing prescribed, but it will likely not be at the exact interval timings.

---

setInterval is a relative of the setTimeout. It functions in a similar manner by providing a mechanism to delay execution of a function by a set period of time. However, with setInterval that function will execute repeatedly on the same interval until clearInterval is called. In the solution above, this was the case that was used to poll in a long running process. In theory you could run an interval on a long poll of 30 seconds, 3 minutes, or every hour and just let the process run. However in the solution, you ran the interval on a short (< 1 second) interval and cleared it after it had executed 15 times.

Both the setInterval and setTimeout methods have two extra methods attached to them. These are unref() and ref(). The unref() method allows the Node.js process to terminate if the timer is the only timer left on the event. loop. The ref() method does the opposite by holding the process until the timer has executed. To see this in action, you can note that immediately after your two-second delay setTimeout method in the solution, you call that timer's unref() method. This means that this timer will never execute. Because the interval from the setInterval is finished and cleared well before the two seconds has elapsed, there remain no other timers on the event loop and the process exits gracefully.

setImmediate is another timing mechanism for Node.js. This is useful for calling near immediate methods, similar to how the process.nextTick() function operates. setImmediate will queue the function to process immediately behind any I/O-bound callbacks that are currently in the event loop. This is slightly varied on how nextTick operates, as it will bump its execution to the front of the event loop. This means that setImmediate is a better way to execute a method that will not lock I/O processes from happening. This is particularly useful if you are running a recursive function that requires some level of CPU usage, as this will not prevent those operations from happening between callbacks.

7-7. Using the V8 Debugger
Problem

You need to step through and debug your Node.js application.

Solution

Node.js runs on Google's V8, which has a built-in debugging mechanism. Because of this, Node.js allows you to debug the source utilizing this tool. You will create a solution that will help you gain an understanding of just how the debugger works and of what insights it can give you to your code. Listing 7-15 shows a simple HTTP server that will require a second module (shown in Listing 7-16).

Listing 7-15. HTTP Server

```
/**
 * Debugging
 */

var http = require('http'),
    mod = require('./7-7-2');

server = http.createServer(function(req, res) {

        if (req.url === '/') {
                debugger;
                mod.doSomething(function(err, data) {
                        if (err) res.end('an error occured');

                        res.end(JSON.stringify(data));
                });
        } else {
                res.end('404');
        }
});

server.listen(8080);
```

Listing 7-16. Required Module

```
/**
 * Debugging
 */

exports.doSomething = function(callback) {
        debugger;
        callback(null, { status: 'okay', data: ['a', 'b', 'c']});
};
```

There are a few things that might be slightly different from your typical Node.js application; in particular you can see some 'debugger;' statements. These will be directives to tell the V8 debug mechanism to pause execution of your program. This process begins by starting your Node.js application with the 'debug' flag.

How It Works

Google designed the V8 JavaScript engine, which powers Node.js, to allow for debugging of the JavaScript that is executing within the engine. Node.js supports V8 debugging in two ways. One way is to implement the V8 debugger protocol in a manner that will create the debugger, listening on a TCP port. This is useful if you are creating or using a third-party debugging tool that is coordinated to utilize the protocol. To do this, start your Node.js application, 7-7-1.js, with the command $ node --debug 7-7-1.js. This will begin the debugger and listen on localhost:5858 for hooks into the debugger. This allows for debugging clients to be created that communicate with the debugger. Fortunately, Node.js comes with its own V8 debugger client. You can access an application that you started in debug mode with the --debug flag by typing $ node debug into the console.

The Node.js built-in debugger can be accessed by starting your Node.js application with the 'debug' parameter.

Listing 7-17. Starting the Node.js debug CLI

```
$ node debug 7-7-1.js
```

This will start your application but with the debugger attached. The output in your console will show you that the debugger has started listening, and it will show the first line of JavaScript code, which the debugger will break by default.

Listing 7-18. Initial State of the Debugger

```
< debugger listening on port 5858
connecting... ok
break in 7-7-1.js:5
  3 */
  4
  5 var http = require('http'),
  6     mod = require('./7-7-2');
  7
debug>
```

You now have a 'debug>' prompt. This is the command-line interface to the debugger. You can walk through the basics of debugging by following the next steps. First, you can add a watch to an object or property in your application. To do this you type 'watch' followed by any expression you wish to watch.

```
debug> watch('expression')
```

So, in your solution you can watch for the request URL by using the watch command and passing 'req.url' as the expression.

```
debug> watch('req.url')
```

You are also able to list all the watchers that are currently active in your debugger session. The results will print the active watchers and their values to the console. The current values are given the immediate context of where the JavaScript code is paused.

```
debug> watchers
  0: req.url = "<error>"
```

Recall that in your application code, you created two places where you called 'debugger;'. It will pause the execution at these points in your application. However, there may be times when you do not wish to add debugger statements and you would just like to set a breakpoint in your code. To do this, the debugger has several breakpoint methods available. To set a breakpoint on the current line, simply type setBreakpoint() into the debug console. Alternatively, you can use the shorthand sb() to set a breakpoint. The setBreakpoint method also accepts a line number, so you can predetermine a line to break on. You can do this in your code by setting a breakpoint on the server.listen(8080) method.

```
debug> sb(21)
  1 /**
  2 * Debugging
  3 */
  4
  5 var http = require('http'),
  6     mod = require('./7-7-2');
  7
  8 server = http.createServer(function(req, res) {
  9     if (req.url === '/') {
 10             debugger;
```

You can also break on another file that will be loaded into your application. To do this, pass the file name and the line number to the setBreakpoint method.

```
debug> sb('7-7-2.js', 5)
Warning: script '7-7-2.js' was not loaded yet.
  1 /**
  2 * Debugging
  3 */
  4
  5 var http = require('http'),
  6     mod = require('./7-7-2');
  7
  8 server = http.createServer(function(req, res) {
  9     if (req.url === '/') {
 10             debugger;
```

Here you see that you have set the breakpoint on the initial line of code in the file 7-7-2.js. Once you continue the execution of the program, the breakpoint will pause the execution of the program again as soon as that line of code is hit.

At this point, you are ready to navigate through your application using the debugger. The debugger, like most debuggers, exposes methods that allow you to step through and continue the execution of your code. The most granular method is the step in command. This is called by typing 'step', or 's', for shorthand. From the beginning of the execution of your debugging instance, if you step, it will move you to the next area of execution. In this instance it has moved into the module.js file and is beginning the process of adding the modules you required in the source.

```
debug> s
break in module.js:380
Watchers:
  0: req.url = "<error>"

 378
 379   function require(path) {
 380     return self.require(path);
 381   }
 382
```

From here you will want to continue. Continuing execution will run until the next breakpoint is hit. If there are no other breakpoints, the application will run normally until you manually pause it with the pause command. A continuation can be triggered by 'cont', or 'c'. In your example, this will move you through the module import code and to the breakpoint, which you set on the '7-7-2.js' file, line 5.

```
debug> c
break in 7-7-2.js:5
Watchers:
  0: req.url = "<error>"

 3 */
 4
 5 exports.doSomething = function(callback) {
 6     debugger;
 7     callback(null, { status: 'okay', data: ['a', 'b', 'c']});
debug> c
break in 7-7-1.js:21
Watchers:
  0: req.url = "<error>"

 19 });
 20
*21 server.listen(8080);
 22
 23
```

Continuing one more time, you will hit the breakpoint you set on line 21 of '7-7-1.js'; this is the last breakpoint you set. However, there are debugger statements that you will hit once a connection is made to your HTTP server. After continuing through this, you can then make a request to your webserver, 'http://localhost:8080/'. Because of the debugger; statement, this will pause the execution at precisely the location in your connection listener callback.

```
debug> c
break in 7-7-1.js:10
Watchers:
  0: req.url = "/"
```

```
 8 server = http.createServer(function(req, res) {
 9     if (req.url === '/') {
10             debugger;
11             mod.doSomething(function(err, data) {
12                     if (err) res.end('an error occured');
```

From here, you can step into the next execution. This is done using the 'next', or 'n', command in the debugger. Performing 'next' twice, you end up at the debugger; statement within your '7-7-2.js' module.

```
debug> n
break in 7-7-1.js:11
Watchers:
  0: req.url = "/"

 9     if (req.url === '/') {
10             debugger;
11             mod.doSomething(function(err, data) {
12                     if (err) res.end('an error occured');
13
debug> n
break in 7-7-2.js:6
Watchers:
  0: req.url = "<error>"

 4
 5 exports.doSomething = function(callback) {
 6     debugger;
 7     callback(null, { status: 'okay', data: ['a', 'b', 'c']});
 8 };
```

You can now step out of this method by using the 'out', or ('o'), command.

```
debug> o
break in 7-7-1.js:19
Watchers:
  0: req.url = "/"

17             res.end('404');
18     }
19 });
20
21 server.listen(8080);
```

Other than step, next, continue, and out, there is the 'pause' command. This will pause the execution of any code that is running at the time.

While you are stepping through your code, it is sometimes necessary to get some more information about what is happening in your application. The debugger has utilities for this as well. First, when you are paused at a breakpoint, if you want to see more of the surrounding code, you can do this by using the 'list(n)' command. This will show the code surrounded by 'n' lines before and after the currently paused location, which can be very useful in gathering more context to what is currently taking place in the debugger. Another useful feature is the 'backtrace' ('bt') command. This will show the trace of execution path for the current point in the program.

Listing 7-19. Example of backtrace from Within the doSomething Method of the 7-7-2.js Module

```
debug> bt
#0 exports.doSomething 7-7-2.js:6:2
#1 7-7-1.js:11:7
```

You can also view the loaded files by using the 'scripts' command. Importantly, if you need to dig deeper into the code, you can use the debugger's read–eval–print loop (REPL) module by using the 'repl' command.

Debugging a Node.js application is treated as a high priority with the built-in command-line interface for debugging your application using the V8 debugger. You will find these tools to be useful when you track down anomalies and bugs in your code.

7-8. Parsing URLs
Problem

You want to be able to parse URLs in your Node.js HTTP server applications.

Solution

Node.js comes with a URL module that can be utilized to parse URLs and gather the information contained within. A solution to see how this works (see Listing 7-20) will show you to parse an arbitrary URL.

Listing 7-20. Parsing an Arbitrary URL

```
/**
 * parse url
 */

var url = require('url');

var theurl = 'http://who:ami@hostname:1234/a/b/c/d/?d=e#f=g';

var urlParsed = url.parse(theurl, true, true);
console.log('protocol', urlParsed.protocol);
console.log('slashes', urlParsed.slashes);
console.log('auth', urlParsed.auth);
console.log('host', urlParsed.host);
console.log('port', urlParsed.port);
console.log('hostname', urlParsed.hostname);
console.log('hash', urlParsed.hash);
console.log('search', urlParsed.search);
console.log('query', urlParsed.query);
console.log('pathname', urlParsed.pathname);
console.log('path', urlParsed.path);
console.log('href', urlParsed.href);

console.log(url.resolve('/a/b/c/', 'd'));
```

Results of 7-20

```
$ node 7-8-2.js
protocol http:
slashes true
auth who:ami
host hostname:1234
port 1234
hostname hostname
hash #f=g
search ?d=e
query { d: 'e' }
pathname /a/b/c/d/
path /a/b/c/d/?d=e
href http://who:ami@hostname:1234/a/b/c/d/?d=e#f=g
/a/b/c/d
```

Using this in practice, you can imagine an HTTP server, not unlike Listing 7-21, that requires the URL to be parsed so that you can coordinate the correct file to serve the client in the HTTP.response().

Listing 7-21. Using the URL Module

```
/**
* Parsing URLS
*/

var http = require('http'),
        fs = require('fs'),
        url = require('url');

var server = http.createServer(function(req, res) {
        var urlParsed = url.parse(req.url,true, true);

        fs.readFile(urlParsed.path.split('/')[1], function(err, data) {
        if (err) {
            res.statusCode = 404;
            res.end(http.STATUS_CODES[404]);
        }

        var ursplit = urlParsed.path.split('.');
        var ext = ursplit[ursplit.length - 1];
        switch(ext) {
            case 'htm':
            case 'html':
                res.writeHead(200, {'Content-Type': 'text/html'});
                res.end(data);
                break;
            case 'js':
                res.writeHead(200, {'Content-Type': 'text/javascript'});
                res.end(data);
                break;
```

```
            case 'css':
                res.writeHead(200, {'Content-Type': 'text/css'});
                res.end(data);
                break;
            case 'json':
                res.writeHead(200, {'Content-Type': 'application/json'});
                res.end(data);
                break;
            default:
                res.writeHead(200, {'Content-Type': 'text/plain'});
                res.end(data);
        }
    });
}).listen(8080);
```

How It Works

Using the URL module provides you with three methods for handling a URL. First you utilized the url.parse()
method. This method takes a URL string and returns a parsed URL object. The parsed URL object can take the
properties shown in Table 7-4.

Table 7-4. *Parsed URL Object Properties*

Property	Description
.auth	The authorization portion of the URL. username:password
.hash	Any fragment that is present in the URL.
.host	Full hostname and port of the URL.
.hostname	The full name of the host in the URL.
.href	The whole URL.
.path	The pathname and search combined.
.pathname	The full pathname following the hostname and port portion of the URL.
.port	The port specified in the URL.
.protocol	The protocol of the request.
.query	The query string without the '?'. Can be parsed as an object.
.search	The query string part of the URL.

The parsed object was used in the HTTP server example to resolve the path so that the server could read in the
file type and serve an appropriate mime-type for the content. There are also great uses for URL routing that could
benefit from parsing the URL.

If you are dealing with a parsed URL, and you would like to turn that object back into a proper URL, whether you
are serving a URL back to the client or some other purpose, you can create a URL from a parsed URL object by calling
the url.format() function on that object. This will reformat the object, excluding the href back to a URL.

The third method that can be used is the url.resolve(from, to) function. This function will attempt to resolve
a path just as a web browser would.

You can see that if you are going to deal with URLs in your Node.js application, you should utilize the features that have been built in with the URL module. It provides the tools needed to parse and format any URLs that you would need in your application.

7-9. Using the Console
Problem

You would like to utilize the console to log details, metrics, and assertions in your Node.js application.

Solution

You are likely familiar with some console functions, as most people utilize at least the console.log() function if they are building a Node.js application, and you have seen it used in many examples in other portions of this book. To see how you can utilize the console, Listing 7-22 shows all the different methods that are available to you as a Node.js developer.

Listing 7-22. Using the Console

```
/**
* Console
*/

console.log('console usage in Node.js');

console.info('console.info writes the', 'same as console.log');

console.error('same as console.log but writes to stderr');

console.warn('same as console.err');

console.time('timer');

setTimeout(console.timeEnd, 2e3, 'timer');

console.dir({ name: 'console.dir', logs: ['the', 'string representation', 'of objects']});

var yo = 'yo';
console.trace(yo);

try {
        console.assert(1 === '1', 'one does not equal one');
} catch(ex) {
        console.error('an error occured: ', ex.message);
}
```

Console Results

```
7|⇒ node 7-9-1.js
console usage in Node.js
console.info writes the same as console.log
same as console.log but writes to stderr
same as console.err
{ name: 'console.dir',
  logs: [ 'the', 'string representation', 'of objects' ] }
Trace: yo
    at Object.<anonymous> (/Users/gack/Dropbox/book/code/7/7-9-1.js:20:9)
    at Module._compile (module.js:456:26)
    at Object.Module._extensions..js (module.js:474:10)
    at Module.load (module.js:356:32)
    at Function.Module._load (module.js:312:12)
    at Function.Module.runMain (module.js:497:10)
    at startup (node.js:119:16)
    at node.js:901:3
an error occured:  one does not equal one
timer: 2001ms
```

How It Works

The console object in Node.js is a method to write to stdout and stderr. The most common console functions are console.log, console.err, console.warn, console.dir, and console.info. These functions deal with logging information directly to provide information to the user and they deal directly with the stdout and stderr of the Node.js process.

Console Object Source

```
Console.prototype.log = function() {
  this._stdout.write(util.format.apply(this, arguments) + '\n');
};
Console.prototype.info = Console.prototype.log;
Console.prototype.warn = function() {
  this._stderr.write(util.format.apply(this, arguments) + '\n');
};
Console.prototype.error = Console.prototype.warn;
Console.prototype.dir = function(object) {
  this._stdout.write(util.inspect(object, { customInspect: false }) + '\n');
};
```

There is not much to implementing these methods in Node.js. There are, however, a few other console methods that can be useful.

One of these is the pair of console.time and console.timeEnd. Each of the functions takes a label, which will tell Node.js to track the time between the call of console.time('label') and console.timeEnd('label'). Once console.timeEnd('label') is called, it will log the number of milliseconds that have elapsed between the events.

```
Console.prototype.time = function(label) {
  this._times[label] = Date.now();
};
```

```
Console.prototype.timeEnd = function(label) {
  var time = this._times[label];
  if (!time) {
    throw new Error('No such label: ' + label);
  }
  var duration = Date.now() - time;
  this.log('%s: %dms', label, duration);
};
```

Console.trace() is a function that will print the current stack trace, applied to an argument that was passed as a label. This happens by creating a new Error object and setting the specifics, based on the current stack.

```
Console.prototype.trace = function() {
  // TODO probably can to do this better with V8's debug object once that is
  // exposed.
  var err = new Error;
  err.name = 'Trace';
  err.message = util.format.apply(this, arguments);
  Error.captureStackTrace(err, arguments.callee);
  this.error(err.stack);
};
```

Console.assert, is a wrapper for assert.ok() that will throw an error if the assertion fails. In the solution for this, you created an assertion that you knew would fail, and you logged the error message when you caught the exception.

CHAPTER 8

■ ■ ■

Creating a WebSocket Server

This chapter begins a departure from the previous chapters in the book. Previously, the chapters concentrated heavily on the Node.js core and its functionality. This was to build a better understanding of the fundamental architecture and platform availabilities that are included with Node.js. However, Node.js is a thriving success because of the ecosystem of third-party modules and the extensibility that they provide. This chapter, and those that follow, will provide you will a taste of the Node.js community and what it can offer you in your application development. This chapter begins by discussing WebSockets.

Before WebSockets, there were many methods for communicating in a WebSocket-like fashion between a client and a server. Many of these used some form of polling from client to server, where the client would connect to the server, which would then either respond with a status directly or hold the HTTP connection open for a long duration waiting for an event. This creates many HTTP requests and is not a fully two-way communication between client and server. So the HTML 5 specification drafted the WebSocket protocol to allow for this two-way communication with a persistent connection.

WebSockets are based on the WebSocket protocol, defined as a two-way communication with a remote host, or bidirectional communication over TCP. WebSocket communication is message-based, which makes it easier to handle than a communication mechanism such as TCP streams. The WebSocket implementation at first glance may appear like an HTTP instance, but the HTTP portion of the interface is just to create a handshake between the client and the server and subsequently upgrade the connection to the WebSocket protocol. Once the handshake is successful, both the client and the server are able to send messages to the other.WebSocket messages are composed of frames, which in terms of the protocol are sections of information that determine what type of message is being sent. These can be the type of content (binary or text), or control frames that can be used to signal that a connection should be closed. WebSocket endpoints are accessed by using the ws:// URI scheme and the wss:// for a Secure Sockets Layer (SSL) connection.

WebSockets thrive in Node.js because of the event-driven nature of Node.js and the ability to quickly and efficiently create a WebSocket server, either manually or through a third-party tool. Because of this natural fit with Node.js, the barrier for entry into the world of WebSockets makes it easy tocreate WebSocket-supported servers with Node.js.

You briefly saw how to create an upgraded WebSocket connection in Chapter 4, but this chapter will showcase utilizing different frameworks and techniques for building a fullyfledged WebSocket application. Some topics you will cover include the following:

- Using third-party modules to build WebSocket servers

- Listening for events on the client

- Building an API with WebSockets

- Communicating events from your server with WebSockets

- Handling these events in the browser and creating two-way communications

- Building a multiuser application with WebSockets

There are several WebSocket implementations that are available to you as a Node.js developer if you do not wish to create your own server. By not creating your own server, you trade off a few things and gain others. You trade off full control of your service from concept to production, but one thing that you gain, if the module you are using is well supported, is the community surrounding the module. This chapter will look at two of these modules: WebSocket-Node and Socket.IO. Both have strong communities to which developers can turn for a sound implementation; however, Socket.IO has become the first place to go for many WebSocket developers.

8-1. Implementing a WebSocket Server with WebSocket-Node
Problem

You would like to begin using the WebSocket-Node module in order to create a WebSocket server.

Solution

When you first turn to WebSocket-Node for your WebSocket needs, you see that you have the opportunity to utilize a framework that is not highly opinionated as to how you format your WebSocket as it is mostly a JavaScript implementation of the WebSocket Protocol.

To get Started utilizing this Node.js module, you first need to install from the npm registry, 'npm install websocket.' Once you have this installed, you are able to use it as shown in Listing 8-1 where you see that you extend a web server to utilize the upgraded WebSockets connection.

Listing 8-1. Upgrading a Web Server to Use WebSockets

```
/**
* using WebSocket-Node
*/

var http = require('http'),
    fs = require('fs'),
    url = require('url'),
    WebSocketServer = require('websocket').server;

var server = http.createServer(function(req, res) {
    var urlParsed = url.parse(req.url,true, true);

    fs.readFile(urlParsed.path.split('/')[1], function(err, data) {
        if (err) {
            res.statusCode = 404;
            res.end(http.STATUS_CODES[404]);
        }
        res.statusCode = 200;
        res.end(data);
    });
}).listen(8080);
```

```
var serverConfig = {
        httpServer: server,
        autoAcceptConnections: false
};

var wsserver = new WebSocketServer();

wsserver.mount(serverConfig);

wsserver.on('connect', function(connection) {
    console.log('connected');
    connection.send('yo');
});

wsserver.on('request', function(req) {
    console.log('request');
        var connection = req.accept('echo-protocol', req.origin);

    connection.on('message', function(message) {
        if (message.type === 'utf8') {
            console.log(message.utf8Data);
        }
        else if (message.type === 'binary') {
            console.log(message.binaryData);
        }
    });
    connection.on('close', function(reasonCode, description) {
        console.log('connection closed', reasonCode, description);
    });
});

wsserver.on('close', function(conn, reason, description) {
    console.log('closing', reason, description);
});
```

How It Works

When you create a WebSocket server with WebSocket-Node, you accomplish quite a few things with a simple-to-use API. First, you are creating an HTTP server. This is a requirement because the HTTP connection must be upgraded in order to successfully create the WebSocket connection via the handshake process. You then need to create a WebSocket server configuration object, serverConfig, in your solution.

This configuration is what will be used to determine the type of WebSocket communication your server will handle. The options that are available to be set on this configuration are shown in Table 8-1. These defaults are merged with the options that you set and used in the WebSocket server.

Table 8-1. *WebSocket Server Configuration Options*

Option	Description
assembleFragments	This tells the server to automatically assemble messages that are fragmented and then the full message is to be emitted on the 'message' event. If this is not true, then the frames are emitted on the 'frame' event and the client will need to assemble these frames together itself. Default: true
.autoAcceptConnections	This tells the server whether or not to accept any WebSocket connection, regardless of the path or the protocol that is specified by the client. This should be avoided in most cases as you are better off inspecting the request to check for allowable origin and protocol. Default: false
.closeTimeout	This is the number of milliseconds to wait after sending a close frame to see if the acknowledgment is returned before closing the socket anyway. Default: 5000
.disableNagleAlgorithm	This will determine if the Nagle algorithm is utilized. This algorithm allows for smaller packets to be aggregated together by inserting a small delay before transmission. Default: true (no delay)
.dropConnectionOnKeepaliveTimeout	This tells the WebSocket server to drop connections to clients that are unable to respond to a keepalive ping within the .keepaliveGracePeriod. Default: true
.fragmentationThreshold	If an outgoing frame is larger than this number, then it will be fragmented. Default: 0x4000 (16KB)
.fragmentOutgoingMessages	This setting tells whether to fragment messages that exceed the fragmentationThreshold option. Default: true
.httpServer	This is the server that you are going to be upgrading the connection to WebSocket protocol. This option is required. Default: null
.keepAlive	This timer will send out a ping to all clients at each specified .keepaliveInterval. Default: true
.keepaliveGracePeriod	This is the amount of time, in milliseconds, to wait after sending the keepalive ping before dropping the connection. Default: 10000
.keepaliveInterval	The amount of time in milliseconds to send a keepalive ping to connected clients. Default: 20000
.maxReceivedFrameSize	This option is to set the maximum frame size threshold for the WebSocket message frames. Default: 0x10000 (hex) = 64 Kilobytes

(continued)

Table 8-1. (*continued*)

Option	Description
.maxReceivedMessageSize	This is to set the maximum size for messages. This only applies if the option .assembleFragments is set to true. Default: 0x100000 (1 MB)
.useNativeKeepalive	This will tell the server to use the TCP keepalive instead of the WebSocket ping and pong packets. The difference is that the TCP keepalive is slightly smaller, reducing bandwidth. If set to true, then .keepaliveGracePeriod and .dropConnectionOnKeepaliveTimeout are ignored. Default: false

Once you have your configuration set with your HTTP server, you can instantiate a new WebSocket server by calling new WebSocketServer([config]), where [config] means you are optionally passing in the configuration options. In your solution you then call the .mount() method of the new WebSocket server, which will merge the options and bind to the 'upgrade' event of the HTTP server.

Another method that is available to the WebSocket server isunmount(), which will remove the ability to upgrade to the WebSocket protocol from the HTTP server but will not affect any existing connections. closeAllConnections() is another method that is a graceful shutdown of all connections; shutdown()closes all connections and unmounts from the server.

There are several events that you are able to listen to as well. In your example, you utilize the 'request', 'connect', and the 'close' event.

The 'request' event is emitted when you do not have the configuration option 'autoAcceptConnections' set to true. This will give you the opportunity to inspect the incoming WebSocket request to guarantee that you are aiming to connect to the desired origin and protocol. You can then either accept() or reject() the request. You saw that in the example the accept()method took parameters. The accept()method can take three parameters: a protocol, an origin, and cookies. The protocol will only accept data from a WebSocket connection of the same protocol. The origin allows you to limit WebSocket communication to a specified host. The cookies in the arguments must be an arrayin which name/value pairs accompany the request.

The 'connect' event is emitted from the server once the request has been accepted. This event will then pass the WebSocketConnection object to be handled in the callback of the handled event.

The 'close' event is emitted when the connection to the WebSocket server is closed for any reason. It will not pass only the WebSocketConnection object, but also a close reason and description to the callback of the event handler.

You have seen how to create a connection to a WebSocket server using WebSocket-Node, a third-party module for WebSocket implementation. You will now investigate two ways to communicate with the WebSocket server by using a Node.js client or from a client on a web application.

■ **Note** WebSockets is not fully available across web browsers. Internet Explorer does not implement the protocol until Internet Explorer version 10. Opera Mini (through version 7.0)and the Android browser (through version 4.2) do not support the protocol. In addition to this, some legacy versions of other browsers do not support the most current implementation. For more information, check http://caniuse.com/#feat=websockets.

8-2. Listening for WebSocket Events on the Client
Problem

You want to be able to communicate with a WebSocket server as a client.

Solution

There are several ways to connect to a WebSocket connection, and you will see two of these methods in this solution. One way to accomplish this is to utilize the third-party framework, WebSocket-Node, to create a client application that will connect to a WebSocket server and communicate between the two endpoints. This is shown in Listing 8-2 and is different than the more typical approach of utilizing a web page (which you will cover in more detail in Section 8-5) to connect to a WebSocket server and continue to communicate using that protocol.

Listing 8-2. Creating a WebSocket Client with WebSocket-Node

```
/**
* A WebSocket Client
*/

var WebSocketClient = require('websocket').client;

var client = new WebSocketClient();

client.on('connectFailed', function(error) {
        console.log('Connect Error: ' + error.toString());
});

client.on('connect', function(connection) {
        console.log('woot: WebSocket client connected');
        connection.on('error', function(error) {
                console.log(error);
        });
        connection.on('close', function() {
                console.log('echo-protocol Connection Closed');
        });
        connection.on('message', function(message) {
                switch (message.type) {
                        case 'utf8':
                                console.log('from server: ', message.utf8Data);
                                break;
                        default:
                                console.log(JSON.stringify(message));
                                break;
                }
        });
        connection.send('heyo');
});

client.connect('ws://localhost:8080/', 'echo-protocol');
```

As an alternative to the WebSocket-Node implementation in Listing 8-2, you could create a WebSocket client that will connect by using an HTML page like the one shown in Listing 8-3.

Listing 8-3. WebSocket Client HTML Page

```
<!doctype html>
<html>
<head>
</head>
<body>
        <h3>WebSockets!</h3>
<script>
window.onload = function() {
        var ws = new WebSocket('ws://localhost:8080', 'echo-protocol');
        ws.onopen = function() {
                console.log('opened');
        };
        ws.onmessage = function(event) {
                console.log(event);
                ws.send(JSON.stringify({ status: 'ok'}));
        };
};
</script>
</body>
</html>
```

How It Works

First, you created a client by using the WebSocketClient that is available to be used in a Node.js application that comes with WebSocket-Node. This client creates the upgraded connection to a WebSocket server for you when you call new WebSocketClient();. This constructor function will accept an options object and extend that with the default options, which are shown in Table 8-2.

Table 8-2. WebSocketClient Options

Option	Description
.assembleFragments	This tells the client to automatically assemble fragmented frames into a complete message. Default: true
.closeTimeout	This is the time to wait, in milliseconds, until the connection is closed after not receiving a response. Default: 5000
.disableNagleAlgorithm	This tells whether to disable the Nagle algorithm, which will set a small delay before sending messages in order to reduce HTTP traffic. Default: true
.fragmentOutgoingMessages	This will cause outgoing messages that are larger than the set .fragmentationThreshold to be fragmented. Default: true

(continued)

Table 8-2. (*continued*)

Option	Description
.fragmentationThreshold	This is the size limit at which to split frames into fragments. Default: 16KB
.webSocketVersion	This is the specified version of the WebSocket protocol to utilize in this connection. Default: 13
.maxReceivedFrameSize	This will set the maximum size of the frames that are received via the WebSocket protocol. Default: 1 MB
.maxReceivedMessageSize	This is the maximum size of the messages received via the protocol. It only applies if the .assembleFragments option is set to true. Default: 8 MB
.tlsOptions	This object can contain Transport Layer Security (TLS) information for secure connections.

Once you have created your WebSocket client, you are able to listen for events and messages that are transported via the connection. In your solution, you listen for a 'connect' event. This event will receive the connection object in the callback, which you will then use to transmit and receive data to the server. The connection is initialized by calling the .connect() function on the WebSocket client. This will accept the URL and the protocol that you wish to bind the endpoints to.

To transmit a message to the WebSocket server, you utilize the connection.send() method. This method will take two arguments: first the data you wish to send, and second, a callback function (which is optional). The data will be processed to check whether the data are a buffer. If the data are a buffer, they will be processed by calling the .sendBytes() method of the connection; otherwise it will attempt to use the connection's .sendUTF() method if the data can be converted with the .toString() method. The .sendBytes() or .sendUTF() methods will be where your callback is passed. You can see the internal workings of the WebSocket-Node implementation of the send method in Listing 8-4.

Listing 8-4. WebSocketClient Send Method

```
WebSocketConnection.prototype.send = function(data, cb) {
    if (Buffer.isBuffer(data)) {
        this.sendBytes(data, cb);
    }
    else if (typeof(data['toString']) === 'function') {
        this.sendUTF(data, cb);
    }
    else {
        throw new Error("Data provided must either be a Node Buffer or implement toString()")
    }
};
```

You were also able to listen to the 'message' event. This event is emitted from the WebSocket server and in your example, you checked to see what type of message is received. Checking the type allows you to process the message appropriately, whether it is a utf8 string or another format. Using the WebSocketClient that comes with WebSocket-Node is a great way to build interprocess communications for your Node.js applications. However, you may want to use an HTML page to create your WebSocket clients.

By utilizing either the WebSocketClient or the native WebSockets available in the WebSocket object in a web browser, you can create a useful client connection to a WebSocket server.

8-3. Building a WebSocket API

Problem

You want to build an application to utilize WebSockets, but you need to create an API that fits well into the WebSocket paradigm.

Solution

Creating an API with WebSockets can seem to be different than another API approach, such as representational state transfer (REST). This is because, though you could conceivably be targeting multiple routes in your application, with WebSockets you lack access to the HTTP verbs that dictate actions in a RESTful design. There are several ways in which you can still build an organized API. In Listing 8-5 you see that you build a WebSocket server, not unlike the server created in the first section of this chapter, which contains some extra handling with the data that are sent in the messages from the client.

Listing 8-5. Route Handling with a WebSocket Server

```
/**
* using WebSocket-Node
*/

var http = require('http'),
    fs = require('fs'),
    url = require('url'),
    WebSocketServer = require('websocket').server;

var server = http.createServer(function(req, res) {
    var urlParsed = url.parse(req.url,true, true);

    fs.readFile(urlParsed.path.split('/')[1], function(err, data) {
        if (err) {
            res.statusCode = 404;
            res.end(http.STATUS_CODES[404]);
        }
        res.statusCode = 200;
        res.end(data);
    });
}).listen(8080);

var serverConfig = {
        httpServer: server,
        autoAcceptConnections: false
};

var wsserver = new WebSocketServer();

wsserver.mount(serverConfig);

wsserver.on('connect', function(connection) {
    connection.send('yo');
});
```

```
wsserver.on('request', function(req) {
    if (req.requestedProtocols[0] == 'echo-protocol') {
        var connection = req.accept('echo-protocol', req.origin);

        connection.on('message', function(message) {
            if (message.type === 'utf8') {
                var rt = JSON.parse(message.utf8Data);
                switch (rt.path) {
                    case 'route_a':
                        console.log('something cool on route a');
                        break;
                    case 'route_b':
                        console.log('something cool on route b', rt);
                        break;
                    default:
                        console.log('something awesome always can happen');
                        break;
                }
            }
            else if (message.type === 'binary') {
                console.log(message.binaryData);
            }
        });
        connection.on('close', function(reasonCode, description) {
            console.log('connection closed', reasonCode, description);
        });
    } else {
        console.log('protocol not acceptable');
    }

});

wsserver.on('close', function(conn, reason, description) {
    console.log('closing', reason, description);
});
```

Once you have this route handling created on your server, you can build a more logical model for sending messages across the WebSocket connection from the client, as shown in Listing 8-6.

Listing 8-6. Manual Routes

```
<!doctype html>
<html>
<head>
</head>
<body>
        <h3>WebSockets!</h3>
```

```
<script>
window.onload = function() {
        var ws = new WebSocket('ws://localhost:8080', 'echo-protocol');
        ws.onopen = function() {
                console.log('opened');
        };
        ws.onmessage = function(event) {
                console.log(event);
                ws.send(JSON.stringify({ status: 'ok', path: 'route_a'}));
                ws.send(JSON.stringify({ status: 'ok', path: 'route_b', action: 'update'}));
        };

};
</script>
</body>
</html>
```

While this is usually a successful strategy for implementing some sort of routing or API design with WebSockets, there are alternatives for this object-routing concept as well. One alternative is shown by utilizing the WebSocket-Node WebSocketRouter object. This object allows you to easily dictate separate routing for different paths or protocols in your WebSocket-based Node.js application. A server of this type is shown in Listing 8-7.

Listing 8-7. A WebSocketRouter Server

```
/**
 * WebSockets API
 */

var http = require('http'),
    fs = require('fs'),
    url = require('url'),
    WebSocketServer = require('websocket').server,
    WebSocketRouter = require('websocket').router;

var server = http.createServer(function(req, res) {
    var urlParsed = url.parse(req.url,true, true);

    fs.readFile(urlParsed.path.split('/')[1], function(err, data) {
        if (err) {
            res.statusCode = 404;
            res.end(http.STATUS_CODES[404]);
        }
        res.statusCode = 200;
        res.end(data);
    });
}).listen(8080);

var serverConfig = {
        httpServer: server,
        autoAcceptConnections: false
};
```

```
var wsserver = new WebSocketServer();

wsserver.mount(serverConfig);

var router = new WebSocketRouter();
router.attachServer(wsserver);

router.mount('*', 'echo-protocol', function(request) {
        console.log('mounted to echo protocol');
        var conn = request.accept(request.origin);

        conn.on('message', function(message) {
                console.log('routed message');
        });

        conn.send('hey');
});

router.mount('*', 'update-protocol', function(request) {
        console.log('mounted to update protocol');
        var conn = request.accept(request.origin);

        conn.on('message', function(message) {
                console.log('update all the things');
        });
});
```

Listing 8-8 shows how you can build an HTTP client within your HTML page that will showcase how you can specify routes from the WebSocketRouter server.

Listing 8-8. WebSocketRouter HTTP Client

```
<!doctype html>
<html>
<head>
</head>
<body>
        <h3>WebSockets!</h3>

<script>
window.onload = function() {
        var ws = new WebSocket('ws://localhost:8080', 'echo-protocol');
        ws.onopen = function() {
                console.log('opened');
        };
        ws.onmessage = function(event) {
                console.log(event);
                ws.send(JSON.stringify({ status: 'ok', path: 'route_a'}));
        };
```

```
        var wsupdate = new WebSocket('ws://localhost:8080', 'update-protocol');

        wsupdate.onopen = function() {
                wsupdate.send('update');
        };
};
</script>
</body>
</html>
```

How It Works

After examining these two types of API implementations with WebSockets, you notice immediately that there is nothing overly complicated about these solutions. The basis for both is to specify an action to be resolved, given a specific message from the server.

In Listing 8-4, you created a server that handled a JavaScript Object Notation (JSON) object that is passed from the client to the server. This requires you to design the routes and actions that you wish to provide for in your API. If you choose, you could even mimic a REST API by providing routes and actions accordingly. For example, if you have a user profile you wish to access via an API, you could build a set of objects that could look like the following:

```
{ route: '/user/profile', action: 'GET' }
{ route: '/user/profile', action: 'POST' }
{ route: '/user/profile', action: 'PUT' }
{ route: '/user/profile', action: 'DELETE'}
```

This would be handled by your server by parsing the incoming message and then handling the routes as you do in the `switch(rt.path) {...}` in the solution. You can see that this solution for building a WebSocket API is very adequate for many needs, especially if you are only implementing a single protocol to handle the API directives. You could, of course, have segregated routing that is handled by different WebSocket protocols. For this, there is a feature in WebSocket-Node that makes accessing differing protocols with a single `WebSocketServer` instance even easier.

This was demonstrated in the solution found in Listing 8-6. Here you create your server again, but you include the .router object from the WebSocket-Node module. To utilize this feature you first create your HTTP server. Then, just as before, you must tell your new WebSocket server that you wish to use this HTTP server for the connection. However, instead of the message and connection handling that you saw before, you now can pass the `WebSocketServer` to be bound to a `WebSocketRouter` instance. This `WebSocketRouter` instance will then allow you to split off the handling of the routes to specific paths and/or protocols from your client.

In your solution, you built a router that can handle any path that is supplied to it (`'*'`), from the client but then can handle differing routes by handling different protocols in isolation. This means that if you have a logical separation in your application, say an API for user updates and an API for product updates, you can keep each of these easily separated with a separate protocol. You would simply create a new WebSocket on the client that points to your server and passes in the specific protocol for each item.

```
var users = new WebSocket('ws://my.wsserver.co', 'users_protocol');
var products = new WebSocket('ws://my.wsserver.co', 'product_protocol');
```

From here you no longer are concerned with all the details of routing in your data, though you will still need to be aware of actions and specific events you wish to drive through the WebSocket connection, but you know that if you are accessing a particular WebSocket protocol, you are isolated to that set of the application logic. In fact the entire route is isolated on the server as you saw in your example. Obviously segregating types of objects is one method, but you can imagine that the possibility to separate each type of update/fetch messaging is possible too. This may be too granular for most cases, but in an example of a chat room, you might have a 'sendmessage_protocol' and a 'getmessage_protocol' and handle the get and send operations completely separately.

There are essentially limitless ways in which you can build an API around your WebSocket connections in your Node.js application, allowing you the freedom to create your application as you see fit.

Most of this chapter to this point has been based around the WebSocket-Node module and its implementations. From here you will investigate Socket.IO, which is another and hugely popular framework for building a WebSocket-based Node.js application.

8-4. Using Socket.IO for WebSocket Communications
Problem

You want to build your WebSocket-based Node.js application by utilizing the Socket.IO module.

Solution

Socket.IO is a fully operational and highly popular framework for utilizing WebSockets with Node.js. Implementations of Socket.IO can take many forms, but the most popular will be to communicate messages between a client and server in a manner similar to the Node.js event model. To get started, you first install Socket.IO via npm with the '$ npm install socket.io' command. To build the Socket.IO server, you can follow the example shown in Listing 8-9, which showcases various methods that are accessible to you as you implement a Node.js Socket.IO server.

Listing 8-9. Implementing a Socket.IO Server

```
/**
 * Socket.io Server
 */

var app = require('http').createServer(connectHandler),
        io = require('socket.io').listen(app),
        fs = require('fs');

app.listen(8080);

function connectHandler (req, res) {
  fs.readFile(__dirname + '/8-4-1.html',
  function (err, data) {
    if (err) {
      res.writeHead(500);
      return res.end('Error loading 8-4-1.html');
    }

    res.writeHead(200);
    res.end(data);
  });
}
// General
io.sockets.on('connection', function (socket) {
socket.broadcast.emit('big_news'); // Emits to all others except this socket.
socket.emit('news', { hello: 'world' });
socket.on('my other event', function (data) {
console.log(data);
});
});
```

```
//namespaced
var users = io.of('/users').on('connection', function(socket) {
                        socket.emit('user message', {
                                that: 'only',
                                '/users': 'will get'
                        });
                        users.emit('users message', {
                                all: 'in',
                                '/users': 'will get'
                        });
                });
```

One of the reasons that Socket.IO has become so popular is that it has a drop-in client module that you can utilize in an HTML page that is bound to your server. This allows for an effortless connection to the WebSocket server that was created using Socket.IO. Implementing this connection requires adding a single JavaScript file reference and then binding to the WebSocket server by using a Socket.IO specific binding as opposed to the new `WebSocket()` instantiation that is part of the web standard.

Listing 8-10. A Socket.IO Client

```
<!doctype html>
<html>
<head>
        <script src="/socket.io/socket.io.js"></script>
        <script>
          var socket = io.connect('http://localhost');
          socket.on('news', function (data) {
        console.log(data);
        socket.emit('my other event', { my: 'data' });
          });

          socket.on('big_news', function(data) {
                console.log('holy cow!');
        });
          var users = io.connect('http://localhost/users');
          users.on('connect', function() {
                users.emit('users yo');
          });
        </script>
</head>
<body>

</body>
</html>
```

How It Works

Socket.IO does many things for you when you are building a WebSocket server, but it also allows the flexibility that you need when building a Node.js application. Just as with WebSocket-Node, it abstracts away the handshake to create the upgraded WebSocket connection not only on the server but also on the client when you include the Socket.IO JavaScript file in your HTML.Socket.IO is also unique because it not only will leverage the power of the WebSocket protocol but also will fall back to other methods of two-way communication, such as Flash sockets, long-polling, and iframes. It will do this so that you can build your application, create a WebSocket communication structure, and still be able to rely on the Socket.IO communication even on older browsers or on those that do not support the WebSocket protocol.

In Listing 8-8 you created a WebSocket server by using Socket.IO. To do this, you first installed the Socket.IO package. You then created a simple HTTP server by using the native Node.js http module; this is to serve the HTML page from Listing 8-9 that you plan to use to connect to the WebSocket server.

When you instantiate Socket.IO in your code, you do so by telling the new object to listen on the HTTP server, `io = require('socket.io').listen(server)`, but you could also just pass in a port on which to listen. Now you have access to the Socket.IO API. On the server there are several events that you utilized to communicate to the client.

First, you listened for the 'connection' event, which is emitted when the server receives a connection from a client. From the callback on this event you gain access to the individual socket that is bound to that particular connection.This socket is where your WebSocket communication can take place.

The first communication that you perform is a broadcasted message. This message is triggered by calling `socket.broadcast.emit('big_news');`, which will send the message 'big_news' to all sockets that are connected to the Socket.IO server with the exception of the connection that is sending the broadcast. Next you emit an event 'news' by using the method `socket.emit('news', { hello: 'world' });`. This event is able to be listened for on the client where you can then process the data that were transmitted with the message. This is similar to the `WebSocket.send()` method that you will see in more detail in the following section.The last method that you utilize inside of the 'connection' event callback is the binding to an arbitrary event message emitted from the client. This is accomplished in the same manner as binding to any event.

You then made a WebSocket connection that was bound to a namespace. This would be useful for creating an API similar to the examples outlined in the previous section. You can bind to a namespace by calling `io.of('/path')`. This will then route any connections that are on that path to the specifiedhandlers. You can name these namespaces as you did in the solution `var users = io.on('/users');`. This is useful because you can then call events on only the user's namespace, such as when you emitted the message to all users by calling `users.emit('users message'...);`.

To receive and transmit messages on the client, you simply start by adding a JavaScript reference to the socket. io.js file. This will give you access to an I/O object, which you can then use to connect to your Socket.IOserver. Once connected, you have an instance of a socket that can listen for and emit events to the server. Again, just as with the server namespacing you are able to connect to a specific route by utilizing a path: `var users = io.connect('http://localhost/users');`.

With this implementation, you are able to see how you can leverage Socket.IO to build a Node.js WebSocket server and client.Socket.IO utilizes its own API for sending and receiving messages. However, if you choose to use the WebSocket standard `.send()` instead of the `.emit()` method, Socket.IO will support that. In the next sections, you will get a closer look at how to utilize the WebSocket object to send and handle messages across connections.

8-5. Handling WebSocket Events in a Browser
Problem

You would like to utilize WebSocket events in the browser.

Solution

Earlier in the chapter you saw how you are able to build a WebSocket client by using the WebSocket-Node module. You have also seen cases where these WebSocket connections can be made either in a web browser or by using Socket.IO in the browser. Listing 8-11shows how you can utilize the WebSocket API directly in the web browser. In this case you should have a WebSocket server running that is similar to the one shown in Listing 8-1.

Listing 8-11. WebSocket API in the Browser

```
<!doctype html>
<html>
<head>
</head>
<body>
<h3>WebSockets!</h3>
<script>
window.onload = function() {
    var ws = new WebSocket('ws://localhost:8080', 'echo-protocol');
    ws.onopen = function() {
        console.log('opened');
    };

    ws.onmessage = function(event) {
      console.log(event);
      ws.send(JSON.stringify({ status: 'ok'}));

      console.log(ws.binaryType);
      console.log(ws.bufferedAmount);
      console.log(ws.protocol);
      console.log(ws.url);
      console.log(ws.readyState);
    };

    ws.onerror = function() {
      console.log('oh no! an error has occured');
    }

    ws.onclose = function() {
      console.log('connection closed');
    }
};
</script>
</body>
</html>
```

How It Works

You were able to create a WebSocket client in HTML by simply binding to the endpoint of your WebSocket server and requesting the correct protocol, which in your case was called 'echo-protocol.'This is accomplished by creating a new WebSocket(<url>, <protocol>); object in your web page's JavaScript. This new WebSocket object has access to several events and attributes. The WebSocket methods that are available are .close() and .send(), which close the connection or send a message, respectively. The events that you bound to in the solution are .onmessage, and .onopen. The .onopen event is emitted as soon as the connection is opened, meaning that the connection is ready to send and receive data. The .onmessage event is the receipt of a message from the WebSocket server. Other event listeners that are available are .onerror, which will receive any error that occurs, and the .onclose event, which is emitted when the state changes to closed.

The WebSocket object in the browser also has access to several attributes. These include the URL and protocol that is being utilized to transport the information, as well as the state and any extensions that are provided by the server. The WebSocket connection also has access to see the types of data that are being transmitted via the connection. This is accessed via the .binaryType property, which can report either "blob" or "arraybuffer" depending on the transported data. The final attribute of the WebSocket on the browser is the .bufferedAmount property. This tells you how many bytes of data have been buffered by using the .send() method.

8-6. Communicating Server Events via WebSockets
Problem

You have seen how to implement WebSocket frameworks and modules. Now you would like tosend server information by using WebSockets.

Solution

When you build your WebSocket server, one of the highly enticing use cases of this two-way freeway of information is to be able to send updates on the status of your server, or events from the server in a low latency way. This is contrary to a standard web server where you would need to poll for information;instead you can simply just send the information on demand, and bind to the message as soon as it arrives.

You can imagine a situation similar to those you have seen in previous sections, but where you have created a WebSocket server that is transmitting data to the client, including connections and client-driven messaging. Here you will handle the WebSocket connections and periodically send updates to all connected clients.

Listing 8-12. Sending Server Events

```
/**
 * server events
 */

var http = require('http'),
    fs = require('fs'),
    url = require('url'),
    WebSocketServer = require('websocket').server;

var server = http.createServer(function(req, res) {
    var urlParsed = url.parse(req.url,true, true);

    fs.readFile(urlParsed.path.split('/')[1], function(err, data) {
        if (err) {
            res.statusCode = 404;
            res.end(http.STATUS_CODES[404]);
        }
        res.statusCode = 200;
        res.end(data);
    });
}).listen(8080);

var serverConfig = {
  httpServer: server,
  autoAcceptConnections: false
};
```

```
var wsserver = new WebSocketServer();

wsserver.mount(serverConfig);

var conns = [];
wsserver.on('connect', function(connection) {
    console.log('connected');
conns.push(connection);
    setInterval(pingClients, 5e3);
});

wsserver.on('request', function(req) {
    console.log('request');
  var connection = req.accept('echo-protocol', req.origin);

    connection.on('message', function(message) {
        if (message.type === 'utf8') {
            console.log(message.utf8Data);
        }
        else if (message.type === 'binary') {
            console.log(message.binaryData);
        }
    });
    connection.on('close', function(reasonCode, description) {
        console.log('connection closed', reasonCode, description);
    });
});
wsserver.on('close', function(conn, reason, description) {
    console.log('closing', reason, description);
    for (var i = 0; i < conns.length; i++) {
      if (conns[i] === conn) {
        conns.splice(i, 1);
      }
    }
});

function pingClients() {
  for (var i =0; i < conns.length; i++) {
    conns[i].send('ping');
  }
}
```

How It Works

In this solution, the server itself is created in the same way as many others you have seen with WebSocket-Node. The difference is highlighted in Listing 8-11, showing that as connections are made, they are added to an array of connections to the server. This way you do not have to remain inside of the connection or request callbacks in order to send messages to the connections. While in this solution, you trivially created a pingClients() method that will loop through all the connections in the array and send them a message on an interval; you can imagine a situation where you have a critical server event to communicate that you are able to distribute to the connected sockets in a similar manner.

The conns array contains the reference to the entire WebSocketConnection object. This means that you have the ability to pick out a single connection from the array and send a message. You see this in the pingClients function, where you iterate over the array and call the .send() method on each individual socket.To clean up after a connection is closed, you simply find the connection that is closed within the array, then remove it with the splice() method.

8-7. Two-way Communications with WebSockets
Problem
You need to be able to utilize WebSockets for two-way communications.

Solution
This solution will allow you to create a simple chat room with WebSockets. You will create the server with Socket.IO and utilize that to transmit data between the client and the server and client. The server is shown in Listing 8-13 and the client web page follows in Listing 8-14.

Listing 8-13. Socket.IO Chat Server

```
/**
 * two-way communications
 */

var app = require('http').createServer(connectHandler),
        io = require('socket.io').listen(app),
        fs = require('fs');

app.listen(8080);

function connectHandler (req, res) {
  fs.readFile(__dirname + '/8-7-1.html',
  function (err, data) {
    if (err) {
      res.writeHead(500);
      return res.end('Error loading 8-7-1.html');
    }

    res.writeHead(200);
    res.end(data);
  });
}

var members = [];
io.sockets.on('connection', function (socket) {
  socket.on('joined', function(data) {
    var mbr = data;
    mbr.id = socket.id;
    members.push(mbr);
    socket.broadcast.emit('joined', data);
    console.log(data.name, 'joined the room');
  });
```

```
  socket.on('message', function(data) {
    // store chat now
    socket.broadcast.emit('message', data);
  });

  socket.on('disconnect', function() {
    for (var i = 0; i < members.length; i++) {
      if (members[i].id === socket.id) {
        socket.broadcast.emit('disconnected', { name: members[i].name });
      }
    }
  });
});
```

Listing 8-14. Chat Client

```html
<!doctype html>
<html>
<head>
        <script src="/socket.io/socket.io.js"></script>
</head>
<body>
        <div id="messages">
        </div>
        <form id="newChat">
                <textarea id="text"></textarea>
                <input type="submit" id="sendMessage" value="Send" />
        </form>
        <script>
                var socket = io.connect('http://localhost');
                var who;

                socket.on('connect', function() {
                        var chatter = prompt('Please enter your name');
                        chatter = (chatter === "" || chatter === null) ? "anon" : chatter;
                        addChatter("you", "Joined");
                        who = chatter;
                        socket.emit('joined', { name: chatter});

                });

                function addChatter(name, message) {
                        var chat = document.getElementById("messages");
                        chat.innerHTML += "<div>" + name + " - " + message + "</div>";
                }

                socket.on('joined', function(data) {
                        console.log(data);
                        addChatter(data.name, ' joined');
                });
```

```javascript
        socket.on('disconnected', function(data) {
                addChatter(data.name, 'disconnected');
        });

        socket.on('message', function(data) {
                addChatter(data.name, data.message);
        });

        var chat = document.getElementById("newChat");

        chat.onsubmit = function() {
                var msg = document.getElementById("text").value;
                socket.emit("message", { name: who, message: msg });
                document.getElementById("text").value = "";
                addChatter(who, msg);
                return false;
        }

    </script>
</body>
</html>
```

How It Works

This solution works by first creating a Socket.IO server. This server will act as a relay between your connected chat clients, and if you were to use this in a production environment you might wish to add some persistence layer to store chats in a database.

Your Socket.IO server performs a relay for three events: joining the chat room, sending a message, and disconnecting a socket.

Joining a chat room is controlled when you input your name on the client. The client will then send a message via socket.emit('joined', { name: <username> });, which tells the server that there was a join event, as well as the name of the user. This is then received on the server, and immediately a broadcast event is emitted to the other clients. These clients then bind to the 'joined' message from the server, which contains the data that they need in order to know who has joined the room. This is then added to the HTML of the web page.

Once you have joined a room, you are able to send a message to the other users in the room. This begins on the client, where you are able to input your chat message into a text area, then you send the message. This occurs with socket.emit('message', {name: <user>, message: <text>}); and again this is immediately broadcast to the other connections where the text is and the user is added to the HTML.

Finally, you want to know if those whom you are chatting with have left the room. To do this, you bind to the 'disconnect' event on the socket and find the username of the socket that is disconnecting; this is accomplished by storing user data in a members[] array on the server. You then broadcast that departure to the remaining clients that are connected to the server.

This is a basic chat server but it illustrates quite clearly how you are able to have low latency two-way communications between the client and server and client with WebSockets. In the next section you will see how you can build a multiuser whiteboard with similar methods, allowing drawn coordinates to be shared between many users in a collaborative way by using WebSockets.

8-8. Building a Multiuser Whiteboard with WebSockets

Problem

Now that you understand the two-way communications of WebSockets, you want to build a multiuser whiteboard application in order to share a drawing in real-time.

Solution

Listing 8-15 shows how you can build a WebSocket server that will act as an intermediary between HTML canvas drawing clients. These clients (HTML; shown in Listing 8-16) and (JavaScript; shown in Listing 8-17) will send and accept WebSocket messages that will provide the ability to share collaborative drawing programs across client instances.

Listing 8-15. A Drawing WebSocket Server with WebSocket-Node

```
var WebSocketServer = require('websocket').server,
    http = require('http'),
    sox = {},
    idx = 0;

var server = http.createServer(function(request, response) {
    response.writeHead(404);
    response.end();
});
server.listen(8080, function() {
});

ws = new WebSocketServer({
    httpServer: server,
    autoAcceptConnections: false
});

function originIsAllowed(origin) {
    //Check here to make sure we're on the right origin
    return true;
}

var getNextId =  (function() {
    var idx = 0;
    return function() { return ++idx; };
})();
ws.on('request', function(request) {
    if (!originIsAllowed(request.origin)) {
        request.reject();
        console.log((new Date()) + ' Connection from origin ' + request.origin + ' rejected.');
        return;
    }
    var connection = request.accept('draw-protocol', request.origin);
    connection.socketid = getNextId();
    connection.sendUTF("socketid_" + connection.socketid);
```

```
        console.log(connection.socketid);
        sox[connection.socketid] = connection;
        connection.on('message', function(message) {

            if (message.type === 'utf8') {
sendToAll(JSON.parse(message.utf8Data), 'utf8');
}
            else if (message.type === 'binary') {
                connection.sendBytes(message.binaryData);
            }
        });
        connection.on('close', function(reasonCode, description) {
            delete sox[connection.socketid];
        });
});

function sendToAll(drawEvt, type) {

    for (var socket in sox) {
        if (type === 'utf8' &&drawEvt.socketid !== socket) {
            sox[socket].sendUTF(JSON.stringify(drawEvt));
        }

    }
}
```

Listing 8-16. Drawing Canvas and HTML Markup

```
<!doctype html>
<html>
<head>
<title>whiteboard</title>
<link rel="stylesheet" type="text/css" href="style.css" />
<script src="jquery_1.10.2.js" type="text/javascript"></script>
<script src="drawings.js" type="text/javascript"></script>
</head>
<body>
<div id="wrapper">
<div class="menu">
<ul>
<li>
<a  id="clear">Clear</a>

</li>
<li>
<li>
<a  id="draw">Draw</a>
<ul id="colors">
<li style="background-color:white;">
<a>White</a>
</li>
```

```
<li style="background-color:red;">
<a>Red</a>
</li>
<li style="background-color:orange;">
<a>Orange</a>
</li>
<li style="background-color:yellow;">
<a>Yellow</a>
</li>
<li style="background-color:green;">
<a>Green</a>
</li>
<li style="background-color:blue;">
<a>Blue</a>
</li>
<li style="background-color:indigo;">
<a>Indigo</a>
</li>
<li style="background-color:violet;">
<a>Violet</a>
</li>
<li style="background-color:black;">
<a>Black</a>
</li>
</ul>

</li>

<label for="sizer">Line Size:</label>
<input name="sizer" id="sizer" type="number" min="5" max="100" step="5" />

</ul>
</div>
<canvas id="canvas" ></canvas>
<canvas id="remotecanvas"></canvas>
</div>
</body>
</html>
```

Listing 8-17. The Drawing Application: WebSockets and Canvas

```
$(document).ready(function() {

    var canvas = document.getElementById("canvas"),
        ctx = canvas.getContext("2d"),
        remotecanvas = document.getElementById("remotecanvas"),
        remotectx = remotecanvas.getContext("2d"),
        $cvs = $("#canvas"),
        top = $cvs.offset().top,
        left = $cvs.offset().left,
        wsc = new WebSocket("ws://localhost:8080", "draw-protocol"),
        mySocketId = -1;
```

```javascript
    var resizeCvs = function() {
        ctx.canvas.width = remotectx.canvas.width = $(window).width();
        ctx.canvas.height = remotectx.canvas.height = $(window).height();
    };

    var initializeCvs = function () {
        ctx.lineCap = remotectx.lineCap = "round";
        resizeCvs();
        ctx.save();
        remotectx.save();
        ctx.clearRect(0, 0, ctx.canvas.width, ctx.canvas.height);
        remotectx.clearRect(0,0, remotectx.canvas.width, remotectx.canvas.height);
        ctx.restore();
        remotectx.restore();
    };

    var draw = {
        isDrawing: false,
        mousedown: function(ctx, coordinates) {
            ctx.beginPath();
            ctx.moveTo(coordinates.x, coordinates.y);
            this.isDrawing = true;
        },
        mousemove: function(ctx, coordinates) {
            if (this.isDrawing) {
                ctx.lineTo(coordinates.x, coordinates.y);
                ctx.stroke();
            }
        },
        mouseup: function(ctx, coordinates) {
            this.isDrawing = false;
            ctx.lineTo(coordinates.x, coordinates.y);
            ctx.stroke();
            ctx.closePath();
        },
        touchstart: function(ctx, coordinates){
            ctx.beginPath();
            ctx.moveTo(coordinates.x, coordinates.y);
            this.isDrawing = true;
        },
        touchmove: function(ctx, coordinates){
            if (this.isDrawing) {
                ctx.lineTo(coordinates.x, coordinates.y);
                ctx.stroke();
            }
        },
        touchend: function(ctx, coordinates){
            if (this.isDrawing) {
                this.touchmove(coordinates);
                this.isDrawing = false;
            }
        }
    }
};
```

```javascript
    // create a function to pass touch events and coordinates to drawer
    function setupDraw(event, isRemote){

        var coordinates = {};
        var evt = {};
        evt.type = event.type;
        evt.socketid = mySocketId;
        evt.lineWidth = ctx.lineWidth;
        evt.strokeStyle = ctx.strokeStyle;
        if (event.type.indexOf("touch") != -1 ){
            evt.targetTouches = [{ pageX: 0, pageY: 0 }];
            evt.targetTouches[0].pageX = event.targetTouches[0].pageX || 0;
evt.targetTouches[0].pageY = event.targetTouches[0].pageY || 0;
coordinates.x = event.targetTouches[0].pageX - left;
            coordinates.y = event.targetTouches[0].pageY - top;
        } else {
            evt.pageX = event.pageX;
            evt.pageY = event.pageY;
            coordinates.x = event.pageX - left;
            coordinates.y = event.pageY - top;
        }
        if (event.strokeStyle) {
            remotectx.strokeStyle = event.strokeStyle;
            remotectx.lineWidth = event.lineWidth;
        }

        if (!isRemote) {
            wsc.send(JSON.stringify(evt));
            draw[event.type](ctx, coordinates);
        } else {
            draw[event.type](remotectx, coordinates);
        }
    }

    window.addEventListener("mousedown", setupDraw, false);
    window.addEventListener("mousemove", setupDraw, false);
    window.addEventListener("mouseup", setupDraw, false);
    canvas.addEventListener('touchstart',setupDraw, false);
    canvas.addEventListener('touchmove',setupDraw, false);
    canvas.addEventListener('touchend',setupDraw, false);

    document.body.addEventListener('touchmove',function(event){
      event.preventDefault();
    },false);

    $('#clear').click(function (e) {
        initializeCvs(true);
        $("#sizer").val("");
    });
```

```javascript
$("#draw").click(function (e) {
    e.preventDefault();
    $("label[for='sizer']").text("Line Size:");
});

    $("#colors li").click(function (e) {
e.preventDefault();
        $("label[for='sizer']").text("Line Size:");
        ctx.strokeStyle = $(this).css("background-color");
    });

    $("#sizer").change(function (e) {
        ctx.lineWidth = parseInt($(this).val(), 10);
    });

    initializeCvs();

    window.onresize = function() {
        resizeCvs();
    };

    wsc.onmessage = function(event) {
        if (event.data.indexOf("socketid_") !== -1) {
            mySocketId = event.data.split("_")[1];
        } else {
var dt = JSON.parse(event.data);
setupDraw(dt, true);
        }

    };
});
```

How It Works

This solution begins again with a straightforward implementation of a WebSocket-Node WebSocket server. This server will only accept connections for the 'draw-protocol'. Once these connections are established, you then must create a new socket identifier in order to deliver the messages to the socket later on. You then bind to the message events that will arrive from the connections. From here, you assume that you will get messages that contain coordinates that will reproduce the drawing from one client to another.You then send these messages to all connected clients by iterating through an object that contains all the sockets that are connected.

```javascript
function sendToAll(text, type) {

    for (var socket in sox) {
        if (type === 'utf8' && text.socketid !== socket) {
            sox[socket].sendUTF(JSON.stringify(text));
        }

    }
}
```

On the client, you create a canvas drawing app that has a few features, but you then extend that in a way that you are able to mimic the entire set of mouse or touch movements from one client to another.You, of course, start by binding to the URL of your WebSocket server and utilizing the 'draw-protocol' required by that server. Then you build out a setupDraw function within your JavaScript. This will parse the mouse or touch events that are occurring on your canvas and send them on to actually draw on the canvas. If the event that instantiates the drawing begins on the client, you will then send the coordinates, styles, and events to the WebSocket server for dispatch.

```
        if (!isRemote) {
wsc.send(JSON.stringify(evt));
            draw[event.type](ctx, coordinates);
        } else {
            draw[event.type](remotectx, coordinates);
        }
```

The sent drawing event is then received on the client. This will then call the setupDraw function again; only this time you are telling the drawing tool that your data are from a remote origin, meaning that you do not need to send the stringified event back to the WebSocket server.

```
    wsc.onmessage = function(event) {
        if (event.data.indexOf("socketid_") !== -1) {
            mySocketId = event.data.split("_")[1];
        } else {
var dt = JSON.parse(event.data);
setupDraw(dt, true);
        }
    };
```

CHAPTER 9

■ ■ ■

Using Web Server Frameworks

Node.js is a natural fit for building a web server. Because of this, many developers have built web server applications. Some of these have gone on to become open source frameworks and available to any developer wishing to develop a Node.js web server. In this chapter you will see examples of utilizing these frameworks in order to build a Node.js web server.

First you will examine one of the most popular Node.js frameworks, Express. You will gain an understanding of how to utilize Express for building a web application. You will also see how to utilize the tools that are packaged with Express to scaffold an application quickly. Express also provides an easy way to route requests that will allow you to create logical routes and build out an API by using the framework.

Aside from Express there are several other frameworks that you will examine in this chapter that allow you to create a Node.js–based web application. The next frameworks that you will investigate are all slightly different in their implementation to Express but will allow you to see that there are various ways in which you can create a Node.js application. These include the following:

- Geddy
- Yahoo! Mojito
- Flatiron

9-1. Getting Started with Express

Problem

You want to get up and running with the Express Node.js application framework.

Solution

There are several methods that you can utilize to get started with Express. In this solution, Listing 9-1, you will build a web server with Express that will perform several tasks.

First, your server will use Express middleware to log requests that are made to the server. Your server will also serve static files from the directory in which the script is being executed. These static files will be compressed with gzip as they are served. In addition to these actions your Express server will be able to perform simple authentication and provide a fallback response to any addresses that cannot be served by static pages.

You will also see how to get and set many Express settings and how to enable and disable them. You will also create a method to set different configurations for your application based on whether you are serving content in development mode or in a production environment. To get started, you must first install the Express framework by using npm. This is done either by running the command $ `npm install express` or globally as $ `npm install -g express`; you will then be able to get started with Express.

Listing 9-1. Getting Started with Express

```
/**
* Getting started with ExpressJS
*/

var express = require('express'),
        app = express();
// use middleware
app.use(express.logger());
app.use(express.compress());
app.use(express.static(__dirname));
app.use(express.basicAuth(function(username, password) {
        return username == 'shire' & password == 'baggins';
}));
// a simple route
app.get('/blah', function(req, res) {
        res.send(app.get('default'));
});
// a default handler
app.use(function(req, res) {
        res.send(app.get('default'));
});

// settings
console.log(app.get('env'));            // development
console.log(app.get('trust proxy')); // undefined
app.disable('trust proxy');
console.log(app.get('trust proxy')); // false
console.log(app.get('jsonp callback name'));
console.log(app.get('json replacer'));
console.log(app.get('json spaces'));
console.log(app.get('case sensitive routing'));
console.log(app.get('strict routing'));
console.log(app.get('view cache'));
console.log(app.get('view engine'));
console.log(app.get('views'));

// configurations
app.configure('development', function() {
        app.set('default', 'express development site');
});

app.configure('production', function() {
        app.set('default', 'express production site');
});
// app.engine('jade', require('jade').__express);
app.listen(8080);                       // same as http.server.listen
```

How It Works

Express is an application framework designed for Node.js. It is a highly flexible framework that allows you to build a Node.js application to suit your needs. In the solution in Listing 9-1 you created a web server that would perform several tasks. In order for this to happen, you first must install the Express Node.js module. This can be done either local to the project you are working on, with $ npm install express, or globally as $ npm install -g express.

Once you have installed Express, you can then incorporate it into your project. You must include the framework – require('express'), and then you tell Express to create an application by instantiating the express object. This creates a reference to the app variable in your solution, which will give access to the Express API.

The first thing you can see with this solution is a cluster of calls to app.use() (see Listing 9-2). This function comes from one of Express's main dependencies—Connect—which is an application middleware framework built for Node.js by Sencha Labs. The following snippet is from the Express implementation of app.use(). This shows you how this .use() call is extended from Connect.

Listing 9-2. app.use in express/lib/application.js

```
app.use = function(route, fn){
  var app;
  // default route to '/'
  if ('string' != typeof route) fn = route, route = '/';

  // express app
  if (fn.handle && fn.set) app = fn;

  // restore .app property on req and res
  if (app) {
    app.route = route;
    fn = function(req, res, next) {
      var orig = req.app;
      app.handle(req, res, function(err){
        req.__proto__ = orig.request;
        res.__proto__ = orig.response;
        next(err);
      });
    };
  }

  connect.proto.use.call(this, route, fn);
  // mounted an app
  if (app) {
    app.parent = this;
    app.emit('mount', this);
  }

  return this;
};
```

You can see from this code that the app.use() method is run through some custom logic, which includes ensuring that the method signature is that which is expected, that the request and response are properly passed along, all before the .use() method from Connect is called.

What this means is that when you call app.use(<function>) in your solution, you are either making available a generic route with a special middleware function or setting an explicit route. In the solution you first use this to call express.logger().

The express.logger() middleware, when added to an Express application, is used to log every request on the server. In this solution, when you run the Express application and navigate to your Express site, the express.logger() application will log something similar to the following:

Listing 9-3. express.logger() in Action

```
< 127.0.0.1 - - [Tue, 16 Jul 2013 00:26:22 GMT] "GET / HTTP/1.1" 401 - "-" "Mozilla/5.0 (Macintosh;
Intel Mac OS X 10.8; rv:22.0) Gecko/20100101 Firefox/22.0"
< 127.0.0.1 - - [Tue, 16 Jul 2013 00:26:27 GMT] "GET / HTTP/1.1" 200 24 "-" "Mozilla/5.0 (Macintosh;
Intel Mac OS X 10.8; rv:22.0) Gecko/20100101 Firefox/22.0"
```

The next middleware that you utilize is express.compress(). This middleware will compress the content with gzip. For example, a JavaScript file that is 1.3 KB (uncompressed) will serve at approximately 518 B when the express.compress() middleware is added.

After express.compress() you add the middleware express.static() to your application. Express uses express.static to point to a directory that you wish to use as a static file handler. For example you can use this to serve your static JavaScript, HTML, and CSS files. The case for express.static() is interesting for discovering the use of app.use(). As shown in the solution, you simply use the functional handler of app.use() and place the static middleware there. However, it may be that the static content you wish to serve is located in an obscure directory in your application, or you simply wish to rename the route to static content to something else. You can do this easily by just naming a route for the static handler. For example, if your static content resides in the subdirectory '/content/shared/static/' and you wish to serve that as '/static', your app.use() would change as follows:

```
//Original
app.use(express.static(__dirname + '/content/shared/static'));
//Altered route
App.use('/static',express.static(__dirname + '/content/shared/static'));
```

The next middleware that you connect to Express is the express.basicAuth() middleware. This middleware will allow you to implement authentication in a rudimentary manner to grant access to your Express application. In this solution you provide a callback, then directly check the credentials within this callback that is provided from the basicAuth() middleware.

The final example of app.use() in your solution is to set the default response for generalized routes for your application. This is where you provide a callback with a request and a response. In the section of the solution you also see the use of app.get().

The Express method app.get() has two main roles. The first role is the routing role. This is app.HTTP_VERB, meaning you will be handling any request that is an HTTP GET request. You will see more about this use of app.get() in later sections. The second role, as you see in the callback for the default route, is to retrieve a setting that you have set for your Express app by using the app.set() method.

The app.set() method is used to alter settings in your application. The signature is app.set(<name>, <value>). In this solution you set a couple of variables. One was the 'default' variable, which set the text that you want to serve from the default route in your web server.

There are a few settings that are used as environment variables for an Express application. Some, like 'jsonp callback name', are set to 'callback' by default but could be set to any value you wish for your JSON with padding (JSONP) methods. Others, such as 'trust proxy', show the state of the setting. In the example you see the default of the 'trust proxy' setting is undefined. You then utilize the app.disable('trust proxy') method to set the value to false. This could also be set to true using the app.enable(). Also, there is the env variable, which is the environment that the Node.js process is running as. You then use to configure options that you wish to keep different in the development and production environments.

This is the basic API that Express provides. You can use this as a web server framework as is shown in this example or you can leverage the command-line capabilities of Express to generate an application as you will see in the following sections.

9-2. Using Express to Generate an Application

Problem

You want to utilize Express's command-line interface to quickly generate an application scaffold.

Solution

Express not only comes with the API that you saw outlined in the previous section but also allows you to create a web server capable of handling many of the boilerplate methods needed in a Node.js server, but it also can be utilized as a command-line application generator. Listing 9-4 demonstrates several methods for Express application generation.

Listing 9-4. Express Application Generation

```
> npm install -g express
> mkdir myapp
> cd myapp
> express -h

      Usage: express [options]
      Options:
        -h, --help           output usage information
        -V, --version        output the version number
        -s, --sessions       add session support
        -e, --ejs            add ejs engine support (defaults to jade)
        -J, --jshtml         add jshtml engine support (defaults to jade)
        -H, --hogan          add hogan.js engine support
        -c, --css <engine>   add stylesheet <engine> support (less|stylus) (defaults to plain css)
        -f, --force          force on non-empty directory
> express
destination is not empty, continue? y
create : .
create : ./package.json
create : ./app.js
create : ./public
create : ./routes
create : ./routes/index.js
create : ./routes/user.js
create : ./public/images
create : ./public/javascripts
create : ./views
create : ./views/layout.jade
create : ./public/stylesheets
create : ./public/stylesheets/style.css

install dependencies:
  $ cd . && npm install
run the app:
  $ node app
> express --sessions --ejs --css less --force
```

```
create : .
create : ./package.json
create : ./app.js
create : ./public
create : ./routes
create : ./routes/index.js
create : ./routes/user.js
create : ./public/images
create : ./public/javascripts
create : ./views
create : ./views/index.ejs
create : ./public/stylesheets
create : ./public/stylesheets/style.less

install dependencies:
  $ cd . && npm install
run the app:
  $ node app
```

How It Works

This command-line utility works by first installing the Express module to your machine with npm install -g express. From here, you now have access to the express command-line utility. When you type 'express', you run a JavaScript file that is found in the bin file of the source.

First, you want to get an idea of what is accessible to you in the Express command-line tool. You do this by typing express -h or express --help. This prints the list of command arguments that can accompany the express command. The first two are general output for the help text and the version of Express that you are utilizing.

The other options are set in the application by parsing the command-line arguments that are passed and added to an object called 'program' by use of a module called 'commander'.

Listing 9-5. Parsing Command-Line Arguments with commander

```
program
  .version(version)
  .option('-s, --sessions', 'add session support')
  .option('-e, --ejs', 'add ejs engine support (defaults to jade)')
  .option('-J, --jshtml', 'add jshtml engine support (defaults to jade)')
  .option('-H, --hogan', 'add hogan.js engine support')
  .option('-c, --css <engine>', 'add stylesheet <engine> support (less|stylus) (defaults to plain css)')
  .option('-f, --force', 'force on non-empty directory')
  .parse(process.argv);
```

Next, you create an Express application by using nothing by the default settings. This is done by navigating to the directory in which you wish to create your application and running the express command with zero arguments. You could also add a single argument naming an application name, express myapp, which will create a child directory by that name from where the script is executed.

When the express command-line application executes, aside from parsing the arguments as you saw above, it will immediately invoke a function that will pass in the path where the application is to be generated.

Listing 9-6. Generate Application

```
(function createApplication(path) {
  emptyDirectory(path, function(empty){
    if (empty || program.force) {
      createApplicationAt(path);
    } else {
      program.confirm('destination is not empty, continue? ', function(ok){
        if (ok) {
          process.stdin.destroy();
          createApplicationAt(path);
        } else {
          abort('aborting');
        }
      });
    }
  });
})(path);
```

This will check to see if the directory in which you are creating your application is empty. It does this by utilizing Node.js and the file system module.

```
function emptyDirectory(path, fn) {
  fs.readdir(path, function(err, files){
    if (err && 'ENOENT' != err.code) throw err;
    fn(!files || !files.length);
  });
}
```

If the directory is not empty, Express will present you with a warning "destination is not empty, continue?" to which you can simply type in 'y' and continue. The application will generate the application structure and scaffolding out your application according to the parameters that you provided. This is done with the createApplicationAt() function.

This method starts by creating the root directory of your application, then all of the directories that are required by your application. You can see that this will utilize the flags that you have set in order to make the application directory tree.

```
mkdir(path, function(){
  mkdir(path + '/public');
  mkdir(path + '/public/javascripts');
  mkdir(path + '/public/images');
  mkdir(path + '/public/stylesheets', function(){
    switch (program.css) {
      case 'less':
        write(path + '/public/stylesheets/style.less', less);
        break;
      case 'stylus':
        write(path + '/public/stylesheets/style.styl', stylus);
        break;
      default:
        write(path + '/public/stylesheets/style.css', css);
    }
  });
```

```
  mkdir(path + '/routes', function(){
    write(path + '/routes/index.js', index);
    write(path + '/routes/user.js', users);
  });

  mkdir(path + '/views', function(){
    switch (program.template) {
      case 'ejs':
        write(path + '/views/index.ejs', ejsIndex);
        break;
      case 'jade':
        write(path + '/views/layout.jade', jadeLayout);
        write(path + '/views/index.jade', jadeIndex);
        break;
      case 'jshtml':
        write(path + '/views/layout.jshtml', jshtmlLayout);
        write(path + '/views/index.jshtml', jshtmlIndex);
        break;
      case 'hjs':
        write(path + '/views/index.hjs', hoganIndex);
        break;

    }
  });
```

After the directory structure is set, the root application JavaScript file will be generated along with a properly configured package.json file. This is done by simply replacing tokens that are set based upon the settings you pass the Express generator on the command line.

```
// CSS Engine support
    switch (program.css) {
      case 'less':
        app = app.replace('{css}', eol + 'app.use(require(\'less-middleware\')({ src: __dirname +
\'/public\' }));');
        break;
      case 'stylus':
        app = app.replace('{css}', eol + 'app.use(require(\'stylus\').middleware(__dirname +
\'/public\'));');
        break;
      default:
        app = app.replace('{css}', ");
    }

    // Session support
    app = app.replace('{sess}', program.sessions
      ? eol + 'app.use(express.cookieParser(\'your secret here\'));' + eol + 'app.use(express.session());'
      : ");

    // Template support
    app = app.replace(':TEMPLATE', program.template);
```

```
// package.json
var pkg = {
    name: 'application-name'
  , version: '0.0.1'
  , private: true
  , scripts: { start: 'node app.js' }
  , dependencies: {
    express: version
  }
}

if (program.template) pkg.dependencies[program.template] = '*';
// CSS Engine support
switch (program.css) {
  case 'less':
    pkg.dependencies['less-middleware'] = '*';
    break;
  default:
    if (program.css) {
      pkg.dependencies[program.css] = '*';
    }
}

write(path + '/package.json', JSON.stringify(pkg, null, 2));
write(path + '/app.js', app);
```

You now have a functioning Express application that has been built via the application's command-line interface tool. You were able to see that the default template rendering that comes with Express is utilizing a framework called Jade. In the next section you will see how you can leverage this tool in order to create minimal and clean HTML templates for your Express application.

9-3. Rendering HTML with Jade

Problem

You have generated an Express application by using the command $ express. By default, this application will utilize the Jade HTML template framework so you need to be able to understand and utilize this framework in your Node.js application.

Solution

Jade was created as a templating language specifically for Node.js. It is used by default with Express so it is important to gain some understanding of it. It is built as a minimalist templating engine; it can be used to build HTML from a very terse template.

In this solution you will examine and build on the default templates that are generated with Express. These are located in <appRoot>/views.

Listing 9-7. /views/layout.jade

```
doctype 5
html
  head
    title= title
    link(rel='stylesheet', href='/stylesheets/style.css')
    //if lt IE 8
      script(src='/old_ie.js')
  body
    block content
```

Listing 9-8. /views/index.jade

```
extends layout

block content
  h1= title
  p.a_class Welcome to #{title}
  #an_id this is a div which has an ID
  label A range slider:
    input(type='range')
  #ckbx
    label A checkbox:
      input(type='checkbox', checked)
  ul
  li.odd: a(href='#', title='one') one
  li.even: a(href='#', title='two') two
  li.odd: a(href='#', title='three') three

  case flag
    when 0: #zero there is no flag
    when 1: #one there is a single flag
    default: #other other

  - if (items.length)
  ul
    - items.forEach(function(item){
      li= item
    - })
```

Listing 9-9. Routes/index.js

```
/*
 * GET home page.
 */

exports.index = function(req, res){
  res.render('index', { title: 'Express', flag: 0, items: ['a', 'b', 'c'] });
};
```

How It Works

Jade works by parsing its own syntax and then rendering that into the appropriate and corresponding HTML output. Take a look at your layout.jade file. This file declares a doctype, specifically the HTML5 doctype. This is done by typing 'doctype 5', or alternatively '!!! 5'. These are the shorthand notations for the document types. While this isn't too drastic of a shortcut for the terse HTML5 document type, you can see from Listing 9-10 that this can become extremely useful if you are utilizing a transitional document type in your Express application.

Listing 9-10. Express.js's Available Document Types

```
var doctypes = exports.doctypes = {
  '5': '<!DOCTYPE html>',
  'default': '<!DOCTYPE html>',
  'xml': '<?xml version="1.0" encoding="utf-8" ?>',
  'transitional': '<!DOCTYPE html PUBLIC "-//W3C//DTD XHTML 1.0 Transitional//EN"
"http://www.w3.org/TR/xhtml1/DTD/xhtml1-transitional.dtd">',
  'strict': '<!DOCTYPE html PUBLIC "-//W3C//DTD XHTML 1.0 Strict//EN"
"http://www.w3.org/TR/xhtml1/DTD/xhtml1-strict.dtd">',
  'frameset': '<!DOCTYPE html PUBLIC "-//W3C//DTD XHTML 1.0 Frameset//EN"
"http://www.w3.org/TR/xhtml1/DTD/xhtml1-frameset.dtd">',
  '1.1': '<!DOCTYPE html PUBLIC "-//W3C//DTD XHTML 1.1//EN" "
http://www.w3.org/TR/xhtml11/DTD/xhtml11.dtd">',
  'basic': '<!DOCTYPE html PUBLIC "-//W3C//DTD XHTML Basic 1.1//EN"
"http://www.w3.org/TR/xhtml-basic/xhtml-basic11.dtd">',
  'mobile': '<!DOCTYPE html PUBLIC "-//WAPFORUM//DTD XHTML Mobile 1.2//EN"
"http://www.openmobilealliance.org/tech/DTD/xhtml-mobile12.dtd">'
};
```

Next you see that HTML elements are written in a shorthand manner, which allows for the highly readable markup. Elements are created and inner content is nested by either two spaces or a tab to indicate they are relative to the parent. You can see this is evident with the title element, nested below the head element. Attributes within an element, such as the 'src' found in the script element, are set within parentheses. Comments are translated from a single line C style comment to an HTML comment so you can see that adding a conditional parameter to test for older versions of Internet Explorer is not complex. Once all the Jade rendering is completed for this HTML block, up to the <body> element, you can see that this relatively short and simple markup is translated to the following HTML:

```
<!DOCTYPE html>
<html>
<head>
        <title>Express</title>
        <link rel="stylesheet" href="/stylesheets/style.css">
        <!--[if lt IE 8]>
                <script src="/zomg_old_ie.js"></script>
                <![endif]-->
</head>
<body>
</body>
</html>
```

As you examine the index.jade file, you see many of the same things as the layout.jade file. You can see that you have named which Jade file this is extending with 'extends layout'. You also have a named block, 'block content', which matches the corresponding block on the layout file.

Also present in this file is a sampling of the template-rendering capabilities of Jade. You have an 'h1= title' snippet. This snippet will create an H1 element in your code but will also take the object from the index render code in the routes/index.js file and add the "title" to the HTML markup. Other portions of the template object that you created were the 'flag' attribute and the 'items' array. These items are also parsed into HTML. The flag, as you can see, you use in a 'case' statement within the code. This allows for conditional markup. Also you can see that you are able to iterate through your array of items and render a list item for each one. When doing this sort of iteration, you must preface the code you are using to iterate with a hyphen. Then you can just write JavaScript behind this hyphen in order to generate the layout you desire. This can greatly improve your markup generation when you are building large lists of things, and it will save you time in your development cycles. The other method to iterate through this array would be to write 'each item in items' and then 'li= item' (indented below).

Jade also has shorthand for adding classes and IDs to your HTML tags. You can see where p.a_class will generate a <p> tag and add the class 'a_class' to that tag. Classes can also be chained together, allowing for any number of class names to be tethered to a tag. Adding an ID to a tag is just as easy. Simply use #, prepended to a string of text and that string of text will become the ID of the tag. However, you can also create a <div> tag with an ID without naming the tag. By simply adding '#an_id', you generate a <div id='an_id'> tag in your markup without the need to type the extra three characters to name the div.

If you create a Node.js application with Express and Jade, you have the power to create clean markup with this powerful template engine.

9-4. Routing with Express
Problem

You have created an application with Express. Your URL structure within your application has grown in complexity so you need a powerful routing mechanism for connecting these URLs to the proper handlers.

Solution

Express allows for an easy method for invoking proper routes in your Node.js application. You are capable of handling routes as external modules or as inline callbacks within the route handlers of your Express application. Listing 9-11 gives examples of both of these types of routing behaviors. This builds on the server file from Section 9-2. You can see that the routes that have been added are highlighted in bold in this listing.

Listing 9-11. Routing with Express

```
/**
 * Module dependencies.
 */

var express = require('express')
  , routes = require('./routes')
  , user = require('./routes/user')
  , http = require('http')
  , path = require('path');

var app = express();
// all environments
app.set('port', process.env.PORT || 3000);
app.set('views', __dirname + '/views');
app.set('view engine', 'jade');
app.use(express.favicon());
```

```
app.use(express.logger('dev'));
app.use(express.bodyParser());
app.use(express.methodOverride());
app.use(app.router);
app.use(express.static(path.join(__dirname, 'public')));

// development only
if ('development' == app.get('env')) {
  app.use(express.errorHandler());
}

app.get('/', routes.index);
app.get('/user/:id', function(req, res) {
        res.send('you supplied param ' + req.params.id);
});
app.get('/users', user.list);
app.post('/user/:id', function(req, res) {
        console.log('update user' + req.params.id);
        res.send('successfully updated');
});

http.createServer(app).listen(app.get('port'), function(){
  console.log('Express server listening on port ' + app.get('port'));
});
```

How It Works

Express handles routes by utilizing an app.VERB paradigm where VERB is an HTTP verb. This means that you can route an application for specific types of HTTP requests, which you will see more of when you build an API with Express in Section 9-6.

The app.VERB methods all behave similarly to the middleware routing that you saw in Section 9-1. They each receive a route, which points to the accessing URL for the request, relative to the application root. They also receive a callback function. If you wish to handle all requests to a certain route a particular way, regardless of the HTTP verb that is supplied, you can use the app.all() function to do just that.

In this solution there are several varieties of routes that are used. First, you see that there is a route for the root path of '/'. This points to a routes module and the index method that resides there. This index method has a request and response object that are then handled by sending a response, which in this case is rendered using Jade, but does not necessarily need to be anything but what an HTTP response could send.

You can also see that routing requests can provide generic parameters. This is evident with the route 'users/:id'. Here, the ':id' is the parameter that you will pass to the route. This is not limited to a singular parameter; in fact you can see from the source code snippet in Listing 9-12 that any number of parameters may be added to a route.

Listing 9-12. Find a Matching Route, then Parse the Remaining to be a Portion of the Parameters

```
Route.prototype.match = function(path){
  var keys = this.keys
    , params = this.params = []
    , m = this.regexp.exec(path);

  if (!m) return false;
  for (var i = 1, len = m.length; i < len; ++i) {
    var key = keys[i - 1];
```

```
    var val = 'string' == typeof m[i]
      ? decodeURIComponent(m[i])
      : m[i];

    if (key) {
      params[key.name] = val;
    } else {
      params.push(val);
    }
  }

  return true;
};
```

This logic depends on the regular expression for the given route as you defined it in your app.js file. For the 'users/:id' route, this regular expression is built and will become that which is shown next.

Listing 9-13. Regular Expression for the 'user/:id' Route

```
/^\\/user\\/(?:([^\\/]+?))\\/?$/
```

This creates a regular expression match of ['/user/1', '1'], if you had supplied the ID of one. If you were to add an additional parameter to this route (for example 'user/:role/:id' or something similar), the regular expression simply grows to look like the following.

Listing 9-14. Regular Expression for '/user/:role/:id'

```
/^\\/user\\/(?:([^\\/]+?))\\/(?:([^\\/]+?))\\/?$/
```

This route produces the regular expression match of ['/user/eng/1', 'eng', '1']. These matches are then added to the params array for the route.

You can use Express to build routes and parameterized routes. In the next section you will get a glimpse of how you might go about handling a failed request in your Node.js application.

9-5. Handling Failed Requests in Your Application
Problem

You have built an Express application in Node.js and have even designated routing and request handling. However, you need to be able to properly handle a failed request in your application.

Solution

Express is a robust framework that allows for you as a developer to handle many aspects of the application development process in your own way. This is evident when you are either building your Express routes or augmenting your settings by adding middleware to your Node.js application. Handling failed requests is also something that Express allows for, but about which it is not overly opinionated.

This failed request handling is shown in Listing 9-15. These handlers must follow a certain pattern but can fit into your application where needed.

Listing 9-15. Failed Request Handling in Express

```
/**
* Getting started with ExpressJS
*/

var express = require('express'),
        app = express();
// use middleware
app.use(express.logger());
app.use(express.compress());
app.use(express.static(__dirname));
app.use(express.basicAuth(function(username, password) {
        return username == 'shire' & password == 'baggins';
}));
// a simple route
app.get('/blah', function(req, res, next) {
        next(new Error('failing route'));
        res.send(app.get('blah'));
});

// a default handler
app.use(function(req, res) {
        res.send(app.get('default'));
});

app.use(function(err, req, res, next){
 console.error(err.stack);
 res.send(500, 'Oh no! Something failed');
});

// configurations
app.configure('development', function() {
        app.set('default', 'express development site');
        app.set('blah', 'blah blah blah');
});

app.configure('production', function() {
        app.set('default', 'express production site');
});
// app.engine('jade', require('jade').__express);
app.listen(8080); // same as http.server.listen
```

How It Works

You built this solution in a similar way to the initial example you had built in Section 9-1. Highlighted in Listing 9-15 are two important parts.

First, in order to simulate a failing route, you build in an error on the route '/blah'. This calls the next() route handler with a new Error() object passed into it. This allows the failed request routing to work, because without this handler the site will break.

The failed request routing is built by using the `app.use()` function. This then uses a default callback that includes an error parameter. When the `next()` function is called with an error, Express will utilize this error handler and utilize it as a failed request handler. In this way you can gracefully handle errors on your Node.js server.

9-6. Designing a RESTful API with ExpressJS
Problem

When designing an API, many times you wish to leverage HTTP and create a representational state transfer (REST) architecture for your application.

Solution

In the previous sections you have seen how to build useful routes in Express. Because of the Express API allowing a route to target a specific HTTP verb, it becomes a natural fit for a REST-like API.

In this solution, you will create a simple REST API to interact with a data model consisting of products. These products are represented by a simple JavaScript object in this example, but they could easily be an object set and retrieved from a data store. The example is shown in Listing 9-16.

Listing 9-16. A REST Interface

```
/**
 * Module dependencies.
 */

var express = require('express')
  , routes = require('./routes')
  , http = require('http')
  , path = require('path');

var app = express();
// all environments
app.set('port', process.env.PORT || 3000);
app.set('views', __dirname + '/views');
app.set('view engine', 'jade');
app.use(express.favicon());
app.use(express.logger('dev'));
app.use(express.bodyParser());
app.use(express.methodOverride());
app.use(app.router);
app.use(express.static(path.join(__dirname, 'public')));

// development only
if ('development' == app.get('env')) {
  app.use(express.errorHandler());
}
var products = [
        { id: 0, name: 'watch', description: 'Tell time with this amazing watch', price: 30.00 },
        { id: 1, name: 'sandals', description: 'Walk in comfort with these sandals', price: 10.00 },
        { id: 2, name: 'sunglasses', description: 'Protect your eyes in style', price: 25.00 }
];
```

```
app.get('/', routes.index);
// curl -X GET http://localhost:3000/products
app.get('/products', function(req, res) {
        res.json(products);
});
// curl -X GET http://localhost:3000/products/2
app.get('/products/:id', function(req, res) {
        if (req.params.id > (products.length - 1) || req.params.id < 0) {
                res.statusCode = 404;
                res.end('Not Found');
        }
        res.json(products[req.params.id]);
});
// curl -X POST -d "name=flops&description=sandals&price=12.00" http://localhost:3000/products
app.post('/products', function(req, res) {
        if (typeof req.body.name === 'undefined') {
                res.statusCode = 400;
                res.end('a product name is required');
        }
        products.push(req.body);
        res.send(req.body);
});
// curl -X PUT -d "name=flipflops&description=sandals&price=12.00" http://localhost:3000/products/3
app.put('/products/:id', function(req, res) {
        if (req.params.id > (products.length -1) || req.params.id < 0) {
                res.statusCode = 404;
                res.end('No product found for that ID');
        }
        products[req.params.id] = req.body;
        res.send(req.body);
});
// curl -X DELETE http://localhost:3000/products/2
app.delete('/products/:id', function(req, res) {
        if (req.params.id > (products.length - 1) || req.params.id < 0) {
                req.statusCode = 404;
                res.end('No product found for that ID');
        }
        products.splice(req.params.id, 1);
        res.json(products);
});

http.createServer(app).listen(app.get('port'), function(){
  console.log('Express server listening on port ' + app.get('port'));
});
```

How It Works

REST is an application architecture pattern that can rely on HTTP requests to perform operations. These operations are typically in the form of common create, read, update, and delete methods on the server.

A typical REST interface will at least use HTTP GET and POST methods to perform these actions on the server. In this solution, however, you actually employed the use of the GET, PUT, POST, and DELETE HTTP verbs in order to create your API. The GET method you utilized to simply retrieve data from a resource. The POST method is used to create data, while the PUT method is used to update existing data. And the DELETE method will remove the data from the data store.

You started by creating a data store of products, which was an array of objects in your code that contains three entries. Once your server is running you can fetch this data by sending an HTTP GET to http://localhost:3000/products.

```
$ CURL -X GET http://localhost:3000/products
[
  {
    "name": "watch",
    "description": "Tell time with this amazing watch",
    "price": 30
  },
  {
    "name": "sandals",
    "description": "Walk in comfort with these sandals",
    "price": 10
  },
  {
    "name": "sunglasses",
    "description": "Protect your eyes in style",
    "price": 25
  }
]
```

Now that you have created and fetched your data, you are able to insert a new record into the products data store. In your REST API you simply send a POST request toward the products route. If successful, and it must at least include a name for the product, it will return the item that you have just added:

```
$ CURL -X POST -d "name=flops&description=sandal%20things&price=12.00"  http://localhost:3000/products
{
  "name": "flops",
  "description": "sandal things",
  "price": "12.00"
}
```

You now have created a new record, but you realize that the name you gave the product was incorrect. To update the name of the product, you need to send a PUT request to the server, but you must also know the :id that you wish to send it to. In your case you know that this is the fourth item in the array, so the :id becomes "3." In order to update the name you can now send the request, which will respond with the updated value in the data store:

```
$ curl -X PUT -d "name=flip%20flops&description=sandals&price=12.00" http://localhost:3000/products/3
{
  "name": "flip flops",
  "description": "sandals",
  "price": "12.00"
}
```

After creating and updating this new record, you realize that the product "sandals" is no longer necessary in your product line. Because of this, you remove it by sending the DELETE HTTP request to that item, which will remove it entirely from the data store. This will also return the list of the products that are now available after removal of this item:

```
$ curl -X DELETE http://localhost:3000/products/1
[
  {
    "name": "watch",
    "description": "Tell time with this amazing watch",
    "price": 30
  },
  {
    "name": "sunglasses",
    "description": "Protect your eyes in style",
    "price": 25
  },
  {
    "name": "flip flops",
    "description": "sandals",
    "price": "12.00"
  }
]
```

9-7. Up and Running with Geddy

Problem

You want to utilize the Geddy application framework for Node.js to build your product.

Solution

To get started with Geddy, you first need to install the module via npm. If you install it globally, as shown in Listing 9-17, you will gain access to the application generators from any directory on your machine.

Listing 9-17. Installing Geddy

```
$ npm install -g geddy
```

Listing 9-18. Generate an Application in a Named Directory

```
$ geddy gen app geddyapp
$ cd geddyapp
```

Listing 9-19. Run the Application

```
$ geddy
```

Listing 9-20. Generate a New Model for the Application and Run the Application

```
$ geddy gen scaffold products name:default description price
$ geddy
```

You can view this application as it is running by navigating in your browser to http://localhost:4000.

How It Works

Geddy works by installing a useful command-line tool that will allow you to generate applications and to scaffold out new functionality quickly and efficiently. Once this command-line tool is installed, you may simply build your first application by typing the command $ geddy gen app <appname>. This will generate a new application for you in the appname directory. The directory structure will look as follows:

```
appname
        -app
                        -controllers
                        -helpers
                        -models
                        -views
        -config
        -lib
        -log
        -node_modules
        -public
                        -css
                        -img
                        -js
        -test
                        -controllers
                        -models
```

You can see that this scaffolds out a working application that will have default models, views, controllers, and helpers within the application, allowing for testing of your application by default. To run the application, you used the command $ geddy, which will start the server running. The server is configured using either a production.js or a development.js file that is contained inside the config directory.

Listing 9-21. Configuration File

```
var config = {
  detailedErrors: true
, debug: true
, hostname: null
, port: 4000
, model: {
    defaultAdapter: 'memory'
  }
```

```
, sessions: {
    store: 'memory'
  , key: 'sid'
  , expiry: 14 * 24 * 60 * 60
  }
};
```

```
module.exports = config;
```

This creates several configuration options for standard features of an HTTP server such as the port and hostname, but it adds features like the adapter for data models, which you see will default to in-memory. Geddy is very robust in that it provides a versatile set of adapters for storage aside from the in-memory option. These options include PostgreSQL, MongoDB, and Riak. Once the application is running, you will see any requests to the server logged in your console.

```
[Sat, 20 Jul 2013 19:47:42 GMT]  127.0.0.1 - - [Sat Jul 20 2013 15:47:42 GMT-0400 (Eastern Daylight
Time)] "GET / 1.1" 200 2645 "-" "Mozilla/5.0 (Windows NT 6.2; WOW64) AppleWebKit/537.36 (KHTML, like
Gecko) Chrome/30.0.1568.2 Safari/537.36"
```

You next generated a scaffold for a products model in your application. This was done with the command $ geddy gen scaffold products name:default description price. This generates corresponding JavaScript or HTML view files in each of the app/models, app/views/, and app/controllers directories. You will notice that you set the 'name' parameter of the products model with the attribute 'default'. This sets it to be a required field in your application, which becomes evident when you view the products model file.

Listing 9-22. Products Model File

```
var Product = function () {

  this.defineProperties({
    name: {type: 'string', required: true},
    description: {type: 'string'},
    price: {type: 'string'}
  });

};
```

```
exports.Product = Product;
```

The scaffolding with Geddy creates a complete create, read, update, and delete (CRUD) controller. With that simple command you now have control over all the CRUD operations that you might need with the application. The controller will direct the application to store, remove, or redirect your view to whichever portion of your model you are trying to reach.

Listing 9-23. Products Controller

```
var Products = function () {
  this.respondsWith = ['html', 'json', 'xml', 'js', 'txt'];
  this.index = function (req, resp, params) {
    var self = this;
```

```javascript
  geddy.model.Product.all(function(err, products) {
    self.respond({params: params, products: products});
  });
};

this.add = function (req, resp, params) {
  this.respond({params: params});
};

this.create = function (req, resp, params) {
  var self = this
    , product = geddy.model.Product.create(params);
  if (!product.isValid()) {
    this.flash.error(product.errors);
    this.redirect({action: 'add'});
  }
  else {
    product.save(function(err, data) {
      if (err) {
        self.flash.error(err);
        self.redirect({action: 'add'});
      }
      else {
        self.redirect({controller: self.name});
      }
    });
  }
};

this.show = function (req, resp, params) {
  var self = this;

  geddy.model.Product.first(params.id, function(err, product) {
    if (!product) {
      var err = new Error();
      err.statusCode = 404;
      self.error(err);
    }
    else {
      self.respond({params: params, product: product.toObj()});
    }
  });
};

this.edit = function (req, resp, params) {
  var self = this;

  geddy.model.Product.first(params.id, function(err, product) {
    if (!product) {
      var err = new Error();
      err.statusCode = 400;
      self.error(err);
    }
```

```
      else {
        self.respond({params: params, product: product});
      }
    });
};

this.update = function (req, resp, params) {
  var self = this;

  geddy.model.Product.first(params.id, function(err, product) {
    product.updateProperties(params);
    if (!product.isValid()) {
      this.flash.error(product.errors);
      this.redirect({action: 'edit'});
    }
    else {
      product.save(function(err, data) {
        if (err) {
          self.flash.error(err);
          self.redirect({action: 'edit'});
        }
        else {
          self.redirect({controller: self.name});
        }
      });
    }
  });
};

this.destroy = function (req, resp, params) {
  var self = this;

  geddy.model.Product.remove(params.id, function(err) {
    if (err) {
      self.flash.error(err);
      self.redirect({action: 'edit'});
    }
    else {
      self.redirect({controller: self.name});
    }
  });
};

};

exports.Products = Products;
```

The controller performs the CRUD operations, in this case in-memory, but with the adapters available you could just as easily store to PostgreSQL or MongoDB for persistence. There are several calls to self.redirect. This function will redirect your application to the views as they are described in the controller. These views are created with EmbeddedJS (EJS) templating by default, but you could utilize Jade by passing that as a command-line parameter when you generate your application.

EmbeddedJS is basically just like it sounds; you can embed JavaScript directly within your view template and that will control the final layout of the page. The embedded JavaScript is simply placed within '<% %>' tags in your markup and that will be stripped out, parsed, and executed as the view is rendered. If you examine the template for adding a product, you see what is shown in Listing 9-24, and the ability to embed a child template.

Listing 9-24. EJS Template: add.html.ejs

```
<div class="hero-unit">
  <form id="product-form" class="form-horizontal" action="/products" method="POST">
    <fieldset>
      <legend>Create a new Product</legend>
      <% if(params.errors) { %>
      <div class="control-group">
        <ul>
        <% for(var err in params.errors) { %>
          <li><%= params.errors[err]; %></li>
        <% } %>
        </ul>
      </div>
      <% } %>

      <%- partial('form', {product: {}}) %>
      <div class="form-actions">
        <%- contentTag('input', 'Add', {type: 'submit', class: 'btn btn-primary'}) %>
      </div>
    </fieldset>
  </form>
</div>
```

Listing 9-25. Partial Child Template .html.ejs

```
<div class="control-group">
  <label for="name" class="control-label">name</label>
  <div class="controls">
    <%- contentTag('input', product.name, {type:'text', class:'span6', name:'name'}) %>
  </div>
</div>
<div class="control-group">
  <label for="description" class="control-label">description</label>
  <div class="controls">
    <%- contentTag('input', product.description, {type:'text', class:'span6', name:'description'}) %>
  </div>
</div>
<div class="control-group">
  <label for="price" class="control-label">price</label>
  <div class="controls">
    <%- contentTag('input', product.price, {type:'text', class:'span6', name:'price'}) %>
  </div>
</div>
```

The EJS templates here utilize a function for creating content from the products model. For example, to create the input field that will become the name of a product, the EJS looks like `<%- contentTag('input', product.name, {type:'text', class:'span6', name:'name'}) %>`, which uses the name of the model item and will assign it back to that model when the form is posted.

Aside from the scaffolding that autogenerates these CRUD methods for you in your application, you can use the `$ geddy gen resource <resourcename>` command. The resource command is less opinionated in that it does not create a specific view for each operation on the model, and the controller is more generalized as follows:

```
var Products = function () {
  this.respondsWith = ['html', 'json', 'xml', 'js', 'txt'];
  this.index = function (req, resp, params) {
    this.respond({params: params});
  };

  this.add = function (req, resp, params) {
    this.respond({params: params});
  };

  this.create = function (req, resp, params) {
    // Save the resource, then display index page
    this.redirect({controller: this.name});
  };

  this.show = function (req, resp, params) {
    this.respond({params: params});
  };

  this.edit = function (req, resp, params) {
    this.respond({params: params});
  };

  this.update = function (req, resp, params) {
    // Save the resource, then display the item page
    this.redirect({controller: this.name, id: params.id});
  };

  this.destroy = function (req, resp, params) {
    this.respond({params: params});
  };

};

exports.Products = Products;
```

Using the resource generator may be more suitable for your application because it is less opinionated and you can easily add your own application-specific logic, without the CRUD boilerplate in the `scaffold` command.

Finally, as you may have already seen in your testing with Geddy, Geddy provides a flexible router. This router is located in the config/router.js file. It can match routes similar to how the Express router performed in Section 9-4. This means that if you had a specific product and you knew the ID and wanted to perform a specific action on that route, you could add this to the router.js file as `router.match('products/:id', 'GET').to(products.handleId);` This will route the specific ID to the `products.handleId` controller method. You do not need to specify the HTTP verb in the `router.match` query, in fact, you could have written that as `router.get('products/:id').to(products.handleId);` and it would perform in the same manner. In this solution you utilize the full resource-based routing, so your router will display as follows:

```
var router = new geddy.RegExpRouter();
router.get('/').to('Main.index');
router.resource('users');
router.resource('products');
exports.router = router;
```

You can swiftly get an application up and running with Geddy. This framework is extremely fast for starting a simple CRUD application and still allows for more creative implementations of your Node.js applications.

9-8. Using Yahoo! Mojito
Problem
You want to create a Node.js application by using the Yahoo! Mojito framework.

Solution

Yahoo! Mojito is another Node.js application development framework. Created by Yahoo!, it allows you to "build high-performance, device-independent HTML5 applications running on both client and server with Node.js."

To get started with Yahoo! Mojito you first must install the command-line interface. This is done through npm. From then you can utilize the command-line interface to build your application, as shown in Listing 9-26.

Listing 9-26. Installing Yahoo! Mojito and Creating an Application

```
$ npm install -g mojito-cli
$ mojito create app mojitoapp
$cd mojitoapp
$ mojito create mojit testmojit
$ mojito test
$ mojito start
http://localhost:8666/@testmojit/index
```

How It Works

When you install Mojito via npm, you do so globally to gain access to the command-line interface throughout your machine. Then you create an application by typing $ `mojito create app mojitoapp`. This creates a directory named "mojitoapp" that has the following structure.

```
mojitoapp
  - artifacts
  - assets
  - mojits
  - node_modules
  application.json
  package.json
  routes.json
  server.js
```

The server.js file controls the Mojito application and is started when you run `mojito start`. In this file you see what appears to be a Mojito version of the Node.js HTTP server.

```
/*jslint anon:true, sloppy:true, nomen:true*/
process.chdir(__dirname);

/*
 * Create the MojitoServer instance we'll interact with. Options can be passed
 * using an object with the desired key/value pairs.
 */
var Mojito = require('mojito');
var app = Mojito.createServer();

// -------------------------------------------------------------------------
// Different hosting environments require different approaches to starting the
// server. Adjust below to match the requirements of your hosting environment.
// -------------------------------------------------------------------------

module.exports = app.listen();
```

From this point you created a "mojit." A "mojit" is a Mojito term that represents a mashup of the names "module" and "widget." This means that when you create a mojit, you can think of it as building a module. By default, a mojit in a Mojito application is accessible via the path `http://localhost:8666/@mojitname/index`. When you navigate to this location in your application, you will see the default mojit page, which is part of the Mojito Model-View-Controller (MVC) framework.

The MVC architecture in Mojito is centered around what is referred to as an "action context," which you will see in the code as 'ac' in most places. The action context of each mojit becomes apparent when you view the source of the controller.server.js file. This file is what registers the mojit with the application and controls the behavior of the views with the models.

```
/*jslint anon:true, sloppy:true, nomen:true*/
YUI.add('testmojit', function(Y, NAME) {

/**
 * The testmojit module.
 *
 * @module testmojit
 */

    /**
     * Constructor for the Controller class.
     *
     * @class Controller
     * @constructor
     */
    Y.namespace('mojito.controllers')[NAME] = {

        /**
         * Method corresponding to the 'index' action.
         *
         * @param ac {Object} The ActionContext that provides access
         *          to the Mojito API.
         */
```

```
        index: function(ac) {
            ac.models.get('testmojitModel').getData(function(err, data) {
                if (err) {
                    ac.error(err);
                    return;
                }
                ac.assets.addCss('./index.css');
                ac.done({
                    status: 'Mojito is working.',
                    data: data
                });
            });
        }

    };

}, '0.0.1', {requires: ['mojito', 'mojito-assets-addon', 'mojito-models-addon', 'testmojitModel']});
```

The action context within the Y.namespace callback is provided in the index handler for this mojit. It will use the appropriate model ac.models.get('testmojitModel') . . . and will then add assets and send data via an ac.done() handler.

The model server is found within the models directory for each mojit and you can see that this follows a similar Yahoo! User Interface (YUI) pattern to generate the model and add it to the application via Y.namespace. This is also where you not only initialize the model with a configuration but also then add methods such as getData.

```
/*jslint anon:true, sloppy:true, nomen:true*/
YUI.add('testmojitModel', function(Y, NAME) {

/**
 * The testmojitModel module.
 *
 * @module testmojit
 */

    /**
     * Constructor for the testmojitModel class.
     *
     * @class testmojitModel
     * @constructor
     */
    Y.namespace('mojito.models')[NAME] = {
        init: function(config) {
            this.config = config;
        },

        /**
         * Method that will be invoked by the mojit controller to obtain data.
         *
         * @param callback {function(err,data)} The callback function to call when the
         *          data has been retrieved.
         */
```

```
        getData: function(callback) {
            callback(null, { some: 'data', even: 'more data' });
        }

    };

}, '0.0.1', {requires: []});
```

Before you look at how the views work with Mojito, you should first understand that you are not limited to leaving your URLs as the default .../@mojitname/index paths. These URLs would be fine from within your application but if a user needs to remember these URLs it is not a great experience. There is a way to make these URLs appear cleaner and more user-friendly.

First, you need to name your new endpoint by adding the name to the application.json file in the root of your application. In this file you name a spec of "test" and direct that to the type of "testmojit," which you created earlier. You then need to name this new route in the routes.json file. This is done by naming "test index" and telling the HTTP GET method on the '/' path to then resolve the .index handler of the testmojit mojit. These files are shown in the following examples.

Listing 9-27. Application.json

```
[
    {
        "settings": [ "master" ],
        "appPort": "8666",
        "specs": {
            "test": {
                "type": "testmojit"
            }

        }
    },
    {
        "settings": [ "environment:development" ],
        "staticHandling": {
            "forceUpdate": true
        }
    }
]
```

Listing 9-28. Routes.json

```
[{
    "settings": [ "master" ],
    "test index": {
        "verbs": ["get"],
        "path": "/",
        "call": "test.index"
    }
//^^ convert http://localhost:8666/@testmojit/index to http://localhost:8666/
}]

$ mojito start
http://localhost:8666/
```

Now that you are serving your mojit on the URL that you desire, you can modify these templates. The templates for Mojito default to using the handlebars template language. Handlebars allow you to insert objects from your models by using simple expressions like you see in the template for the testmojit you created.

Listing 9-29. Templating with Handlebars

```
<div id="{{mojit_view_id}}">
    <dl>
        <dt>status</dt>
        <dd id="dd_status">{{status}}</dd>
        <dt>data</dt>
        <dd id="dd_data">
            <b>some:</b> {{#data}}{{some}}{{/data}}
            <span>event:</b>{{#data}}{{even}}{{/data}}
        </dd>
    </dl>
</div>
```

Building a Node.js application by using the Yahoo! Mojito application framework can allow for a versatile MVC application.

9-9. Building a Flatiron Application
Problem

You want to build a Node.js server by utilizing the Flatiron application framework.

Solution

To get started with Flatiron, just like many of the other frameworks you have seen in this chapter, you need to install the framework and doing so globally allows for universal access to the command-line interface. The command-line interface, as you can see in Listing 9-30, allows you to quickly scaffold a Flatiron application.

Listing 9-30. Installing Flatiron and Generating an Application

```
$ npm install  -g flatiron
```

```
$ flatiron create flatironapp
```

Once you have created your application, you can install dependencies from within the generated directory $ cd flatironapp. Then, in order to utilize your Flatiron app, you simply start the app.js file.

```
$ npm install
$ node app.js # starts your app on localhost:3000
```

How It Works

When you first generate an application with Flatiron, you utilize the cli/create.js file that creates the application. This will prompt you for the author and a description of the application you are going to make.

```
$ flatiron create flatironapp
info:    Creating application flatironapp
info:    Using http scaffold.
prompt: author: cgack
prompt: description:  test application
test application
prompt: homepage:
info:    Creating directory config
info:    Creating directory lib
info:    Creating directory test
info:    Writing package.json
info:    Writing file app.js
info:    Writing file config/config.json
info:    Application flatiron is now ready
```

Once you provide this information, you now have generated the app.js file, the configuration files, and the package.json file. The package.json file includes the dependencies needed to run the app. This means all you need to do is navigate to your application directory and install dependencies with npm. This will then give you access to the main Flatiron application, which, by default, will use the HTTP plugin, flatiron.plugins.http.

```
var flatiron = require('flatiron'),
    path = require('path'),
    app = flatiron.app;

app.config.file({ file: path.join(__dirname, 'config', 'config.json') });
app.use(flatiron.plugins.http);
app.router.get('/', function () {
  this.res.json({ 'hello': 'world' })
});

app.start(3000);
```

This application has a router built into it, which uses the syntax app.router.VERB('/path', callback); in order to provide the routes and the handlers for those routes. There is no default templating language included for your views in a Flatiron application but the documentation suggests that you can utilize the language 'Plates – npm install plates –save-dev' in order to create simple, template-language-free templates. These templates only use a binding between unique HTML ID attributes and would look similar to what is shown here.

```
var flatiron = require('flatiron'),
    path = require('path'),
    plates = require('plates'),
    app = flatiron.app;

app.config.file({ file: path.join(__dirname, 'config', 'config.json') });
app.use(flatiron.plugins.http);
app.router.get('/', function () {
  this.res.json({ 'hello': 'world' })
});
```

```
app.router.get('/test', function() {
        var html = '<div id="bind"></div>';
        var data = { "bind": "Bound data" };

        var output = plates.bind(html, data);
        this.res.end(output);
});

app.start(3000);
```

Flatiron has an openness and an API syntax that are similar to the Express framework. It is quick to get up and running with and you should find that it is flexible and extensible. It, like many of the frameworks you have seen in this chapter, provides a way to build a Node.js web server application in a way that allows for swift generation and flexible scalability.

CHAPTER 10

■ ■ ■

Connecting to a Data Store

If you are building an application with Node.js, you are almost inevitably going to need some form of data storage. This can be as simple as in-memory storage or any number of data storage solutions. The Node.js community has created many drivers and connectivity bridges for nearly any data store you might encounter in your application development. In this chapter you will investigate how to use Node.js to connect to many of these, including the following:

- MySQL
- Microsoft SQL Server
- PostgreSQL
- MongoDB
- CouchDB
- Redis
- Cassandra

■ **Note**　This chapter contains a wide variety of databases to utilize with Node.js. It may not be in your best interest to spend your time installing each of these databases on your local machines or environments. This chapter focuses on the Node.js communication with these databases and not the installation and initialization of each database. Because this book is designed to focus on Node.js and how it can operate in various use cases and with all of these database types, you are encouraged to find the recipe that suits your specific database needs.

10-1. Connecting to MySQL

Problem

Many developers are first introduced to database programming via MySQL. Because of this, many also want to bring this familiarity, or bridge, from an existing application into a Node.js application. Because of this, you want to be able to connect to a MySQL database from within your Node.js code.

Solution

When you begin to integrate MySQL to your application, you must decide on a Node.js framework that you wish to use as the MySQL driver. If you choose to use npm and search for MySQL, you will likely see the mysql package listed at or near the top. You then install that package with the $ npm install mysql command.

Once the package is installed, you are ready to use MySQL in your Node.js application. To connect and execute queries, you can use a module similar to the one that you see in Listing 10-1. In this example you can utilize the MySQL sample database, Sakila, which you can install from the instructions found at http://dev.mysql.com/doc/sakila/en/sakila-installation.html.

Listing 10-1. Connecting and Querying MySQL

```
/**
 * mysql
 */

var mysql = require('mysql');

var connectionConfig = {
        host: 'localhost',
        user: 'root',
        password: '',
        database: 'sakila'
};

var connection = mysql.createConnection(connectionConfig);

connection.connect(function(err) {
        console.log('connection::connected');
});

connection.query('SELECT * FROM actor', function(err, rows, fields) {
  if (err) throw err;

  rows.forEach(function(row) {
        console.log(row.first_name, row.last_name);
  });
});

var actor = { first_name: 'Wil', last_name: 'Wheaton' };
connection.query('INSERT INTO actor SET ?', actor, function(err, results) {
        if (err) throw err;

        console.log(results);
});

connection.end(function(err) {
        console.log('connection::end');
});
```

How It Works

Using the mysql module to connect to MySQL begins with a connection configuration object. The connection object in your solution simply provides the host, user, password, and database to which you wish to connect. These are the basic settings, but there are other options that can be configured on this object, as you see in Table 10-1.

Table 10-1. Connection Options for MySQL

Option	Description
bigNumberStrings	When used with supportBigNumbers, Big Numbers will be represented by strings in your JavaScript. Default: False
Charset	Names the charset that you want to use for the connection. Default: UTF8_GENERAL_CI
Database	Lists the name of the database on the MySQL server.
Debug	Prints details using stdout. Default: False
Flags	Lists nondefault connection flags to be used.
Host	Provides the hostname of the database server to which you are connecting. Default: Localhost
insecureAuth	Allows connecting to insecure (older) server authentication methods. Default: False
multipleStatements	Allows more than one statement per query. This could allow for SQL injection attacks. Default: False
Password	Lists the password of the MySQL user.
Port	Gives the port number on the machine where the MySQL server instance resides. Default: 3306
queryFormat	Creates a custom query function.
socketPath	Provides the path to a Unix socket. This will cause the host and port to be ignored.
stringifyObjects	Will stringify objects instead of converting their values. Default: False
supportBigNumbers	Use this when using BIGINT or DECIMAL in your columns. Default: False
Timezone	Lists the time zone for local dates. Default: Local
typecast	Converts types to native JavaScript types. Default: True
User	Lists the MySQL user to utilize for authentication.

Once you create your connection object, you are then able to instantiate a new connection to your MySQL server. This is done by calling `mysql.createConnection(config)`, which will then instantiate the connection object and pass to it the `ConnectionConfig()` object.

You can see in Listing 10-2 that the connection object will actually attempt to create the connection in the Protocol module, which performs the necessary MySQL handshake in order to connect to the server.

Listing 10-2. Connecting in the MySQL Module

```
module.exports = Connection;
Util.inherits(Connection, EventEmitter);
function Connection(options) {
  EventEmitter.call(this);

  this.config = options.config;

  this._socket         = options.socket;
  this._protocol       = new Protocol({config: this.config, connection: this});
  this._connectCalled  = false;
  this.state           = "disconnected";
}
```

Now that you have a connection to the MySQL server, you are able to query by using that connection. In the solution you were able to perform two distinct types of queries.

The first query was an explicit select statement from the actor table in your database. This required nothing more than properly forming the query as a string to the first parameter of the connection.query method. The connection.query method can accept up to three arguments: sql, values, and a callback. If the values parameter is not present, it is detected by checking if it is a function, then just the SQL is enqueued to be executed on the server. The callback will be returned once the query has completed.

In the second query, you pass in some values that you wish to have set within the database. These values are in the form of a JavaScript object, and they are passed in to the '?' placeholder on your INSERT query. One of the great things about using this method is that the mysql module will attempt to safely escape all of the data that you are loading into your database. It does this in order to mitigate SQL injection attacks. There is an escape matrix that will perform different types of escaping for different value types in the mysql module (see Table 10-2).

Table 10-2. *Escape Matrix*

Value Type	How It Is Converted
Arrays	Turned to a list ['a', 'b'] => 'a', 'b'
Boolean	'True' / 'false' strings
Buffers	Hex strings
Dates	'YYYY-mm-dd HH:ii:ss' strings
NaN/Infinity	As is, because MySQL has nothing to convert them to
Nested Arrays	Grouped lists [['a','b'], ['c','d']] => ('a', 'b'), ('c', 'd')
Numbers	None
Objects	Key-'value' pairs are generated; nested objects turn to strings
Strings	Safely escaped
Undefined/null	NULL

This is just a basic example for connecting and executing queries with MySQL by using the mysql module. There are other methods that you can utilize as well. You can stream the response from a query and bind to the events in order to perform specific actions on a row as it is returned, before continuing to the next. An example of this would be as shown in Listing 10-3.

Listing 10-3. Streaming a Query

```
/**
 * mysql
 */

var mysql = require('mysql');

var connectionConfig = {
        host: 'localhost',
        user: 'root',
        password: '',
        database: 'sakila'
};

var connection = mysql.createConnection(connectionConfig);


connection.connect(function(err) {
        console.log('connection::connected');
});

var query = connection.query('SELECT * FROM actor');

query.on('error', function(err) {

        console.log(err);

}).on('fields', function(fields) {

        console.log(fields);

}).on('result', function(row) {
        connection.pause();
        console.log(row);
        connection.resume();
}).on('end', function(err) {
        console.log('connection::end');
});
```

Here you see that the query itself does not change; instead of passing a callback to the query method, we are binding to the events that are emitted from the query while it executes. So as the fields are parsed they are processed. Then for each row you process that data before moving on to the next record. This is done by using the `connection.pause()` function, then performing your actions, followed by the `connection.resume()` method.

Connecting and using MySQL in Node.js is straightforward when you use a framework such as the mysql module. If MySQL is your database of choice, it should not limit your ability to choose Node.js as your data access server.

10-2. Connecting to Microsoft SQL Server
Problem

You want to integrate your Node.js application into a Microsoft SQL Server instance.

Solution

Just as with MySQL, there are several solutions for finding a driver for Microsoft SQL Server with Node.js. One of the most popular packages is "tedious," named after the Tabular Data Stream (TDS) protocol for connecting to SQL Server. You first install this package via npm with the $ `npm install tedious` command.

You then build a set of modules that interact with SQL Server. The first portion of this solution, Listing 10-4, utilizes tedious to create a connection to your SQL Server instance. The second part, as seen in Listing 10-5, is the module that contains the interaction with the data on your SQL Server instance.

■ **Note**   SQL Server is a Microsoft product. As such, the following implementation will work only if your server is running Windows and SQL Server.

Listing 10-4. Connecting to Your SQL Server Instance

```
/*
* Using MS SQL
*/

var TDS = require('tedious'),
        Conn = TDS.Connection,
        aModel = require('./10-2-1.js');

var conn = new Conn({
                username: 'sa',
                password: 'pass',
        server: 'localhost',
        options: {
            database: 'Northwind',
            rowCollectionOnRequestCompletion: true
        });

function handleResult(err, res) {
        if (err) throw err;
        console.log(res);
}

conn.on('connect', function(err) {
        if (err) throw err;

        aModel.getByParameter(conn, 'parameter', handleResult);

        aModel.getByParameterSP(conn, 'parameter', handleResult);
});
```

Listing 10-5. Querying Microsoft SQL Server

```
var TDS = require('tedious'),
        TYPES = TDS.TYPES,
        Request = TDS.Request;
var aModel = module.exports = {
        // Use vanilla SQL
        getByParameter: function(conn, parm, callback) {
                var q = 'select * from model (NOLOCK) where identifier = @parm';

                var req = new Request(q, function(err, rowcount, rows) {
                        callback( err, rows );
                });
                req.addParameter('parm', TYPES.UniqueIdentifierN, parm);

                conn.execSql(req);
        },
        // Use a Store Procedure
        getByParameterSP: function(conn, parm, callback) {
                var q = 'exec sp_getModelByParameter @parm';
                var req = new Request(q, function(err, rowcount, rows) {
                        callback( err, rows );
                });
                req.addParameter('parm', TYPES.UniqueIdentifierN, parm);

                conn.execSql(req);
        }
};
```

How It Works

When you first connect to a Microsoft SQL Server by using the tedious module, you first need to create a connection. This is done by using the TDS.Connection object and instantiating it with a configuration object. In your solution, to create the connection you send a username, password, server name, and a set of options to be used in the connection. There are a number of options that can be passed into this object, as shown in Table 10-3.

Table 10-3. *TDS.Connection Configuration*

Setting	Description
options.cancelTimeout	Time until a cancel request times out. Default: 5 seconds
options.connectTimeout	Time to wait until the connection attempt times out. Default: 15 seconds
options.cryptoCredentialsDetails	Object that will contain any credentials required for encryption. Default: Empty Object '{}'
options.database	The name of the database to connect to
options.debug.data	Boolean telling whether debug information about packet data is sent. Default: False

(*continued*)

Table 10-3. (*continued*)

Setting	Description
options.debug.packet	Boolean telling whether debug information about packets will be sent. Default: False
options.debug.payload	Boolean telling whether debug information about packet payload is sent. Default: False
options.debug.token	Boolean telling whether debug information about stream tokens is sent. Default: False
options.encrypt	Sets whether or not to encrypt requests. Default: False
options.instanceName	The named instance to connect to.
options.isolationLevel	The level of isolation on the server, or when the server will allow data to be seen from another operation. Default: Read Uncommitted (This is known as "dirty reads," or the lowest level of isolation. A given transaction can see uncommitted transactions from another transaction.)
options.packetSize	The size limit for packets that are sent to and from the server. Default: 4 KB
options.port	The port on which to connect. This option is mutually exclusive with options.instanceName. Default: 1433
options.requestTimeout	Time until a given request times out. Default: 15 seconds
options.rowCollectionOnDone	Boolean that states that a row collection will be received when the 'done,' 'doneInProc,' and 'doneProc' events are emitted. Default: False
options.rowCollectionOnRequestCompletion	Boolean that, when true, will provide a row collection in the Request callback. Default: False
options.tdsVersion	The version of the TDS protocol that the connection is to use. Default: 7_2
options.textsize	Sets the maximum width of any column for text data types. Default: 2147483647
.password	The password associated with the username
.server	The name or IP address of the server to which you wish to connect
.userName	Username to use for connecting to the MS SQL Server instance (Note: Windows authentication connections are not supported.)

Once you have passed these options to the connection object, which is a Node.js `EventEmitter`, you then bind to the 'connect' event. There are several ways in which the 'connect' event can be emitted from the connection as described below:

- A successful connection

- A login failure

- After `connectTimeout` has elapsed

- After a socket error occurs during connection

Once you have successfully connected to SQL Server, you then call your module that contains your requests. `TDS.Request` is an `EventEmitter` that allows you to execute SQL either by a plain T-SQL string or a stored procedure. The request also accepts a callback, which will either be called directly, or the result will be applied to the 'requestCompleted' event.

Just as with many SQL Server implementations, you can pass parameters to the SQL that you wish to execute. In both of the examples from your solution (one an SQL text and one a stored procedure), you pass a named parameter. This named parameter is added to the request by using the `Request.addParameter()` method. The `addParameter()` method accepts up to four arguments: name, type, value, and an options object. The type that is used when adding a parameter can be any type in the `TDS.Types` object that is allowed to be part of a parameter. These are Bit, TinyInt, SmallInt, Int, BigInt, Float, Real, SmallDateTime, DateTime, VarChar, Text, NVarChar, Null, UniqueIdentifier, and UniqueIdentifierN.

Once you have made the request object, and you added the parameters that you need, you can then execute the SQL statement by calling `connection.execSql(<Request>)` where you pass the request to the method. When the request completes, your callback executes and you can handle the result and the rows accordingly.

You now understand how to implement a connection to MS SQL Server by using Node.js and the tedious package to manage TDS connections.

10-3. Using PostgreSQL with Node.js

Problem

You are going to use PostgreSQL for your database and need to utilize this in your Node.js application.

Solution

There are several packages that can be used for connecting to PostgreSQL. This solution will be utilizing the node-postgres module, which is a low-level implementation of PostgreSQL. Listing 10-6 shows a simple example of connecting to a PostgreSQL instance and executing a simple query, then logging the result.

Listing 10-6. Connecting to PostgreSQL and Executing a Query

```
/**
* PostgreSQL
*/

var pg = require('pg');

var connectionString = 'tcp://postgres:pass@localhost/postgres';

var client = new pg.Client(connectionString);
```

```
client.connect(function(err) {
        if (err) throw err;

        client.query('SELECT EXTRACT(CENTURY FROM TIMESTAMP "2011-11-11 11:11:11")', function(err,
result) {
                if (err)  throw err;

                console.log(result.rows[0]);

                client.end();
        });
});
```

How It Works

This solution begins by installing the node-postgres module by using $ `npm install pg`. You then can add this to your Node.js code. You then create a connection to your PostgreSQL instance by instantiating a new client. The client constructor can parse the connection string parameters, and you can then create a connection as seen in Listing 10-7.

Listing 10-7. Client Construct of node-postgres

```
var Client = function(config) {
  EventEmitter.call(this);

  this.connectionParameters = new ConnectionParameters(config);
  this.user = this.connectionParameters.user;
  this.database = this.connectionParameters.database;
  this.port = this.connectionParameters.port;
  this.host = this.connectionParameters.host;
  this.password = this.connectionParameters.password;

  var c = config || {};

  this.connection = c.connection || new Connection({
    stream: c.stream,
    ssl: c.ssl
  });
  this.queryQueue = [];
  this.binary = c.binary || defaults.binary;
  this.encoding = 'utf8';
  this.processID = null;
  this.secretKey = null;
  this.ssl = c.ssl || false;
};
```

Once you have created this connection, you next execute a query. This is done by calling `client.query()` and passing an SQL string as the first parameter. The second parameter can either be an array of values to be applied to the query, like you saw in Section 10-1, or the callback. The callback function will pass two arguments, an error if one exists, or the results of the query. The results, as you see, will contain an array of the rows returned. Once you have handled the results, you are able to then close the client connection by calling `client.end()`. The `.end()` method will close the connection via the `connection.end()` method.

Your example used a plaintext SQL statement for node-postgres to execute. There are two other methods for executing a query with node-postgres: parameterized, and a prepared statement.

Parameterized queries allow you to pass parameters to the query such as `'select description from products where name=$1', ['sandals']`. By using parameterized queries, you provide a greater level of protection from SQL injection attacks. They also perform more slowly than plaintext queries, because before each execution these statements are prepared and then executed.

The final type of query that you are able to execute with node-postgres is a prepared statement. One of these will be prepared once, and then for each session connection to postgres, the execution plan for this SQL query is cached so that if it is executed more than once it becomes the most efficient way to execute SQL with node-postgres. Like the parameterized queries, a prepared statement also provides a similar barrier to SQL injection attacks. The prepared statement is created by passing an object to the query method that has a name, text, and a values attribute. You can then call these prepared statements by the names that you provided for them.

Utilizing node-postgres allows you to interact directly and efficiently with PostgreSQL from your Node.js application. The next sections will be a departure from the traditional SQL interfaces with Node.js, and you will begin to investigate several no SQL options for connecting to Node.js.

10-4. Using Mongoose to Connect to MongoDB
Problem

You want to be able to utilize MongoDB in your Node.js application. To do this, you choose to integrate with Mongoose.

Solution

When you use MongoDB with your Node.js application, there are many drivers you can choose from to connect to your data store. However, what is likely the most widely used solution is to integrate your MongoDB instance with the Mongoose module. After installing with `$ npm install mongoose`, you can then create a connection to MongoDB by using the connection methods outlined in Listing 10-8.

Listing 10-8. Connecting to MongoDB with Mongoose

```
/**
 * Connecting to MongoDB with Mongoose
 */

var mongoose = require('mongoose');

// simple connection string
// mongoose.connect('mongodb://localhost/test');
mongoose.connect('mongodb://localhost/test', {
        db: { native_parser: false },
        server: { poolSize: 1 }
        // replset:  { rs_name : 'myReplicaSetName' },
        // user: 'username',
        // pass: 'password'
});
```

```
// using authentication
// mongoose.connect('mongodb://username:password@host/collection')

mongoose.connection.on('open', function() {
        console.log('huzzah! connection open');
});

mongoose.connection.on('connecting', function() {
        console.log('connecting');
});

mongoose.connection.on('connected', function() {
        console.log('connected');
});

mongoose.connection.on('reconnected', function() {
        console.log('reconnected');
});

mongoose.connection.on('disconnecting', function() {
        console.log('disconnecting');
});

mongoose.connection.on('disconnected', function() {
        console.log('disconnected');
});

mongoose.connection.on('error', function(error) {
        console.log('error', error);
});

mongoose.connection.on('close', function() {
        console.log('connection closed');
});
```

How It Works

Connecting to MongoDB in general is not complex. It requires a MongoDB-specific uniform resource identifier (URI) scheme, which will point to a server (or servers) that can host your MongoDB data. In Mongoose, the same URI scheme is used, as seen in Listing 10-9, with the addition of several options that you saw in Listing 10-8.

Listing 10-9. MongoDB Connection String

```
mongodb://[username:password@]host[:port][[,host2[:port2]...[,hostN[:portN][/database][?options]
```

For Mongoose, you use the mongoose.connect(<uri>, <options>) method. The options that you set in Mongoose can be set like any of those listed in Table 10-4.

Table 10-4. Mongoose Connection Options

Option	Description
.auth	The authentication mechanism options, including the source and type of mechanism to use.
.db	Passed to the connection .db instance (e.g., {native_parser: true} will use native binary JSON [BSON] parsing).
.mongos	Boolean that says to use the high-availability option for your .mongos. This should be set to true if connecting to multiple instances of Mongoose.
.pass	The password associated with the username.
.replset	This is the name of the replica set to use, assuming that the Mongoose instance you are connecting to is a member of a set.
.server	Passed to the connection server instance (e.g., {poolSize: 1} number of pools).
.user	The username to be used for authentication.

The connection object inherits for the Node.js EventEmitter, so you can see from your solution that there are many events that you are able to subscribe to by using Mongoose. These events are outlined and described in Table 10-5.

Table 10-5. Mongoose Connection Events

Event	Description
'close'	Emitted after disconnected and 'onClose' are executed on all connections.
'connected'	Emitted once the successful connection to the database occurs.
'connecting'	Emitted when connection.open or connection.openSet is executed on the connection.
'disconnected'	Emitted after disconnecting.
'disconnecting'	Emitted when the connection.close() event is executed.
'error'	Emitted when an error occurs (i.e., when a Mongo instance is dropped).
'fullsetup'	Emitted in a replica set when all nodes are connected.
'open'	Emitted once the connection is opened to the MongoDB instance.
'reconnected'	Emitted after a subsequent connection.

This is the basic scenario and setup for connecting to MongoDB by using Mongoose. In the next section you will investigate how to use Mongoose to smartly model a data store and retrieve it in MongoDB.

10-5. Modeling Data for Mongoose
Problem

You want to model your MongoDB data with Mongoose in your Node.js application.

Solution

When you model data with Mongoose, you need to utilize the `mongoose.model()` method. You do not necessarily need the `mongoose.Schema` method, but for the model created in Listing 10-10 it is utilized to build the schema for the model.

Listing 10-10. Creating a Model with Mongoose

```
/**
* Modeling data with Mongoose
*/

var mongoose = require('mongoose'),
        Schema = mongoose.Schema,
        ObjectId = Schema.ObjectId;

mongoose.connect('mongodb://localhost/test');

var productModel = new Schema({
        productId: ObjectId,
        name: String,
        description: String,
        price: Number
});

var Product = mongoose.model('Product', productModel);

var sandal = new Product({name: 'sandal', description: 'something to wear', price: 12});

sandal.save(function(err) {
        if (err) console.log(err);

        console.log('sandal created');
});

Product.find({name: 'sandal'}).exec(function(err, product) {
        if (err) console.log(err);

        console.log(product);
});
```

How It Works

One of the reasons why Mongoose has become a high priority for anyone utilizing MongoDB in a Node.js application is due to the fact that Mongoose naturally models data. This means that you only need to generate a schema model once for your data and then you can use the model to fetch, update, and remove data from MongoDB.

In your solution, start by importing the `mongoose.Schema` object. The schema is created by passing a JavaScript object that contains the actual schema you wish to model, as well as an optional second parameter that contains the options for your model. The schema not only allows you to create the names of the fields in your model but also provides you with the opportunity to name specific types for the values in your schema. The types that are implemented in the schema instantiation appear as `{ <fieldname> : <DataType> }`. The available types are the following:

- Array
- BooleanBuffer
- Date
- Mixed
- Number
- ObjectId

StringThe options that you create for your schema are any that are shown in Table 10-6.

Table 10-6. *Options for mongoose.Schema*

Option	Description
autoIndex	Boolean that determines whether MongoDB will autogenerate an index.
	Default: True
bufferCommands	Boolean that determines whether the commands are buffered when a connection is lost, until a reconnect occurs.
	Default: True
capped	Sets the MongoDB to be capped—meaning that the collection is a fixed size.
	Default: False
Collection	String that sets the collection name.
id	Returns the document's _id field—or the hexString of the object. If set to false, this will be undefined.
	Default: True
_id	Tells whether MongoDB will create the _id field when the model object is created.
	Default: True
read	Sets query.read options on the schema. This string determines whether your application will read from the primary, secondary, or nearest Mongo in a replicated set.
	Options: 'primary' 'primaryPreferred' 'secondary' 'secondaryPreferred' 'nearest'
safe	Boolean that sets whether an error is passed to the callback.
	Default: True
shardKey	Sets which sharded collection to target.

(continued)

Table 10-6. (*continued*)

Option	Description
strict	Boolean that ensures that nonmodel values passed to the constructor aren't saved. Default: True
toJSON	Converts the model to JavaScript Object Notation (JSON).
toObject	Converts the model to a plain JavaScript object.
versionKey	Sets the version of the schema when the model is created. Default: __v: 0

When you create your "product" schema, you create a simple object that contains a productId, which imports the ObjectId or the hexString of the product. Your model will also create a name as a string, a description as a string, and a price as a number for the products you wish to store and retrieve.

From the schema object, you now actually create a Mongoose model by using the mongoose.model() method and passing the name you chose for your model and the schema model itself. You are now able to use this new product model to create a product. You do this by passing the object that you wish to model in the document on your MongoDB server. In this solution, you create a sandal object. This is then saved by using the sandal.save() method, which takes a callback.

You can also find and remove data from your model. In this solution you query your model by using Product.find({ name: 'sandal' }), which will search for all products named "sandal" and return that in the exec() callback. From within the callback you have access to the array of all the products named "sandal." If you wish to remove all or some of these, you could loop through these results and remove them individually, as shown in Listing 10-11.

Listing 10-11. Using Mongoose to Remove Records

```
Product.find({name: 'sandal'}).exec(function(err, products) {
        if (err) console.log(err);
        console.log(products);
        for (var i = 0; i < products.length; i++) {
                if (i >= 3) {
                        products[i].remove(function() {
                                console.log('removing');
                        });
                }
        }
});
```

You have seen how to connect to and implement a schema with Mongoose in your Node.js application. The Mongoose object model allows for clean implementation of your models to the MongoDB document database.

10-6. Connecting to CouchDB
Problem

You want to utilize CouchDB in your Node.js application.

Solution

CouchDB is a database that utilizes JSON documents, HTTP for its application programming interface (API), and JavaScript for MapReduce. Because of this, it has become a natural fit for many Node.js developers. There are several modules that can be used to build your Node.js application using CouchDB. In this solution you will utilize Nano, which is a lightweight module that supports CouchDB. It can be installed by using $ npm install nano.

In Listing 10-12, you will create a database and insert a document into that database. Next, you will update that document in the database. You will then, in Listing 10-13, retrieve the document and remove it from the database.

Listing 10-12. Creating a Database and Documents in CouchDB with Nano

```
/**
* CouchDB
*/

var nano = require('nano')('http://localhost:5984');

nano.db.create('products', function(err, body, header) {
        if (err) console.log(err);

        console.log(body, header);
});

var products = nano.db.use('products', function(err, body, header) {
        if (err) console.log(err);

        console.log(body, header);
});

products.insert({ name: 'sandals', description: 'for your feet', price: 12.00}, 'sandals',
function(err, body, header) {
        if (err) console.log(err);

        console.log(body, header);
});

products.get('sandals', {ref_info: true}, function(err, body, header) {
        if (err) console.log(err);

        console.log(body, header);
});

// Updating in couchDB with Nano.
products.get('sandals', function(err, body, header) {
        if (!err) {
                products.insert({name: 'sandals', description: 'flip flops', price: 12.50, _rev:
body._rev }, 'sandals', function(err, body, header) {
                        if (!err) {
                                console.log(body, header);
                        }
                });
        }
});
```

Listing 10-13. Removing a Document from a CouchDB Database

```
var nano = require('nano')('http://localhost:5984');

var products = nano.db.use('products');
// deleting in couchDB with Nano.
products.get('sandals', function(err, body, header) {
        if (!err) {
                products.destroy( 'sandals', body._rev, function(err, body, header) {
                        if (!err) {
                                console.log(body, header);
                        }
                        nano.db.destroy('products');
                });
        }
});
```

You can also create requests to CouchDB by using Nano through a single nano.request() interface, as shown in Listing 10-14.

Listing 10-14. Using nano.request()

```
nano.request({
        db: 'products',
        doc: 'sandals',
        method: 'get'
}, function(err, body, header) {
        if (err) console.log('request::err', err);
        console.log('request::body', body);
});
```

How It Works

Using CouchDB is a natural fit for many Node.js applications. The Nano module was designed to be a "minimalistic CouchDB driver for Node.js." Not only is Nano minimalistic, but it also supports using pipes, and you get direct access to errors from CouchDB.

In Listing 10-12 you first required the Nano module and connected to your server. Connecting to a server is as simple as pointing to a host and port that contain the CouchDB instance that is running. Next, you create a database on your CouchDB server that will hold all of the products that you wish to create. When you call any method with Nano, you can add a callback that will receive an error, body, and header parameter. When you first create a database with Nano, you will see the body and the request response JSON that looks like Listing 10-15.

Listing 10-15. Callback after Creating "Products"

```
Body: { ok: true }
Header: { location: 'http://localhost:5984/products',
  date: 'Sun, 28 Jul 2013 14:34:01 GMT',
  'content-type': 'application/json',
  'cache-control': 'must-revalidate',
  'status-code': 201,
  uri: 'http://localhost:5984/products' }
```

Once you have created your database, you then create your first product document. You create the "sandals" document by passing a JavaScript object that contains the information about the product to the `products.insert()` method. The second argument is the name that you want to associate with this document. The body and header responses will let you know that the insert was okay, as seen in Listing 10-16.

Listing 10-16. Inserting a Product

```
Body: { ok: true,
  id: 'sandals',
  rev: '1-e62b89a561374872bab560cef58d1d61' }
Header: { location: 'http://localhost:5984/products/sandals',
  etag: '"1-e62b89a561374872bab560cef58d1d61"',
  date: 'Sun, 28 Jul 2013 14:34:01 GMT',
  'content-type': 'application/json',
  'cache-control': 'must-revalidate',
  'status-code': 201,
  uri: 'http://localhost:5984/products/sandals' }
```

If you want to update a document in CouchDB with Nano, you need to get the revision identifier for the particular document you wish to update and then call the `nano.insert()` function again, passing in the revision identifier to that particular document you wish to update. In your solution you did this by using the `nano.get()` method, then using the `body._rev` revision identifier from the callback to update the document (see Listing 10-17).

Listing 10-17. Updating an Existing Document

```
products.get('sandals', function(err, body, header) {
        if (!err) {
                products.insert({name: 'sandals', description: 'flip flops', price: 12.50, _rev:
body._rev }, 'sandals', function(err, body, header) {
                        if (!err) {
                                console.log(body, header);
                        }
                });
        }
});
```

After you have created, inserted, and updated a document, you will likely want to be able to remove items from time to time. To do this, you also need a reference to the revision of the document that you are planning to remove. This means that you can first fetch the document with `nano.get()` and use the `body._rev` identifier from the callback to be passed into the `nano.destroy()` method. This will remove the document from your database. However, if you want to remove your database you can destroy a database in its entirety by calling `nano.db.destroy(<DBNAME>);`.

The key to the Nano framework is that all of these functions are really wrappers around the `nano.request()` method that you saw in Listing 10-14. In Listing 10-14 your request was made to the "sandals" document in the "products" database as an HTTP GET. This is the same as `nano.get()`. The equivalent for a destroy action is to use the HTTP Verb DELETE, so in the instance of your `nano.db.destroy('products')`, you are essentially writing `nano.request({db: 'products', method: 'DELETE'}, callback);`.

10-7. Using Redis
Problem

You want to utilize the Redis key-value store in your Node.js application.

Solution

Redis is an extremely powerful and popular key-value data store. Because it is so popular, there are many implementations for Node.js to choose from. Some are utilized to connect to the Express web server framework, and others are just as specified. One implementation that is recommended on the Redis website is node_redis, found at https://github.com/mranney/node_redis. To install node_redis, you can utilize npm as follows: `$ npm install redis`.

Using redis_node is simple for those familiar with Redis because the API is the same. All of your get, set, hget, and hgetall commands are able to be executed as they would be directly from Redis itself. A simple example of getting and setting values and hash values is shown in Listing 10-18.

Listing 10-18. Getting and Setting String and Hash Key-Value Pairs with node_redis

```
/**
 * Redis
 */

var redis = require("redis"),
    client = redis.createClient();

client.on("error", function (err) {
    console.log("Error " + err);
});

client.set("key", "value", redis.print);

client.hset("hash key", "hashtest 1", "some value", redis.print);
client.hset(["hash key", "hashtest 2", "some other value"], redis.print);
client.hkeys("hash key", function (err, replies) {
    console.log(replies.length + " replies:");
    replies.forEach(function (reply, i) {
        console.log("    " + i + ": " + reply);
    });
    client.quit();
});

client.hgetall('hash key', function(err, replies) {
    replies.forEach(function(reply) {
        console.log(reply);
    });
});

client.get("key", function(err, reply) {
    if (err) console.log(err);

    console.log(reply);
});
```

Other times, instead of just storing hashes for session-level key-value storage, you may want to implement a loosely coupled publish and subscribe paradigm. This can be a very familiar method to many developers of Node.js applications who are already familiar with event-driven development but who want to leverage Redis for these purposes. An example of using publish and subscribe is shown in Listing 10-19.

Listing 10-19. Publish and Subscribe Example

```
/**
 * Pub/Sub

 */

var redis = require("redis"),
    subscriber = redis.createClient(),
    publisher = redis.createClient();

subscriber.on("subscribe", function (topic, count) {
    publisher.publish("event topic", "your event has occured");
});

subscriber.on("message", function (topic, message) {
    console.log("message recieved:: " + topic + ": " + message);
    subscriber.end();
    publisher.end();
});

subscriber.subscribe("event topic");
```

How It Works

Once you install node_redis via $ npm install redis, you have access to the full implementation of Redis in Node.js. As you saw in Listing 10-18, you can easily create a new client by utilizing redis.createClient(). The createClient() method will create a connection to the port and host of the Redis instance, which defaults to http://127.0.0.1:6379, and will then instantiate a RedisClient object, as shown in Listing 10-20.

Listing 10-20. Node_redis createClient

```
exports.createClient = function (port_arg, host_arg, options) {
    var port = port_arg || default_port,
        host = host_arg || default_host,
        redis_client, net_client;

    net_client = net.createConnection(port, host);

    redis_client = new RedisClient(net_client, options);

    redis_client.port = port;
    redis_client.host = host;

    return redis_client;
};
```

The RedisClient inherits the Node.js EventEmitter and will emit several events, as shown in Table 10-7.

Table 10-7. *RedisClient Events*

Event	Description
'connect'	This event will be emitted at the same time as 'ready' unless the client option 'no_ready_check' is set to true, in which case only once the connection is established will this be emitted. Then you are free to send commands to Redis.
'drain'	The RedisClient will emit 'drain' when the Transmission Control Protocol (TCP) connection to the Redis server has been buffering but is once again writable.
'end'	Once the client connection to the Redis server has closed, this event is emitted.
'error'	The RedisClient will emit 'error' when there is an exception from the Redis server.
'idle'	The RedisClient will emit 'idle' once there are no outstanding messages that are awaiting a response.
'ready'	The client will emit the 'ready' event once a connection is established to the Redis server *and* the server reports that it is ready to receive commands. If you send commands before the 'ready' event, they will be queued and executed just before this event is emitted.

In your solution, you then set a string value and a hash value. String values are set and retrieved by using `client.set` and `client.get`. You also used `client.hset`, `client.hkeys`, and `client.hgetall` in order to deal with hashes. These methods are directly equivalent with entering the commands directly (see Listing 10-21).

Listing 10-21. Redis set, get, hset, hkeys, and hgetall

```
> set key value
OK
> get key
"value"
> hset 'hash key' 'hashtest 1' 'blah'
(integer) 0
> hset 'hash key' 'hashtest 2' 'cheese'
(integer) 0
> hkeys 'hash key'
1) "hashtest 1"
2) "hashtest 2"
> hgetall 'hash key'
1) "hashtest 1"
2) "blah"
3) "hashtest 2"
4) "cheese"
```

You then created a publish and subscribe solution. This can be utilized alongside the Node.js's event model in order to create a loosely coupled integration between segregated portions of your application. To get started, you created two RedisClients called publisher and subscriber. First, you call `subscriber.subscribe()` on the topic you wish to listen for, then actually emit that event, using `publisher.publish(<event name>)`, once the subscriber's 'subscribe' event has been emitted. You then can bind the subscriber to the message event and perform some variety of action once this event has been published.

You have now utilized Redis to store key-value pairs, as well as hashed keys in a data store with node_redis. You also have performed publish and subscribe methods by using Redis to power these messages.

10-8. Connecting to Cassandra

Problem

You are utilizing Cassandra to log events from your application and you would like to implement this logging with Node.js.

Solution

There are many different drivers for Cassandra across different programming languages. For Node.js, the package, "helenus," installed with $ npm install helenus, is at the forefront because it provides bindings to both the thrift protocol and the Cassandra Query Language (CQL).

In Listing 10-22 you will create a logging mechanism that will log events that are occurring on your Node.js server.

Listing 10-22. Using helenus to Create a Logging Application for Cassandra

```
var helenus = require('helenus'),
  pool = new helenus.ConnectionPool({
    hosts      : ['127.0.0.1:9160'],
    keyspace   : 'my_ks',
    user       : 'username',
    password   : 'pass',
    timeout    : 3000//,
    //cqlVersion : '3.0.0' // specify this if you're using Cassandra 1.1 and want to use CQL 3
});

var logger = module.exports = {
    /**
    * Logs data to the Cassandra cluster
    *
    * @param status     the status event that you want to log
    * @param message     the detailed message of the event
    * @param stack       the stack trace of the event
    * @param callback    optional callback
    */
    log: function(status, message, stack, callback) {
        pool.connect(function(err, keyspace){
            console.log('connected');
            keyspace.get('logger', function(err, cf) {
                var dt = Date.parse(new Date());
                //Create a column
                var column = {};
                column['time'] = dt;
                column['status'] = status;
                column['message'] = message;
                column['stack'] = stack;

                var timeUUID = helenus.TimeUUID.fromTimestamp(new Date());

                cf.insert(timeUUID, column, function(err) {
                    if (err) {
                        console.log('error', err);
                    }
```

```
                    Console.log('insert complete');
                    if (callback) {
                        callback();
                    } else {
                        return;
                    }

                });
            });
        });
    }
};
```

How It Works

The helenus module is a robust solution for connecting to the Cassandra database. In your solution, after importing the helenus module, you connect to Cassandra. This is done by passing a simple object to `helenus.connectionPool()`. The object that creates this connection pool contains several options, as outlined in Table 10-8.

Table 10-8. *Connection Pool Options*

Option	Description
.cqlVersion	Names the version of CQL you wish to utilize.
.hosts	Provides an array of values that are the IP address and port for all the Cassandra instances in your cluster.
.keyspace	Lists the keyspace on the Cassandra cluster that you wish to connect to initially.
.password	Provides the password that you wish to use to connect to the node.
.timeout	Is the timeout in milliseconds.
.user	Gives the username for connecting to the node.

Once you have a connection, you can then call `pool.connect()`. Once the connect has occurred, the callback will provide a reference to the default keyspace that you configured in your connection pool. There is, however, another way in which you can connect to a keyspace by using the `pool.use('keyspacename', function(err, keyspace) {});` method.

You now have access to a keyspace on your Cassandra cluster. To gain access to the logger column family, you call `keyspace.get('logger'...)`, which will fetch the column family and return a reference so that you can then operate on the column family directly.

Now that you have gained access to the column family to which you wish to write data, you can create the column that you want to insert. In this solution, assume that your logger column family has a row key that is a TimeUUID type, creating a unique timestamp for each entry. Helenus allows you to use this type of key easily because TimeUUID is a built-in type. You can access this type and create a new TimeUUID by using the `fromTimestamp` method on the object, as seen in Listing 10-23. You will also see that, if needed, helenus provides a way to generate UUID types.

Listing 10-23. Creating a New TimeUUID

```
> helenus.TimeUUID.fromTimestamp(new Date());
c19515c0-f7c4-11e2-9257-fd79518d2700

> new helenus.UUID();
7b451d58-548f-4602-a26e-2ecc78bae57c
```

Aside from the row key in your logger column family, you simply pass the timestamp, status, message, and stack trace of the event you wish to log. These all become parts of an object you named "column." Now that you have the row key and the column values, you can insert them into Cassandra by calling the `cf.insert` method on your column family.

This solution leveraged JavaScript and objects to generate a model-like implementation that was converted to the Cassandra Thrift protocol in order to insert data. Helenus allows for other methods of inserting data by using the CQL language. A similar implementation to the one seen in Listing 10-22 but that utilizes CQL is shown in Listing 10-24. The step to retrieve the column family is omitted because CQL operates directly on the keyspace.

Listing 10-24. Using CQL to Log Data to Cassandra

```
var helenus = require('helenus'),
    pool = new helenus.ConnectionPool({
        hosts      : ['127.0.0.1:9160'],
        keyspace   : 'my_ks',
        user       : 'username',
        password   : 'pass',
        timeout    : 3000//,
        //cqlVersion : '3.0.0' // specify this if you're using Cassandra 1.1 and want to use CQL 3
    });

var logger = module.exports = {
    /**
     * Logs data to the Cassandra cluster
     *
     * @param status    the status event that you want to log
     * @param message   the detailed message of the event
     * @param stack     the stack trace of the event
     * @param callback  optional callback
     */
    log: function(status, message, stack, callback) {
        pool.connect(function(err, keyspace){
            keyspace.get('logger', function(err, cf) {
                var dt = Date.parse(new Date());
                //Create a column
                var column = {};
                column['time'] = dt;
                column['status'] = status;
                column['message'] = message;
                column['stack'] = stack;

                var timeUUID = helenus.TimeUUID.fromTimestamp(new Date());
                var cqlInsert = 'INSERT INTO logger (log_time, time, status, message,stack)' +
                                'VALUES ( %s, %s, %s, %s, %s )';

                var cqlParams = [ timeUUID, column.time, column.status, column.message, column.stack ];
                pool.cql(cqlInsert, cqlParams, function(err, results) {
                    if (err) logger.log('ERROR', JSON.stringify(err), err.stack);
                });
            });
        });
    }
};
```

```
var queueObj = {};
var timeUUID = helenus.TimeUUID.fromTimestamp(new Date()) + '';
                    var cqlInsert = 'INSERT INTO hx_services_pha_card (card_id, card_definition_id,
pig_query, display_template, tokens, trigger)' +
                                    'VALUES ( %s, %s, %s, %s, %s, %s )';

                    var cqlParams = [ timeUUID, queueObj.card_definition_id, queueObj.pig_query,
queueObj.display_template, tokens.join(','), queueObj.trigger ];
                    pool.cql(cqlInsert, cqlParams, function(err, results) {
                        if (err) logger.log('ERROR', JSON.stringify(err), err.stack);
                    });
```

10-9. Using Riak with Node.js

Problem

You want to be able to utilize the highly scalable distributed database, Riak, with your Node.js application.

Solution

Riak is designed for high availability across distributed systems. It is designed to be fast and scalable, which makes it a good fit for many Node.js applications. In Listing 10-25, you will once again create a data store that will create, update, and retrieve your product data.

■ **Note**   Riak is not supported on Windows machines currently. The following implementation should work on Linux or OSX.

Listing 10-25. Using Riak with Node.js

```
/**
* RIAK
*/

var db = require('riak-js').getClient();

db.exists('products', 'huaraches', function(err, exists, meta) {
        if (exists) {
                db.remove('products', 'huaraches', function(err, value, meta) {
                        if (err) console.log(err);
                        console.log('removed huaraches');
                });
        }
});

db.save('products', 'flops', { name: 'flip flops', description: 'super for your feet', price: 12.50},
function(err) {
        if (err) console.log(err);
        console.log('flip flops created');
        process.emit('prod');
});
```

```
db.save('products', 'flops', { name: 'flip flops', description: 'fun for your feet', price: 12.00},
function(err) {
        if (err) console.log(err);
        console.log('flip flops created');
        process.emit('prod');
});

db.save('products', 'huaraches', {name: 'huaraches', description: 'more fun for your feet', price: 20.00},
function(err) {
        if (err) console.log(err);

        console.log('huaraches created');
        process.emit('prod');

        db.get('products', 'huaraches', function(err, value, meta) {
                if (err) console.log(err);
                console.log(value);
        });

});

process.on('prod', function() {

        db.getAll('products', function(err, value, meta) {
                if (err) console.log(err);
                console.log(value);
        });

});
```

How It Works

To create this solution, you started with the Node.js module riak-js, installed by using $ npm install riak-js.
You then connected to the server by using the getClient() method. This method, when left alone, will find the
default client running on the local machine but can also be configured with an options object.

You are now connected to the Riak instance by using the db object. First, you see that the API is concise as you
encounter db.exists(<bucket>, <key>, callback). This callback will return a value of true if the key exists in the
bucket on your Riak node. If the bucket key did exist, you removed that particular set of data by simply pointing to that
bucket key and using the db.remove() method.

Next, you saved some data to your Riak node by using the db.save method. This method accepts a bucket, key,
and a value you wish to set for the bucket key. This can be a JavaScript object, a number, or a string that you wish to store
for the key's value. You also, as with all requests with riak-js, gain access to the callback function. The callbacks have three
values: an error if one occurred, a value that is passed as the result of the riak-js method, and the meta object.

After you save your huaraches to the products bucket, you then retrieve this key by utilizing the db.get()
function. Again, this method takes the bucket and the key in order to determine which data on your node you wish to
retrieve. And the callback can contain the values and the meta associated with the data. There is one other way that
you can access data by using riak-js. This is used to retrieve all the values for a given bucket. The resultant value in the
callback will be an array of data associated with the bucket.

You have used riak-js to interact with your Riak cluster in Node.js. This provides a simple API to insert, read, update, and remove data on your node. Riak is a powerful distributed database solution that, aside from these simple tasks, can also perform more complex searches by using map and reduce functions through a similar API. In order to do this, you could search all products in your node by running the following commands (see Listing 10-26).

Listing 10-26. Map Reduce with riak-js

```
db.mapreduce
        .add('products')
        .map(function(v) {
                return [Riak.mapValuesJson(v)[0]];
        })
        .run(function(err, value, meta) {
                console.log(value);
        });
```

CHAPTER 11

Testing in Node.js

Testing allows you the peace of mind to know that the code you wrote is actually performing the operations that it was intended to do. Node.js offers a native implementation for writing some form of unit tests, and the Node.js community has created several robust libraries to aid you in your test-driven development process.

In this chapter you will investigate how to decide on a testing framework for your Node.js application, and you will also see a variety of techniques and testing mechanisms that you can use to create a fully tested application. Once you have built the tests that you need for your Node.js application, you will learn how to report on the tests that you have created and integrate them into your workflow.

There are a plethora of options for you to utilize when you are creating a Node.js testing implementation. In this chapter you will get a chance to see a small sampling of the number of frameworks, including the following:

- Node.js assert
- Nodeunit
- Mocha
- Chai.js
- Vows.js
- Should.js

The ones that are used in this chapter feature more prominently in the community, but by all means this is not an exhaustive list. This chapter is designed to inform you enough to create a full test suite for your Node.js application, but I will attempt to remain agnostic about which framework you might eventually choose.

11-1. Choosing a Framework for Test-Driven Development or Behavior-Driven Development

You want to implement testing into your Node.js development process. To do this, you need to discover the best testing solution available to meet your testing needs.

The first thing that you should consider when you are choosing a testing framework is the types of tests you are trying to make. There are two generic categories to describe testing styles, which can then be broken down into smaller categories.

First, there is the classic test-driven development (TDD). TDD is useful because you take a code requirement, write a failing test for that aspect of the requirement, then create the code that will allow that test to pass. The evolution of TDD is behavior-driven development (BDD). BDD takes not only a functional unit of code that can be tested, but also a business use case that can be tested, protecting both the code and the end user's experience.

Your framework choice depends not only on the style of testing that you would prefer, but also on the types of testing that you wish to encounter. You might want to do some simple assertion testing only on critical values in your application. You may want to provide a code coverage summary to let you know where you can refactor and remove extraneous code from your application.

In this chapter you will see many implementations that each offer a unique take on testing in Node.js. It is not an exhaustive list but is meant to help you to gain a perspective on how to pick a testing framework that will work for you.

Some work seamlessly with asynchronous code; others perform better on a large-scale test project. These decisions are up to you, the developer, to decide which suits your need. Should you choose any or none of these frameworks is not as important as getting testing into your workflow and building a Node.js application that you know is well tested.

11-2. Creating Tests with the Node.js assert Module
Problem

You want to utilize Node.js's native assert module to test your Node.js application.

Solution

There are many options for creating basic tests in Node.js. The basis for many tests derives from the Node.js assert module. This module is used internally for Node.js testing and is a good model for TDD.

Listing 11-1 shows you how to implement a basic set of tests with the Node.js assert module.

Listing 11-1. Node.js assert Basics

```
var assert = require('assert');

/*11-2*/
var three = 3;

assert.equal(three, '3', '3 equals "3"');

assert.strictEqual('3', three.toString(), '3 and "3" are not strictly equal');

assert.notEqual(three, 'three', '3 not equals three');

// assert.ok(false, 'not truthy ');
assert.ok(true, 'truthy');
```

The Node.js assert module can also be utilized to test asynchronous code, as shown in Listing 11-2.

Listing 11-2. Testing Function to Square a Number Asynchronously

```
var squareAsync = function(a, cb) {
    result = a * a;
    cb(result);
};

var assert = require('assert');
```

```
squareAsync(three, function(result) {
        assert.equal(result, 9, '3 squared is nine');
});

squareAsync('three', function(result) {
        assert.ok(isNaN(result), '"Three squared is NaN');
});
```

Normally in Node.js, you create code that is asynchronous as you saw above. However, there are times when you may have some code of a synchronous nature that you would like to test. You can test synchronous code with the assert module by following the example shown in Listing 11-3.

Listing 11-3. Synchronous with Node.js assert

```
var square = function(a) {
    if (typeof a !== 'number') return false;
    return a * a;
};

var assert = require('assert');

assert.equal(square(three), 9, '3 squared equals 9');

assert.equal(square('three'), false, 'should fail because "three" is not a number');
```

How It Works

The Node.js assert testing module, imported using require('assert'), is utilized for internal Node.js tests and has become the basis for many third-party testing implementations. The assert module is created in such a way that if a particular condition is not met for your testing needs, it will throw an assertion error. If all passes, the Node.js process will exit as expected.

In this solution you saw that you can validate truthy or falsey values, equality, and nonequality by using a smaller portion of the assert module's application programming interface (API). The full listing of what the API is capable of asserting is shown in Table 11-1.

Table 11-1. *API Methods for the assert Module*

Method	Description
assert.deepEqual(actual, expected, message)	Tests for deep equality. This tests beyond the '===' operator and checks dates, regular expressions, objects, and buffers in the comparison.
assert.doesNotThrow(block, [error], [message])	Expects that the provided code block will not throw an error.
assert.equal(actual, expected, message)	Tests to see if the actual value is equal to the expected value by using the '==' operator.
assert.fail(actual, expected, message, operator)	Throws an assertion exception by showing the message and the actual and expected values separated by the operator.
assert.ifError(value)	Tests to see if the value is not false, and throws an assertion exception if it is. This is used to test if an error argument is provided by a callback.

(continued)

Table 11-1. (*continued*)

Method	Description
assert.notDeepEqual(actual, expected, message)	Tests for deep nonequality. This tests beyond the '!==' operator and checks dates, regular expressions, objects, and buffers in the comparison.
assert.notEqual(actual, expected, message)	Tests to see that the actual value is not equal to the expected value by using the '!=' operator.
assert.notStrictEqual(actual, expected, message)	Same as .notEqual with the exception that this compares the values with the '!==' operator.
assert.ok(value, message)	Tests to see if the value passed is a truthy value. If not, the message will be logged with the assertion exception.
assert.strictEqual(actual, expected, message)	Same as .equal with the exception that this compares the values by using the '===' operator.
assert.throws(block, [error], [message])	Expects the provided block to throw an error.

11-3. Creating Tests with Nodeunit
Problem

You want to utilize the nodeunit unit-testing module to test your Node.js application.

Solution

The nodeunit testing module builds off of the assert module's API and is shown in Listing 11-4.

Listing 11-4. Using nodeunit for Testing

```
var test = require('nodeunit');

module.exports = {
        '11-2': {
                'equal': function(test) {
                        test.equal(3, '3', '3 equals "3"');
                        test.done();
                },
                'strictEqual': function(test) {
                        test.strictEqual('3', 3, '3 and "3" are not strictly equal');
                        test.done();
                },
                'notEqual' : function(test) {
                        test.notEqual(3, 'three', '3 not equals three');
                        test.done();
                },
                'ok' : function(test) {
                        test.ok(false, 'not truthy ');
                        test.done();
                }
        }
};
```

Listing 11-5 demonstrates the solution for utilizing the nodeunit testing framework for creating tests of asynchronous methods.

Listing 11-5. Nodeunit Asynchronous Test

```
var squareAsync = function(a, cb) {
    result = a * a;
    cb(result);
};

module.exports = {
    '11-4': {
        'squareAsync': function(test) {
            test.expect(2);
            squareAsync(three, function(result) {
                test.equal(result, 9, 'three squared is nine');
            });
            squareAsync('three', function(result) {
                test.ok(isNaN(result), 'squaring a string returns NaN');
            });
            test.done();
        }
    }
};
```

Nodeunit also allows for synchronous testing (shown in Listing 11-6).

Listing 11-6. Nodeunit Synchronous Test

```
var square = function(a) {
    if (typeof a !== 'number') return false;
    return a * a;
};

var test = require('nodeunit');
module.exports = {
    '11-3': {
        'squareSync': function(test) {
            test.equal(square(three), 9, 'three squared is nine');
            test.equal(square('three'), false, 'cannot square a non number');
            test.done();
        }
    }
};
```

How It Works

Nodeunit provides the same API as the assert module with the addition of two methods. First, add the .done() method, which tells nodeunit that you have finished that test and it is time to move on to the next one. The second addition that nodeunit brings is the .expect(amount) method. This method allows you to instruct nodeunit as to how many tests you plan to implement and to ensure that all tests have executed. If you had instructed nodeunit to run two tests using expect(2), and only ran one, the tests will fail with the message: `Error: Expected 2 assertions, 1 ran.` You will see in the next section that being able to use the expect() and done() methods allows for a great way to test asynchronous code.

To implement a test with nodeunit you need to export the tests from a module. As you saw previously you first require the nodeunit module and then export your tests. The format of this export can help you to group your tests. You can see in the solution that you grouped all the tests for this section under the 11-2 heading. You then created each test separately, calling the assertions for each test, then calling `test.done()`.

To call a nodeunit test, you must first install nodeunit with `npm install -g nodeunit`. Then target the module you wish to test. If you used a file named nodeunit.js, you would call `$ nodeunit nodeunit.js` and the tests would execute and produce a result similar to what you see in Listing 11-7, with checkmarks to indicate passing tests and an "X" for failures.

Listing 11-7. Nodeunit Results

```
nodeunit.js
✔ 11-2 - equal
✔ 11-2 - strictEqual
✔ 11-2 - notEqual
✖ 11-2 – ok
```

11-4. Creating Tests with Mocha
Problem

You need to utilize Mocha to create tests for your Node.js application.

Solution

A prominent framework for writing Node.js tests is Mocha. An example of how it can be used is shown in Listing 11-8.

Listing 11-8. Using the Mocha Framework

```
var assert = require('assert');

var three = 3;
describe('11-2', function() {
        describe('#equal', function() {
                it('should return true that 3 equals "3"', function() {
                        assert.equal(three, '3', '3 equals "3"');
                })
        })
        describe("#strictEqual", function() {
                it('"3" only strictly equals 3.toString()', function() {
                        assert.strictEqual('3', three.toString(), '3 and "3" are not strictly equal');
                })
        })
        describe("#notEqual", function() {
                it('should be that 3 is not equal to three', function() {
                        assert.notEqual(three, 'three', '3 not equals three');
                })
        })
```

```
        describe("#ok", function() {
                it('should return that false is not truthy', function() {
                        assert.ok(false, 'not truthy ');
                })
        })
        describe("#ok", function() {
                it('should be true that true is truthy', function() {
                        assert.ok(true, 'truthy');
                })
        })
});
```

Mocha can also test asynchronous code, as shown in Listing 11-9.

Listing 11-9. Mocha Asynchronous Tests

```
var squareAsync = function(a, cb) {
    result = a * a;
    cb(result);
};

squareAsync(three, function(result) {
        result.should.equal(9, 'three squared is nine');
});

squareAsync('three', function(result) {
        // NaN !== NaN
        result.should.not.equal(result);
});
```

On occasion, you will want to test code that has been written synchronously. Mocha can test code like this, as shown in Listing 11-10.

Listing 11-10. Mocha Synchronous Test

```
var square = function(a) {
    if (typeof a !== 'number') return false;
    return a * a;
};

describe('11-3 sync', function() {
    describe('square a number', function() {
        it('should do this syncronously', function() {
            square(three).should.equal(9);
        });
        it('should fail when the target is not a number', function() {
            square('three').should.be.false;
        });
    });
});
```

How It Works

Mocha is a testing framework that can utilize any assertion module that you choose. For this example you utilized the Node.js assert module to manage your simple assertions. However, in order for these assertions to work, you had to wrap your assertions in a Mocha-specific description. This allows you to name your test suite and specific case in order to see the desired output from your tests.

The way in which you create a description for your tests is to wrap them in the function 'describe'. This function will take a name and a callback function. A test suite nests the individual test cases inside of its callback. In general this should look like the example shown in Listing 11-11.

Listing 11-11. Building a Test Suite with Mocha

```
describe('Test suite', function() {
    describe('test-case', function() {
        // tests go here
    });
});
```

A test in Mocha can contain a description of what the expected outcome is to be, which is used when you encounter an assertion error. The syntax reads almost like a sentence, as you see in Listing 11-12, where you describe what the test should result to, and the test itself is contained within the callback. The test description will only appear if the test fails.

Listing 11-12. Test Failure Description

```
it('should return true that 3 equals "3"', function() {
        assert.equal(three, '3', '3 equals "3"');
});
```

There are two main ways in which you can tell Mocha to perform its tests once you have installed Mocha globally via $ npm install -g mocha. Mocha can be called on a file directly, by calling $ mocha filename.js. This is valuable if you are testing an individual test file, but if you want to test more than one you simply can create a test/ directory and move your Mocha test files into that directory. Once you have done this, simply call $ mocha, and it will find that directory and traverse it, executing the tests as they are encountered.

11-5. Creating Tests with Chai.js
Problem

You want to create tests with the Chai.js testing framework.

Solution

Another example of a testing framework that incorporates the Node.js assert module's API is the Chai.js testing framework. An example of the same basic testing structure is shown in Listing 11-13.

Listing 11-13. Testing with Chai.js

```
/**
 * chaijs
 */

var chai = require('chai');

/* 11-2 simple */
var assert = chai.assert;
var three = 3;

assert.equal(three, '3', '3 equals "3"');

assert.strictEqual('3', three.toString(), '3 and "3" are not strictly equal');

assert.notEqual(three, 'three', '3 not equals three');

assert.ok(true, 'truthy');

//assert.isFalse(true, 'true is false');

var expect = chai.expect;

expect(three).to.be.a('number');

var should = chai.should();

three.should.be.a('number');
```

Next, you can create asynchronous tests with the Chai.js framework. These are shown in Listing 11-14.

Listing 11-14. Chai.js Asynchronous Tests

```
var squareAsync = function(a, cb) {
    result = a * a;
    cb(result);
};

squareAsync(three, function(result) {
        result.should.equal(9, 'three squared is nine');
});

squareAsync('three', function(result) {
        // NaN !== NaN
        expect(result).to.not.eql(result);
});
```

Listing 11-15 shows how you implement synchronous tests with Chai.js.

Listing 11-15. Chai.js Synchronous Test

```
var square = function(a) {
    if (typeof a !== 'number') return false;
    return a * a;
};

var chai = require('chai');

var should = chai.should();

square(three).should.equal(9);

square('three').should.be.false;
```

How It Works

Chai.js can be used as a test driver, accompanied by any Node.js assertion module. You begin testing with Chai by installing the Chai.js module and importing it locally. You then can build your assertions in any of the several styles that Chai.js offers.

There are two methods for BDD-style assertions that Chai.js offers. First is the 'expect' style. The expect style creates a sentence-like structure to describe how you expect your code to be. You can build a statement that looks like the following: `expect('cheese').to.be.a('string');`. This type of testing will throw assertion errors when you encounter a statement such as `expect(3).to.be.a('string')`, or `expect(3).to.equal(6);`.

The second type of BDD style is 'should'. 'Should' resembles the 'expect' module in many respects, although implementing the 'should' module requires you to execute the 'should' function, `chai.should()`, instead of a reference to the function as in `chai.expect`. This is because when you call 'expect', you invoke the function with the object that you are testing: `expect(three)`. In 'should' style, you start with the object that you are testing, then describe the behavior that should occur.

The 'should' and 'expect' styles share the same API, as shown in Table 11-2. They also provide a nontesting set of methods that are used to build the sentence-like structure in a chainable way. These methods are to, be, been, is, that, and, have, with, at, of, and some.

Table 11-2. *API Methods for 'should' and 'expect' Modules*

Method	Description
.above(value)	Asserts that the target is greater than the value.
.arguments	The target must be an arguments object.
.a(type)	Determines that the preceding object should be of the type 'type'.
.below(value)	The target is less than the value.
.closeTo(expected, delta)	The target value is within a given expected value plus or minus a delta.
.contain(value)	Asserts that the preceding contain the value given, that is, expect('cheese').to.contain('he').
.deep	This should be used with a following equal or property method. Will perform a deep equal check on the assertion.
.empty	Asserts that the target has length 0, or there are no enumerable keys in an object.

(continued)

Table 11-2. *(continued)*

Method	Description
.eql(value)	The target must be deep equal.
.equal(value)	The target must be strict equal. If the deep method precedes it, this performs a deep equal check.
.exist	The target must not be null or undefined.
.false	The target must be false.
.include(value)	Asserts that the preceding includes the value given, i that is, expect([1,2,4]). to.include(2);.
.instanceof(constructor)	The target must be an instance of the constructor.
.itself	Sets the itself flag to be later used by the respondTo method.
.keys(key1, [key2],...,[keyN])	The target contains exactly the provided keys.
.least(value)	The target must be greater than or equal to the value, ..is.at.least(value).
.length(value)	The target must have length of value.
.match(regex)	The target matches the regular expression.
.members(set)	The target has the same members of set, or is a superset of the set.
.most(value)	The target is less than or equal to the value.
.not	Negates any assertions that follow in the chain.
.null	The target must be null.
.ok	Ensures that the target is truthy.
.ownProperty(name)	The target will have its own property name.
.property(name, [value])	The target will have the property name, and optionally the value must match.
.respondTo(method)	The target will respond to the method.
.satisfy(method)	The target passes the given truth test.
.string(string)	The string target must contain the string.
.throw(constructor)	The function target should throw an exception.
.true	The target must be true.
.undefined	The target must be undefined.
.within(start, finish)	The target must fall between the start and finish range.

Also in this example was the classic TDD style that is used in the Chai.js assert module. This module resembles the Node.js assert module, but it incorporates even more methods to the assert API, as shown in Table 11-3.

Table 11-3. *Chai.js assert*

Method	Description
.closeTo(actual, expected, delta, [message])	The actual value will be within the delta of the expected.
.deepEqual(actual, expected, [message])	The actual value must be deep equal to the expected.
.deepProperty(object, property, [message])	The object must contain the property and can be deeply nested.
.deepPropertyNotVal(object, property, value, [message])	The object must contain the deep property but the value is not the value.
.deepPropertyVal(object, property, value, [message])	The object must contain the deep property with the value.
.doesNotThrow(function, [constructor/regexp], [message])	The function will not error as an instance of constructor or matching the regular expression.
.equal(actual, expected, [message])	The actual value must be nonstrict equal (==) to the expected.
.fail(actual, expected, [message], [operator])	Throws a failure.
.include(haystack, needle, [message])	The haystack contains a needle. This can be used for strings (contains) or arrays.
.includeMembers(superset, subset, [message])	The subset must be included in the superset.
.instanceOf(object, constructor, [message])	The object must be an instance of the constructor.
.isArray(value, [message])	The value must be an array.
.isBoolean(value, [message])	The value must be a boolean.
.isDefined(value, [message])	The value must not be undefined.
.isFalse(value, [message])	The value must be false.
.isFunction(value, [message])	The value must be a function.
.isNotArray(value, [message])	The value must not be an array.
.isNotBoolean(value, [message])	The value must not be a boolean.
.isNotFunction(value, [message])	The value must not be a function.
.isNotNull(value, [message])	The value must not be null.
.isNotNumber(value, [message])	The value must not be a number.
.isNotObject(value, [message])	The value must not be an object.
.isNotString(value, [message])	The value must not be a string.
.isNull(value, [message])	The value must be null.
.isNumber(value, [message])	The value must be a number.
.isObject(value, [message])	The value must be an object.
.isString(value, [message])	The value must be a string.
.isTrue(value, [message])	The value must be true.

(continued)

Table 11-3. (*continued*)

Method	Description
.isUndefined(value, [message])	The value must be undefined.
.lengthOf(object, length, [message])	The object must have the given length.
.match(value, regexp, [message])	The value must match the regular expression.
.notDeepEqual(actual, expected, [message])	The actual value must be not deep equal to the expected.
.notDeepProperty(object, property, [message])	The object must not contain the deep property.
.notEqual(actual, expected, [message])	The actual value must be nonstrict inequal (!=) to the expected.
.notIncluded(haystack, needle, [message])	The haystack does not contain a needle.
.notInstanceOf(object, constructor, [message])	The object must not be an instance of the constructor.
.notMatch(value, regexp, [message])	The value must not match the regular expression.
.notOk(object, [message])	The object must not be truthy.
.notProperty(object, property, [message])	The object must not contain property.
.notStrictEqual(actual, expected, [message])	The actual value must be strict inequal (!==) to the expected.
.notTypeOf(value, name, [message])	The value is not a type of name.
.ok(object, [message])	The object must be truthy.
.operator(val1, operator, val2, [message])	The val1 will have the relation to val2 that is determined by the operator, that is, operator(3, '>', 0).
.propertyNotVal(object, property, value, [message])	The object must contain the property but the value is not the value.
.property(object, property, [message])	The object must contain the property.
.propertyVal(object, property, value, [message])	The object must contain the property with the value.
.sameMembers(set1, set2, [message])	Set1 and set2 must have the same members.
.strictEqual(actual, expected, [message])	The actual value must be strict equal (===) to the expected.
.throws(function, [constructor/string/regexp], [string/regexp], [message])	The function will error as an instance of the constructor, or it will throw an error with a matching regexp/string.
.typeOf(value, name, [message])	The value must be of the type name.

11-6. Creating Tests with Vows
Problem

You need to create tests for your Node.js application by using the Vows testing framework.

Solution

Vows is a popular testing framework that is popular with Node.js developers because it works great with Node.js's asynchronous nature. You can see the basic solution for using this framework in Listing 11-16.

Listing 11-16. Using Vows.js for Testing

```
var vows = require('vows'),
       assert = require('assert');

var three = 3;
vows.describe('vows testing').addBatch({
        '11-2': {
                'basic testing': {
                        topic: three,

                        ' 3 equals "3"': function(topic) {
                                assert.equal(three, '3');
                        },
                        ' 3 and "3" are not strictly equal': function(topic) {
                                assert.strictEqual('3', three.toString());
                        },
                        ' 3 notEqual "three"' : function(topic) {
                                assert.notEqual(three, 'three');
                        },
                        ' false is truthy? ' : function(topic) {
                                assert.ok(false);
                        },
                        ' true is truthy? ' : function(topic) {
                                assert.ok(true);
                        }
                }
        }
}).export(module);
```

Listing 11-17. Vows.js Synchronous Tests

```
var square = function(a) {
    if (typeof a !== 'number') return false;
    return a * a;
};

var vows = require('vows'),
    assert = require('assert');
```

```
vows.describe('vows testing').addBatch({
        '11-3': {
                'sync': {
                        topic: function(a) { return 3 * 3; },
                        'squared': function(topic) {
                                assert.equal(topic, 9);
                        }
                }
        }
});
```

How It Works

Vows is arguably the greatest departure in style from the previous testing frameworks. Vows is a testing framework that is built for testing asynchronous code, and therefore it is a great fit for Node.js.

In Vows, and in your solution using Vows, you begin by describing a test suite. In our case this was the 'vows testing' suite created with calling `vows.describe(<suite name>)`. You then group a set of tests in a batch and add that to the suite by calling the .addBatch() method, which accepts an object literal: the test batch.

The batches are then divided into groups; in this case, the 11-2 group was created and further subdivided with 'basic testing'. Next, you break up your tests into individual topics. Here you deal with the variable 'three', which points to the value 3. Within the topic, you build your tests, first describing the outcome you wish to see, then executing the test by passing the topic to the callback function. Within this callback you utilize the Node.js assert module in order to validate your tests. The output of your tests from this solution using Vows can be generated in two ways, as shown in Listing 11-18.

Listing 11-18. Vows Output Options

```
$ vows vows.js
...?.

  11-2 basic testing
    ?  false is truthy?
      » expected expression to evaluate to true, but was false // vows.js:24
  ? Broken » 4 honored · 1 broken

$ vows vows.js --spec

  ? vows testing

  11-2 basic testing
    √  3 equals "3"
    √  3 and "3" are not strictly equal
    √  3 notEqual "three"
    ?  false is truthy?
      » expected expression to evaluate to true, but was false // vows.js:24
    √  true is truthy?

? Broken » 4 honored · 1 broken
```

Simply calling the Vows method will run the tests, but by adding the --spec parameter to the call, you are able to get a more verbose output of the results. It will then print the number of vows that were "honored": tests passed, or broken, meaning failed tests.

Setting up tests with any of these frameworks should not be a limitation in your Node.js development. These frameworks should become a part of your development cycle and can allow you to build a more proven and sound Node.js application. In the coming sections you will see how to test for certain points of synchronous methods, and more commonly how to fit these testing frameworks into your asynchronous applications build with Node.js.

11-7. Creating Tests with Should.js
Problem

You have created a Node.js application that you need to create tests for by using the Should.js framework.

Solution

Should.js is a testing framework that uses a very friendly and chainable BDD syntax for testing. A basic example using Should.js is shown in Listing 11-19.

Listing 11-19. Using Should.js

```
var should = require('should');
var three = 3;

should.equal(three, '3', '3 equals "3"');

should.strictEqual('3', three.toString(), '3 and "3" are not strictly equal');

should.notEqual(three, 'three', '3 not equals three');

true.should.be.ok;
false.should.not.be.ok;

three.should.be.a('number');
```

Should.js can also be utilized for asynchronous and synchronous tests, as shown in Listings 11-20 and 11-21.

Listing 11-20. Should.js Asynchronous Tests

```
var squareAsync = function(a, cb) {
    result = a * a;
    cb(result);
};

squareAsync(three, function(result) {
        result.should.equal(9, 'three squared is nine');
});

squareAsync('three', function(result) {
        // NaN !== NaN
        result.should.not.equal(result);
});
```

Listing 11-21. Should.js Synchronous Tests

```
var square = function(a) {
    if (typeof a !== 'number') return false;
    return a * a;
};

var should = require('should');

square(three).should.equal(9);

square('three').should.be.false;
```

How It Works

When you begin to test with Should.js, you note that it begins as an extension of the Node.js assert module. This means that you are able to implement all of the items of the assert API just as you would normally. Should.js also expands this module to include a method named .exists() that is the same as .ok().

Should.js, like the Chai.js 'should' style, allows the chaining of tests. This not only helps to better describe the behavior, but also allows the testing framework to become a self-documenting piece of code. The chainable syntax allows chaining methods like an, and, be, have, and with. These methods do not actually manipulate the tests but are convenient for chaining and readability. The API for Should.js contains the methods that are shown in Table 11-4.

Table 11-4. Should.js API

Method	Description
.a	The target should be of the type declared.
.above	The target must have a numeric value above the expected.
.arguments	The target is an arguments array-like object.
.below	The target must have a numeric value below the expected.
.empty	The target must have length 0.
.eql	Checks for equality.
.equal	Is of strict equality.
.false	The target must === false.
.header(field, [value])	The target must be the specified field with an optional value equality check.
.html	The target must be 'text/html, charset=utf-8'.
.includeEql(obj)	The object 'obj' must be present and equal.
.include(obj)	The 'obj' object must be present in the indexOf. Works for strings, arrays, and objects.
.instanceOf	The target should be an instance of the declared.
.json	The target must be 'application/json, charset=utf-8'.
.keys	The target must have the keys specified.
.length	The target must be of the length specified.

(continued)

Table 11-4. (*continued*)

Method	Description
.match	The target must match the regular expression.
.ok	The target must be truthy.
.ownProperty	The target must have its own property specified.
.property	The target must contain the property specified.
.status(code)	The target statusCode must be that specified.
.throw and .throwError	Ensures that an exception is thrown. throwError is to be used if your JavaScript Linter does not parse kindly the .throw nomenclature.
.true	The target must === true.
.within	The target should be within a numeric range.

You can see that this API is similar to the 'should' and 'expect' API that the Chai.js framework uses. This is because the chaining syntax of this type of testing lends to many of these features being present in the API.

In Listing 11-6, you built some simple tests using the assert module syntax. You then stepped into the BDD model by using the chainable Should.js syntax: `true.should.be.ok;`, was an example of this.

11-8. Reporting Code Coverage with Node-cover
Problem

You have built some tests for your Node.js application. Now you would like to analyze whether the code that you have written will be covered in full by using the node-cover module.

Solution

There are several libraries that are available to use for reporting code coverage in your Node.js application. For this solution you will examine one of these: node-cover. This library can be installed globally by using npm: `$ npm install cover -g`. Once you have it installed, you will then be able to run coverage tests and reports on your Node.js application.

For this section you will create a simple Node.js application that will purposefully test your code coverage and that will help to highlight the strengths of the Node.js coverage libraries. This example code is shown in Listing 11-22.

Listing 11-22. Code Coverage Example App

```
/**
* coverage tests
*/

function add(a, b, callback) {
        callback(a + b);
}

function subtract(a, b, callback) {
        callback(a - b);
}
```

```
add(2, 3, function(result) {
        console.log(result);
});

//subtract(3, 2, function(result) {
        // console.log(result);
// });
```

You are now able to begin your code coverage tests for this block of code. To get started, install node-cover first, then run the coverage tests, as shown in Listing 11-23.

Listing 11-23. Installing node-cover and Running a Coverage Test

```
$ npm install -g cover

$ cover run 11-5-1.js
```

You now have successfully executed a coverage test for your code. With node-cover there are two ways in which you can view the report of this coverage. First, Listing 11-24 shows how to view the coverage directly in your command prompt/terminal.

Listing 11-24. Node-cover Report in the Terminal

```
> cover run 11-5-1.js
path.existsSync is now called `fs.existsSync`.
5
```

Once you have viewed the report in the terminal, you may decide that to better view the results, or to publish them to other parties with vested interest in your coverage, you should view the report in an HTML mode. Node-cover makes reporting in HTML simple, as shown in Listing 11-25. Here, the module will generate a cover-html directory and allow you to navigate to /cover_html/index.html in your browser in order to view the reports shown in Figures 11-1 and 11-2.

Listing 11-25. Reporting node-cover Coverage in HTML.

```
$ cover report html
```

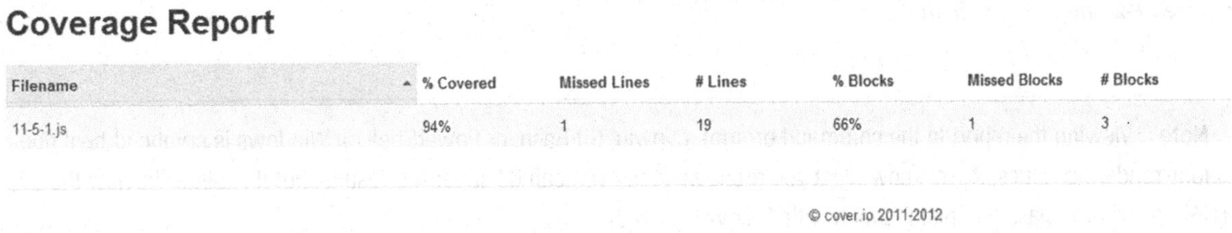

Coverage Report

Filename	% Covered	Missed Lines	# Lines	% Blocks	Missed Blocks	# Blocks
11-5-1.js	94%	1	19	66%	1	3

© cover.io 2011-2012

Figure 11-1. *node_cover index.html*

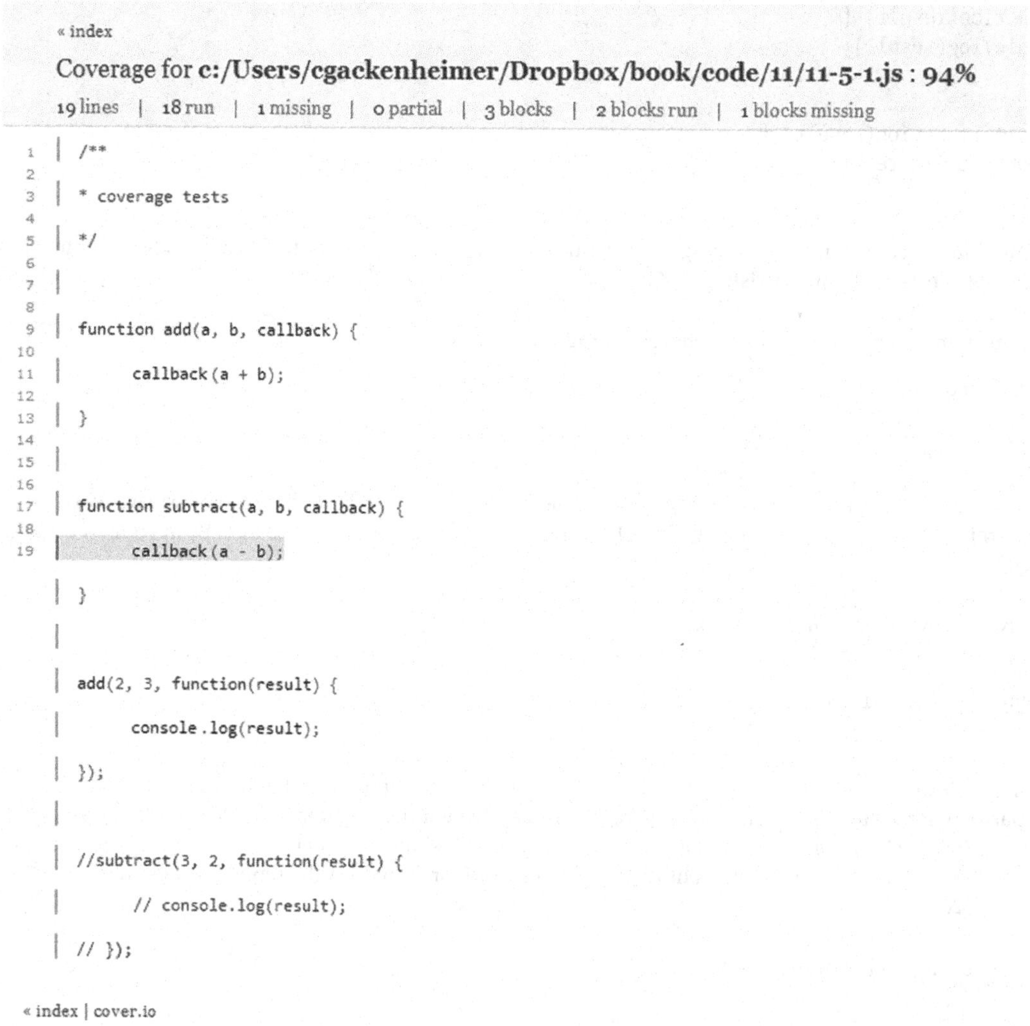

« index

Coverage for c:/Users/cgackenheimer/Dropbox/book/code/11/11-5-1.js : 94%

19 lines | 18 run | 1 missing | 0 partial | 3 blocks | 2 blocks run | 1 blocks missing

```
 1   /**
 2
 3    * coverage tests
 4
 5    */
 6
 7
 8
 9   function add(a, b, callback) {
10
11       callback(a + b);
12
13   }
14
15
16
17   function subtract(a, b, callback) {
18
19       callback(a - b);

     }


     add(2, 3, function(result) {

         console.log(result);

     });


     //subtract(3, 2, function(result) {

     //  console.log(result);

     // });
```

« index | cover.io

Figure 11-2. node_cover detail

■ **Note** Viewing the report in the command prompt, Cygwin, Git Bash, or PowerShell on Windows is cryptic at best due to font-rendering issues. If you know what you are looking for, you can decipher the results, but it is better to view the HTML report or to pass the 'plain' option with $ `cover report plain`.

How It Works

Testing for code coverage is important because it can highlight unnecessary or underused code in your application. In this solution you saw how you could leverage the node-cover framework in order to view your code coverage.

The node-cover framework is installed globally, allowing you to simply use the cover method in your terminal or shell wherever your Node.js application resides and where you wish to run coverage tests. To run a test, use the command $ `cover run <file>`.

After running, you now have a reference to the code coverage. To view this access you need to see the results via the command $ `cover results [type] [file]`. The type can be 'cli', which is the default and attempts to generate an ASCII graphical layout in your terminal. This works decently in Mac or Linux, but for Windows users the command-line interface (CLI) output is nearly impossible to read. Fortunately there are three other options for output. The first is plain, which will just output the line or lines of your code that are not covered. For more graphical reports you can use the 'html' option, which will generate a full report that can be viewed in the browser. Alternatively, if you would like to manage your own implementation, or would like to view the data in a custom reporting service, you could choose the JSON output type for the report. The JSON output contains all of the relevant details for the report and the original source code of the code on which you have executed the coverage test.

11-9. Reporting Code Coverage with istanbul

Problem

You want to analyze the coverage of your code by utilizing the istanbul code coverage framework.

Solution

There are several libraries that are available for reporting code coverage in your Node.js application. For this solution, you will examine istanbul.

For this section you will create a simple Node.js application that will purposefully test your code coverage and that will help to highlight the strengths of the Node.js coverage libraries. This example code is shown in Listing 11-26.

Listing 11-26. Code Coverage Example App

```
/**
* coverage tests
*/

function add(a, b, callback) {
        callback(a + b);
}

function subtract(a, b, callback) {
        callback(a - b);
}

add(2, 3, function(result) {
        console.log(result);
});

//subtract(3, 2, function(result) {
        // console.log(result);
// });
```

The code coverage module that you will utilize to show code coverage for this set of code is istanbul. Istanbul is installed globally by using $ npm install -g istanbul. You can then run coverage tests for your module, as shown in Listing 11-27.

Listing 11-27. Coverage Test with istanbul

```
$ istanbul cover 11-5-1.js
5
==============================================================================
Writing coverage object [c:\Users\cgackenheimer\Dropbox\book\code\11\coverage\coverage.json]
Writing coverage reports at [c:\Users\cgackenheimer\Dropbox\book\code\11\coverage]
==============================================================================

============================= Coverage summary ==============================
Statements   : 83.33% ( 5/6 )
Branches     : 100% ( 0/0 )
Functions    : 66.67% ( 2/3 )
Lines        : 83.33% ( 5/6 )
==============================================================================
```

Istanbul will automatically generate an HTML report for you. It will place this inside of the coverage directory in a directory named lcov-report. The results of the coverage test above can be viewed in a browser. The summary page is shown in Figure 11-3 with the coverage detail in Figure 11-4.

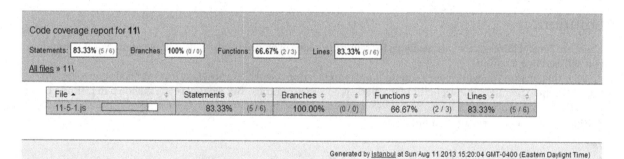

Figure 11-3. istanbul cover summary

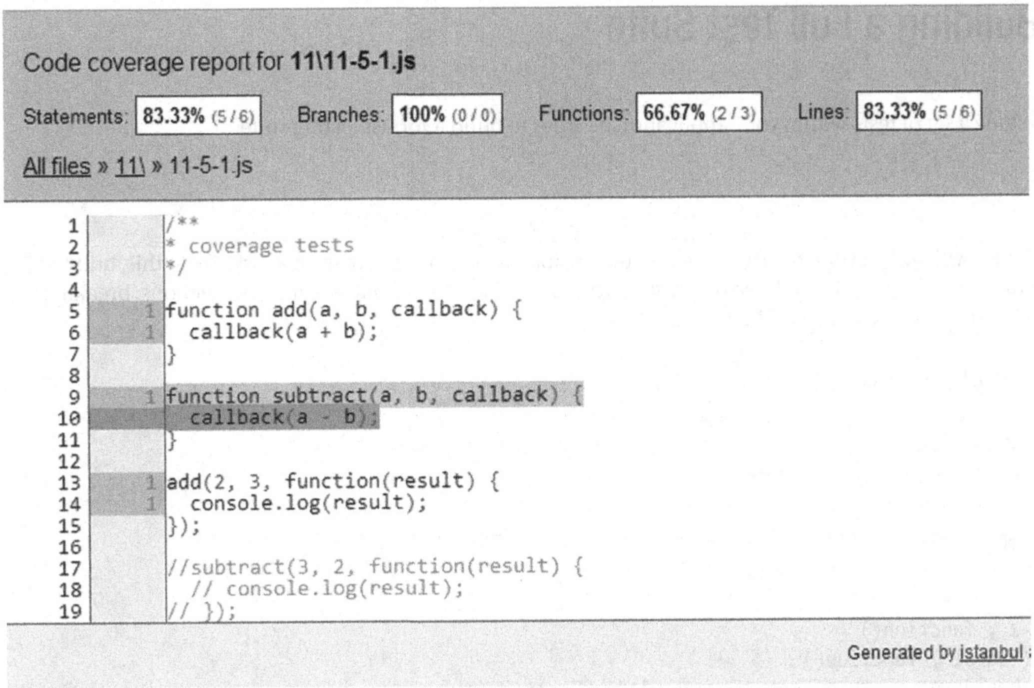

Code coverage report for **11\11-5-1.js**

Statements: **83.33%** (5 / 6)   Branches: **100%** (0 / 0)   Functions: **66.67%** (2 / 3)   Lines: **83.33%** (5 / 6)

All files » 11\ » 11-5-1.js

```
 1    /**
 2     * coverage tests
 3     */
 4
 5  1 function add(a, b, callback) {
 6  1   callback(a + b);
 7    }
 8
 9  1 function subtract(a, b, callback) {
10      callback(a - b);
11    }
12
13  1 add(2, 3, function(result) {
14  1   console.log(result);
15    });
16
17    //subtract(3, 2, function(result) {
18    // console.log(result);
19    // });
```

Generated by istanbul

Figure 11-4. *istanbul cover detail*

How It Works

You utilized istanbul as a module to generate code coverage tests. Istanbul is also installed globally for ease of use with the command line throughout your projects. To generate a coverage test with istanbul, simply run `$ istanbul cover <file>`. This will run the test coverage for you.

When you run a coverage test with istanbul, you also get the reports automatically. There is not a secondary step like with node-cover to generate the test results. Running the cover command will also produce a clean summary of the coverage directly in your CLI. It will also produce a JSON output and the HTML. As you saw in Figure 11-4, the detailed summary of the coverage in HTML will highlight the statements that aren't covered in red. The functions that are not covered are highlighted in an orange hue.

Adding these reports to your testing workflow can be extremely helpful for analyzing your coding, especially if you are adding large modules to your implementation. If you have been in the process of refactoring, you may likely see that there are a great number of gaps in your code coverage. This allows for a more informed form of refactoring your code for the next iteration.

11-10. Building a Full Test Suite

Problem

You want to include a set of tests within your application in order to build a robust testing suite.

Solution

In this solution, you will build a suite of tests to be executed using the Mocha testing framework. To do this, build all your tests into the tests directory. For this example, you can utilize all the tests from the previous sections, breaking them up into a few files (see Listings 11-28 and 11-29).

Listing 11-28. First Test/Mocha.js File

```
/**
* mocha
*/

var assert = require('assert');

var three = 3;
describe('11-2', function() {
    describe('equal', function() {
        it('should return true that 3 equals "3"', function() {
            assert.equal('three', '3', '3 equals "3"');
        });
    });
    describe("strictEqual", function() {
        it('"3" only strictly equals 3.toString()', function() {
            assert.strictEqual('3', three.toString(), '3 and "3" are not strictly equal');
        });
    });

    describe("notEqual", function() {
        it('should be that 3 is not equal to three', function() {
            assert.notEqual(three, 'three', '3 not equals three');
        });
    });
    describe("ok", function() {
        it('should return that false is not truthy', function() {
            assert.ok(false, 'not truthy ');
        });
    });
    describe("ok", function() {
        it('should be true that true is truthy', function() {
            assert.ok(true, 'truthy');
        });
    });
});
```

Listing 11-29. Second Test/Mocha.2.js

```
/**
 * mocha
 */

var three = 3;

var should = require('should');

var square = function(a) {
    if (typeof a !== 'number') return false;
    return a * a;
};

describe('11-3 sync', function() {
    describe('square a number', function() {
        it('should do this syncronously', function() {
            square(three).should.equal(9);
        });
        it('should fail when the target is not a number', function() {
            square('three').should.be.false;
        });
    });
});

var squareAsync = function(a, cb) {
    result = a * a;
    cb(result);
};

describe('11-4 async', function() {
    describe('square a number', function() {
        it('should perform async', function() {
            squareAsync(three, function(result) {
                result.should.equal(9);
            });
        });
        it('should fail', function() {
            squareAsync('three', function(result) {
                result.should.not.be.a('number');
            });
        });
    });
});
```

How It Works

This is a simple test suite, but it shows the power of a tool like Mocha, which allows you to utilize a single command to execute an entire folder of tests.

When you execute the `mocha` command, it will look for the files that reside in the test directory and execute the Mocha tests on each one. The `mocha` command will only execute on files that are formatted for at least one Mocha test. This means that a directory that has a number of files that use only the Node.js assert methods for testing code will still only run the tests for files that contain Mocha tests. The entire file is not required to contain only Mocha tests; in fact only a single `mocha describe` needs to be present in the file in order to get the Mocha command line to find the file and execute the test, adding the result to the aggregate total.

11-11. Implementing Testing into Your Workflow

Problem

You want to implement testing as a part of your workflow when developing a Node.js application.

Solution

Adding testing to your workflow can be done in any number of ways. What is important is that you are able to add tests to your process. One way to implement tests is to simply invoke the test framework of your choosing at each time you create new code for your Node.js application. This can be a manual process or, as you will see in the next section, an automated task.

Another way you can implement testing is to add a test command to the scripts section in your package.json file, as shown in Listing 11-30.

Listing 11-30. Package.json for npm Test

```
{
  "name": "Ch11",
  "version": "0.0.0",
  "description": "chapter 11",
  "main": "mocha.js",
  "directories": {
    "test": "test"
  },
  "dependencies": {
    "chai": "~1.7.2",
    "nodeunit": "~0.8.1",
    "should": "~1.2.2",
    "vows": "~0.7.0"
  },
  "devDependencies": {
    "mocha": "~1.12.0"
  },
  "scripts": {
    "test": "mocha"
  },
  "author": "cgack"
}
```

Here you would simply invoke $ `npm test` each time that you want to run your tests. This allows you to have a uniform test call for each module that you wish to test, regardless of the underlying testing infrastructure.

How It Works

You saw previously in this chapter how to execute tests using the framework of your choosing, so implementing this into your workflow is straightforward and works just the same as invoking the frameworks.

Adding the ability to test your modules using npm test is a useful trick. This works because the npm command line has the ability to parse your test directory and use the test script that you have supplied for your npm package. json file that describes your Node.js module.

There are many ways to implement testing into your workflow, but, as you will see in the next section, automating your testing is the easiest way to ensure that you never miss an opportunity to test your code.

11-12. Automating Your Testing

Problem

You need to automate your tests so you can always be assured that your Node.js is tested and passing each time a change is made to your code.

Solution

There are a number of ways to automate your testing solution. One of the easiest methods, if you are utilizing Mocha, is to use the Mocha watch functionality. To do this, invoke Mocha as shown in Listing 11-31.

Listing 11-31. Mocha Watch

```
$ mocha -w

. . . . . . . . . . .

  11 passing (9 ms)
  1 failing

  1) calc tests simple maths should be easy to subtract:
     AssertionError: four minus 2 is two
       at Context.<anonymous> (c:\Users\cgackenheimer\Dropbox\book\code\11\test\calc_test.js:14:11)
       at Test.Runnable.run
(c:\Users\cgackenheimer\AppData\Roaming\npm\node_modules\mocha\lib\runnable.js:211:32)
       at Runner.runTest (c:\Users\cgackenheimer\AppData\Roaming\npm\node_modules\mocha\lib\runner.js:355:10)
       at c:\Users\cgackenheimer\AppData\Roaming\npm\node_modules\mocha\lib\runner.js:401:12
       at next (c:\Users\cgackenheimer\AppData\Roaming\npm\node_modules\mocha\lib\runner.js:281:14)
       at c:\Users\cgackenheimer\AppData\Roaming\npm\node_modules\mocha\lib\runner.js:290:7
       at next (c:\Users\cgackenheimer\AppData\Roaming\npm\node_modules\mocha\lib\runner.js:234:23)
       at Object._onImmediate
(c:\Users\cgackenheimer\AppData\Roaming\npm\node_modules\mocha\lib\runner.js:258:5)
       at processImmediate [as _immediateCallback] (timers.js:330:15)

. . . . . . . . . . .

  12 passing (16 ms)

\ watching
```

Another test automation method is to utilize the Grunt.js task runner to drive tests. One of the more popular integrations with Grunt is the grunt-contrib-nodeunit module. This allows you to group and run all of your nodeunit tests together with a single command.

To configure the Grunt nodeunit, you need to install the Grunt command line with `$ npm install -g grunt-cli`. You will then install the `grunt-contrib-nodeunit` module by entering `$ npm install grunt-contrib-nodeunit`. Next you need to add a reference to Grunt and grunt-contrib-nodeunit to your package.json file. When these dependencies are installed, install Grunt to the project named `$ npm install grunt -save-dev`.

Now you need to create a Gruntfile.js file that will export the tasks that you desire for Grunt to execute. A simple Grunt file to use for the nodeunit tests that you had previously created would look like the example in Listing 11-32.

Listing 11-32. Gruntfile.js for nodeunit

```
module.exports = function(grunt) {

        grunt.initConfig({
                nodeunit: {
                        all: ['nodeunit.js']
                }
        });

        grunt.loadNpmTasks('grunt-contrib-nodeunit');
};
```

You can now execute any nodeunit test by running the `grunt nodeunit` command, as shown in Listing 11-33.

Listing 11-33. Executing grunt nodeunit

```
$ grunt nodeunit
Running "nodeunit:all" (nodeunit) task
Testing nodeunit.js......OK
>> 8 assertions passed (7ms)

Done, without errors.
```

How It Works

Watching a file with the built-in file watcher for the Mocha command line will run the tests initially, a single time, and then watch the files in the directory for any alterations.

In this solution, you started by creating a calc.js module (see Listing 11-34) that had erroneously placed a multiplication operator where the subtraction operator was located in the subtract method.

Listing 11-34. Erroneous calc.js Module

```
/**
* calc
*/

var calc = module.exports = {
        add: function(a, b) {
                return a + b;
        },
        subtract: function(a, b) {
                return a * b;
        }
};
```

You invoked the mocha -w, watcher on the tests that you wrote, expecting that the subtraction would work, but they failed on the subtraction test. Watch the files in the directory for changes. You then need to correct the file to properly subtract b from a, and the file watcher picks up the change. Once the file changes, Mocha runs the tests again—this time passing—and continues to watch the files for changes. Having this continual feedback on tests is very beneficial, and it can help motivate you to write your tests first.

You next saw how to integrate nodeunit testing into your testing workflow by automating these tests to the Grunt. js task-runner framework. The key here is that you are able to design your gruntfile.js so that you can cover all the tests in a directory or the tests that fit a certain file structure. In your case you provided a single file; however, the Grunt task configuration for nodeunit can accept a variety of named tests, not just the 'all' seen here, but you could break them down to the submodule as well. The nodeunit configuration also allows for the implementation of wildcards, so that you could target all files in the test directory with 'test/*.js', or a similar pattern.

Allowing testing to become a natural and automated part of your Node.js development process can be critical, especially as the scale of your project grows. You have seen two methods for implementing testing automatically, which eases the burden of running tests as your project grows in size.

CHAPTER 12

■ ■ ■

Debugging and Deploying Your Application

In this book you have seen a great deal of what you are capable of producing with Node.js. You have created an application, or you are envisioning an application that you will want to publish. This means you will need to become familiar with the process of deploying your code to several destinations for your code. In addition to deploying your code, you will revisit and expand on some of the debugging techniques from Chapter 7 when encountering the V8 debugging module.

There are several methods and platforms that are available to you as a Node.js developer that will allow you to deploy your code. In this chapter you will examine techniques that range from self-deployment on a machine that you own to deploying on a cloud-based platform as a service solution. You will also learn how to publish your modules to npm.

At the time of this writing there is an enormous variety in cloud-based platforms as service hosting solutions for your Node.js applications. This chapter is not a catalog of every possible hosting solution, but it looks at several common and practical methods you can utilize to host Node.js applications.

12-1. Logging Information to the Console

Problem

You need to be able to gather important information about your application by logging information to your console window.

Solution

The easiest way to log information to the command line when you are debugging your code is to use the console module that is native to Node.js. In this solution you see there are various methods that can be used to log data to the console by using this module as shown in Listing 12-1.

Listing 12-1. Logging to the Console

```
/**
 * Logging information to your console.
 */

console.time('timer');
console.log('hey %s', 'there');
console.info('info');
```

```
console.warn('warn');
console.error('error');
console.dir(console);
console.trace(console.error('traced'));
console.assert(true !== false, 'true equals false');
console.timeEnd('timer');
```

How It Works

The console module relies on Node.js's use of stdout and stderr. The console object in the Node.js source is created by accepting those two streams as arguments (see Listing 12-2).

Listing 12-2. Instantiating the Console

```
function Console(stdout, stderr) {
  if (!(this instanceof Console)) {
    return new Console(stdout, stderr);
  }
  if (!stdout || !util.isFunction(stdout.write)) {
    throw new TypeError('Console expects a writable stream instance');
  }
  if (!stderr) {
    stderr = stdout;
  }
  var prop = {
    writable: true,
    enumerable: false,
    configurable: true
  };
  prop.value = stdout;
  Object.defineProperty(this, '_stdout', prop);
  prop.value = stderr;
  Object.defineProperty(this, '_stderr', prop);
  prop.value = {};
  Object.defineProperty(this, '_times', prop);

  // bind the prototype functions to this Console instance
  Object.keys(Console.prototype).forEach(function(k) {
    this[k] = this[k].bind(this);
  }, this);
}
```

Once the object is instantiated, the stderr and stdout properties are converted to properties on the console object itself by using the Object.defineProperty() method.

In your solution, you utilized each of the core methods that are exposed on the console object. First, and most common, is the console.log() method. This method accepts any number of arguments, formats them together using the util module as shown in Listing 12-3, and writes the result to stdout. The console.info method is the same as the console.log method and formats the arguments in the same way.

Listing 12-3. Console.log as a stdout.write

```
Console.prototype.log = function() {
  this._stdout.write(util.format.apply(this, arguments) + '\n');
};

Console.prototype.info = Console.prototype.log;
```

The next console method you will encounter is the `console.error()` method. This is the same as the `console.warn()` method. These methods are similar to the `console.log()` and `console.info()` methods with the difference being that they write to the `stderr` instead of `stdout`, as shown in Listing 12-4.

Listing 12-4. Console.error and console.warn

```
Console.prototype.warn = function() {
  this._stderr.write(util.format.apply(this, arguments) + '\n');
};

Console.prototype.error = Console.prototype.warn;
```

Next you utilize the `console.dir()` method. This function uses the `util.inspect()` method to describe the object that is passed to it (see Listing 12-5). In this case you inspect the console object itself.

Listing 12-5. Console.dir()

```
Console.prototype.dir = function(object) {
  this._stdout.write(util.inspect(object, { customInspect: false }) + '\n');
};
```

The output of the `console.dir(console);` call is shown in Listing 12-6.

Listing 12-6. Console.dir(console);

```
{ log: [Function],
  info: [Function],
  warn: [Function],
  error: [Function],
  dir: [Function],
  time: [Function],
  timeEnd: [Function],
  trace: [Function],
  assert: [Function],
  Console: [Function: Console] }
```

Next, ran `console.trace()` to log any error to `stderr` a stack trace. This method's source is shown in Listing 12-7. You can see that the error is logged via the `console.error()` method once the name has been changed to demonstrate that it is a 'Trace';.

Listing 12-7. Console.trace() Source

```
Console.prototype.trace = function() {
  // TODO probably can to do this better with V8's debug object once that is
  // exposed.
  var err = new Error;
  err.name = 'Trace';
  err.message = util.format.apply(this, arguments);
  Error.captureStackTrace(err, arguments.callee);
  this.error(err.stack);
};
```

The final console method that you will use is the `console.assert()` method. This method leverages the assert module to log the results of the `assert.ok()` method. You can see how this works internally in Listing 12-8.

Listing 12-8. Console.assert()

```
Console.prototype.assert = function(expression) {
  if (!expression) {
    var arr = Array.prototype.slice.call(arguments, 1);
    require('assert').ok(false, util.format.apply(this, arr));
  }
};
```

12-2. Using a Graphical Debugging Tool
Problem

You would like to utilize a tool that will allow you to debug your Node.js application in an integrated development environment (IDE)-like debugging tool. This means you want to have graphical access to your Node.js debugging environment.

Solution

One of the most basic yet most consistent cross-platform debugging tools for Node.js applications is an npm package called node-inspector. This package is used to bind the debugger that comes with a Blink-based browser, such as Google Chrome or the latest versions of Opera. You will then gain access to the native debugging tools for these browsers but it will allow you to navigate the code and debug your Node.js application in an IDE-like setting.

To get started with node-inspector, install it globally via npm. This gains you access to the node-inspector command that will allow you to start the debugger listening from any directory on your machine, as shown in Listing 12-9.

Listing 12-9. Node-inspector Install and Implementation

```
$ npm install -g node-inspector

$ node-inspector
Node Inspector v0.3.1
   info  - socket.io started
Visit http://127.0.0.1:8080/debug?port=5858 to start debugging.
```

Once the inspector is running, you can begin a new instance of your Node.js application. For this example assume that a simple HTTP server responds with the text "hello world". When you start this Node.js application you need to enable the debugging hooks by passing the parameter –debug to the command. This looks like what you see in Listing 12-10.

Listing 12-10. Beginning Node Inspection by Creating a Server

```
$ node --debug 12-2-1.js
debugger listening on port 5858
```

How It Works

Now that you have a debugger listening on the proper port and the inspector is running, you can experience the fun of using a graphical debugger by navigating to http://127.0.0.1:8080/debug?port=5858. This is where the node-inspector has Blink developer tools opened and will allow you to debug your code. This initial interface will look similar to that shown in Figure 12-1.

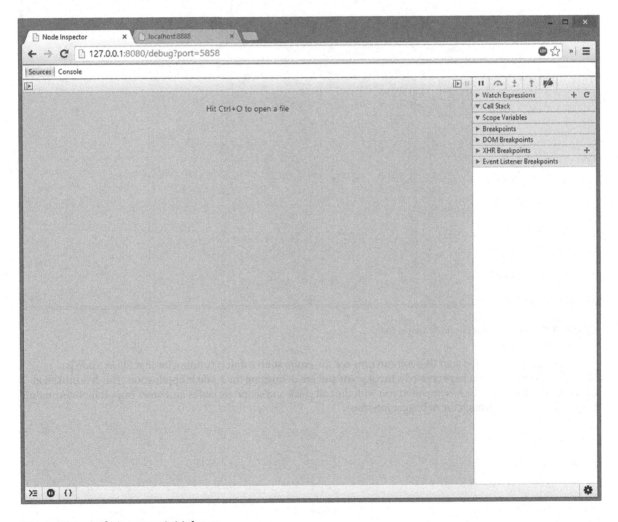

Figure 12-1. node-inspector initial state

From here you now have the ability to open up the Sources panel and view the source files that are available to you. This is shown in Figure 12-2; you can select the file you wish to debug.

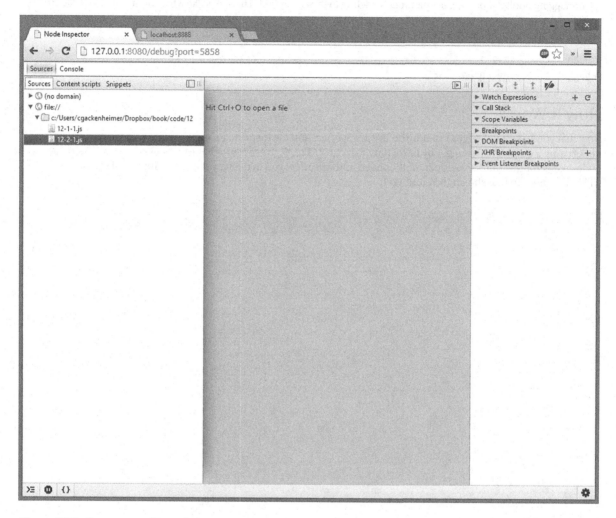

Figure 12-2. *Sources panel in node-inspector*

Once you have selected your file, you can now see the entire source that is running for that file in Node.js. Figure 12-3 shows how you have created a breakpoint and are debugging the Node.js application. This has broken at that point and the inspector has provided you with the call stack and scope variables and other important information that can be accessed through the debugger interface.

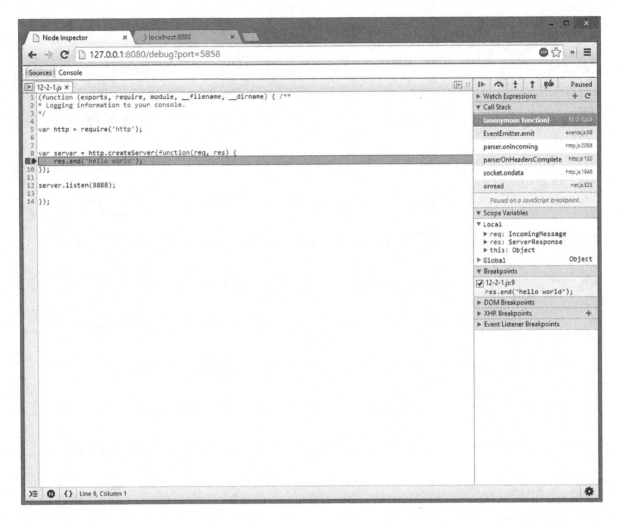

Figure 12-3. *node-inspector viewing a source file*

Finally, node-inspector also gives you access to more detail about objects in your source code by providing hover-over information. This information gives you more detail about the object that is being inspected (see Figure 12-4).

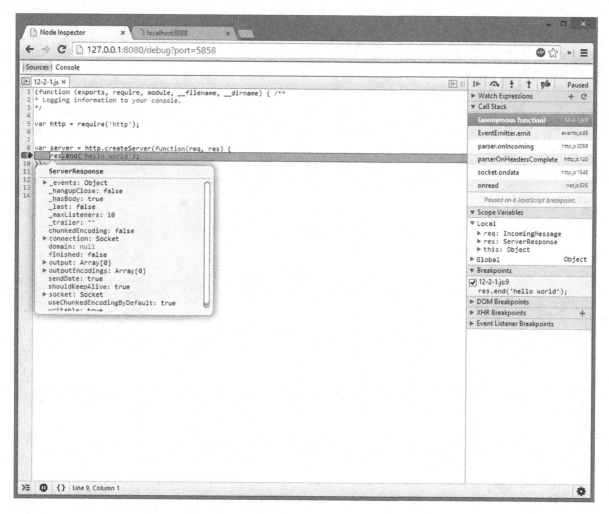

Figure 12-4. *Hovering over an object with node-inspector*

12-3. Debugging Your Application in a Production Environment

Problem

You have a Node.js application running on a production server that is behaving in a manner that prompts you to step into the code and see what is happening. You need to be able to attach a debugger to the production process in order to debug your application.

Solution

Connecting to a Node.js process that is currently running is built into the Node.js debugging functionality. This will attach the V8 debugger to your application in the same way that starting your application with the debug flag will.

You first need to run a Node.js process. For this example you can start a simple HTTP server that you created for debugging in Section 12-2. Once you have this running, you need to find the process identifier on your operating system that is running this Node.js process. You can do this through an activity monitor, task manager on Windows, or the shell using grep - $ ps ax | grep node.

Once you have the process identifier, you can then tell the debugger to connect to the process, as shown in Listing 12-11.

Listing 12-11. Connecting the Debugger to a Node.js Process

```
$ node debug -p 6284
connecting... ok
debug>
```

You now have the V8 debugger prompt, which is connected to your Node.js process (shown on your original command line as shown in Listing 12-12).

Listing 12-12. Debugger Connected

```
$ node 12-2-1.js
Starting debugger agent.
debugger listening on port 5858
```

Once you are connected to the process, from the debug> prompt you might like to know at what point in the process the current state of your application resides. You can do this by either pausing the application using debug> pause or by processing a step into debug> s or the next debug> n.

You can now debug your application on production, to pinpoint where you are encountering issues in your application.

How It Works

Debugging using the Node.js debugger was covered in detail in Chapter 7, and using the command $ node debug -p <pid> to bind to a Node.js process will give you access to the same commands that you saw in Chapter 7. This is the V8 debugger that runs the debug terminal.

When you begin debugging, as mentioned above, you are able to see where you are at in the code by typing debug> n (see Listing 12-13).

Listing 12-13. The Next Step in V8 Debugger

```
connecting... ok
debug> n
break in net.js:1153
 1151
 1152 function onconnection(clientHandle) {
 1153   var handle = this;
 1154   var self = handle.owner;
 1155
```

This listing is just an example of where you may find yourself in the code. In your case you may be anywhere inside of your application or the modules that are imported to your application. You can then continue to execute your program by typing debug> c, as shown in Listing 12-14. This example shows that by continuing you were able to run the code until it encountered the debugger; command. This command tells the V8 debugger to stop executing and to wait.

Listing 12-14. Continue to Debugger

```
debug> c
break in c:\Users\cgackenheimer\Dropbox\book\code\12\12-2-1.js:7
  5
  6 var server = http.createServer(function(req, res) {
  7     debugger;
  8     res.end('hello world');
  9 });
```

You are now able to debug your application and you did not need to start Node.js with the debug command passed to it. You only needed to find the process that was running and bind the V8 debugger to the application by using the process identifier.

12-4. Continuously Running Your Server with Forever
Problem

You want to ensure that your Node.js process will continuously run and be able to restart after unexpected failures on your production machine.

Solution

To keep a Node.js process running, there are several choices that you have as a developer for doing so. In this solution you will examine how to utilize the forever module to keep your processes alive and running continuously.

To get started you must first install the forever module. The module source is located at https://github.com/nodejitsu/forever and can be installed as a global command-line module, as shown in Listing 12-15.

Listing 12-15. Installing forever

```
$ npm install -g forever
```

Once you have forever installed from the command line, you are now able to run your Node.js process utilizing the command-line interface (CLI). In order to start your Node.js process utilizing the forever module, you must start the script by using the forever start command, as shown in Listing 12-16.

Listing 12-16. forever start

```
$ forever start app.js
warn:    --minUptime not set. Defaulting to: 1000ms
warn:    --spinSleepTime not set. Your script will exit if it does not stay up for at least 1000ms
info:    Forever processing file: app.js
```

You can then check to see the status of any running applications that forever is serving by using the forever list command (see Listing 12-17).

Listing 12-17. forever list

```
$ forever list
info:    No forever processes running

# Once a task is running.
```

```
$ forever list
info:    Forever processes running
data:        uid  command                 script    forever pid  logfile                          uptime
data:    [0] UJVS /usr/local/bin/node 12-2-1.js 41659   41660 /Users/gack/.forever/UJVS.log 0:0:2:46.801
data:    [1] VVX7 /usr/local/bin/node app.js 41757    41758 /Users/gack/.forever/VVX7.log 0:0:0:3.444
```

You may have noticed some warnings that state you have not specified spinSleepTime or minUptime forever options. To set these flags, they must be set before you tell forever to start. This will look like the example shown in Listing 12-18, in which you specify a minimum uptime and spin sleeptime of 20 milliseconds each.

Listing 12-18. Setting forever Flags

```
$ forever --minUptime 10 --spinSleepTime 10 start app.js
info:    Forever processing file: app.js
```

How It Works

Forever is a Node.js module that ensures that the script you have told it to execute will run continuously. When you start an application with forever, you are actually creating a monitor instance that will attempt to spawn your script as a child process. It does this so that forever will be able to monitor the process of the child and restart the process if the child is interrupted. The process of starting the monitor is shown in Listing 12-19, which is the forever source for the monitor.

Listing 12-19. Starting a forever Monitor

```
Monitor.prototype.start = function (restart) {
  var self = this,
      child;

  if (this.running && !restart) {
    process.nextTick(function () {
      self.emit('error', new Error('Cannot start process that is already running.'));
    });
    return this;
  }

  child = this.trySpawn();
  if (!child) {
    process.nextTick(function () {
      self.emit('error', new Error('Target script does not exist: ' + self.args[0]));
    });
    return this;
  }

  this.ctime = Date.now();
  this.child = child;
  this.running = true;
  process.nextTick(function () {
    self.emit(restart ? 'restart' : 'start', self, self.data);
  });
```

```
  function onMessage(msg) {
    self.emit('message', msg);
  }

  // Re-emit messages from the child process
  this.child.on('message', onMessage);

  child.on('exit', function (code, signal) {
    var spinning = Date.now() - self.ctime < self.minUptime;
    child.removeListener('message', onMessage);
    self.emit('exit:code', code, signal);

    function letChildDie() {
      self.running = false;
      self.forceStop = false;
      self.emit('exit', self, spinning);
    }

    function restartChild() {
      self.forceRestart = false;
      process.nextTick(function () {
        self.start(true);
      });
    }

    self.times++;

    if (self.forceStop || (self.times >= self.max && !self.forceRestart)
        || (spinning && typeof self.spinSleepTime !== 'number') && !self.forceRestart) {
      letChildDie();
    }
    else if (spinning) {
      setTimeout(restartChild, self.spinSleepTime);
    }
    else {
      restartChild();
    }
  });

  return this;
};
```

Once the child process has started, an event listener is bound to the process, listening for events. When the 'exit' event is emitted, forever will check to see if the process is spinning and then restart the process. This is the foundation of forever: catching exiting processes and restarting them continuously.

As you built your solution you were able to see a few of the parameters that are used to manipulate the way in which forever executes. The full list of available parameters and options that can be used with forever is shown in Table 12-1.

Table 12-1. *Options and Parameters for the forever Module*

Name	Type	Description
Cleanlogs	Action	Deletes *all* forever log files.
Clear <key>	Action	Remotes the set key.
Columns add <col>	Action	Adds the specified column to the forever list output.
Columns rm <col>	Action	Removes the specified column from the forever list output.
Columns set <col>	Action	Set all columns for the forever list output.
Start	Action	Starts a Node.js script.
Config	Action	Lists all forever configurations.
List	Action	Lists all running processes.
Logs	Action	Lists the log files for all the forever processes.
Logs <script|index>	Action	Lists the log file for the specified script or index.
Restart	Action	Restarts a script.
Restartall	Action	Restarts all scripts.
Set <key> <val>	Action	Sets an option specified by the key and the value.
Stop	Action	Stops the script execution.
Stopall	Action	Stops all the forever scripts.
-a –append	Option	Appends the logs.
-c Command	Option	This is the command to be executed—this defaults to 'node'.
-d, --debug	Option	Log debug output.
-e ERRFILE	Option	Specifies a named error file.
-f –fifo	Option	Stream logs to stdout.
-h, --help	Option	Shows help.
-l LOGFILE	Option	Specifies a named log file.
-m MAX	Option	Runs the script for only a maximum number of times.
-o OUTFILE	Option	Specifies a named out file.
-p PATH	Option	Specifies the log file path.
-s, --silent	Option	Silences stdout and stderr on the child script.
-v, --verbose	Option	Turns on verbose messages from forever.
-w, --watch	Option	Watches for file changes, restarting if detected.
--minUptime	Option	Sets the minimum uptime in milliseconds that the script is considered "spinning."
--pidFILE	Option	Lists the pid file.
--plain	Option	Disables command-line coloring.
--sourceDir	Option	Lists the source directory that the SCRIPT is relative to.
--spinSleepTime	Option	Lists the time in milliseconds to wait between launches of the "spinning" script.
--watchDirectory	Option	Lists the top-level watch directory.

12-5. Deploying Your Application on Your Own Server

Problem

You have a server that you have dedicated to hosting your Node.js application and you need to be able to deploy your application to that server.

Solution

Deploying your application to your own server requires a few steps to happen. To do this, you can manually copy the files over to your destination server, install the npm dependencies, and start the script, but there are more automated ways for doing this (as you can see in Listing 12-20). This solution will utilize a Git process to install dependencies and start your Node.js application.

Listing 12-20. Deploying with Git

```
## Initialize the repository
$ git init
## add your files
$ git add .
## make a change to your source on the development machine
$ git commit -am "I made an important change"
$ git push origin
```

This will push the changes to the Git repository that is located on your remote production machine and it will then use a Git post-receive hook to install dependencies and start your Node.js application.

How It Works

The key to this process is the nature of Git's post-receive hooks. This will execute a bash script each time that a change is received in the repository. To get started you need to build a post-receive file in the 'hooks' directory of your production Git repository. A basic deploy script would look like the one shown in Listing 12-21.

Listing 12-21. Basic repo.git/hooks/post-receive File

```
#!/bin/sh
echo "processing post receive hook"
echo "installing npm dependencies"
npm install
echo "starting application"
node app.js
```

This will utilize the package.json file that is part of your repository, and it will utilize npm to install any dependencies that your code requires. After these are installed it will begin the node process by running the node app.js command. However, as you saw in the previous section, you may want to accommodate for failures and run this script by using forever. Assuming that you have already installed forever on your production machine globally, you can alter your script to look like what is shown in Listing 12-22.

Listing 12-22. Post-receive Hook Using forever

```
#!/bin/sh
echo "processing post receive hook"
forever stop app.js
echo "installing npm dependencies"
npm install
echo "starting application"
forever start app.js
```

■ **Note** Running your post-receive hook in this manner will stop your server for the entirety of your npm install. In a volatile production environment it is best to segregate these events so that you do not limit production uptime.

By using the post-receive hooks you can deploy your code as you would normally, targeting a production repository, and then have Git initialize the build-and-deploy process on the target machine.

12-6. Publishing Your Code to npm

Problem

You have built a Node.js module that you would like to share with the greater Node.js community. In order to do this you will want to deploy your module to npm.

Solution

With npm, it is simple to create and publish a module to the registry. To do this, you simply use the npm publish command shown in Listing 12-23.

Listing 12-23. Publishing to npm

```
$ npm publish /path/to/your/module
```

How It Works

This solution works by leveraging the npm command-line tool. This will read the directory that you have specified, which alternatively could be a tarball of the module. Once this is read, it will read the package.json file that is associated with the file and determine if the module is eligible for publication. The name and the version of the package must be unique or the publication will fail.

Once it is determined that the publication is allowed, the package will be added to the npm registry and will be discoverable by Node.js developers everywhere.

12-7. Using Amazon Web Services to Host Your Application
Problem

You want to deploy your Node.js application to be hosted on the Amazon Web Services (AWS) hosting platform.

Solution

For deploying to AWS, you first need to create an AWS account found at http://aws.amazon.com. From there you can then create an Elastic Compute Cloud (EC2) instance; in this solution Ubuntu Server 12.04 was utilized. Once you have your EC2 instance provisioned you can then connect with Secure Shell (SSH) into that instance by using the key pair that you downloaded when you created the instance.

If you are planning to host a web application on your EC2 instance, you need to ensure that the "Security Group" which the EC2 instance is utilizing has opened port 80 so that the web content can be served.

Once you are remotely connected to your Ubuntu instance, you will want to install Node.js. You can use the Ubuntu package by Chris Lea for this, or you can install from the source shown in Listing 12-24. Once you have Node. js and npm installed, then the next step is to get your source code to the remote server on AWS.

Listing 12-24. Installing node.js

```
$ sudo apt-get update
$ sudo apt-get install build-essential libssl-dev
$ git clone https://github.com/joyent/node.git
$ ./configure
$ make
$ sudo make install
```

Now that you have Node.js installed, you can run a simple web application by running a node app with an HTTP server bound on port 80, $ sudo node app.js. However, you likely will have code from another location you would like to serve from the server. There are several ways that you can do this, but it has become increasingly popular to utilize a GitHub or other Git repository in order to transfer your code to your server. Again, simply clone this repository, ensure that you have the source configured to listen on port 80, and you can start your Node.js application on the server.

This can also work the other way, just as you saw in Section 12-5, where you can create a production Git repository on your EC2 instance with a post-receive hook installed and you will be able to deploy directly to that repository from your local development environment.

How It Works

Utilizing the AWS EC2 works because it provisions a virtual instance of a real Ubuntu server. This means that you are able to run everything that you would on a typical Ubuntu server (or another type of EC2 server instance) installation; thus you are able to run Node.js. EC2 provides you with granular control over security and provisioning for your server so that you can tell it to open port 80 and provision new instances with the click of a button.

Once you have Node.js installed, you are able to run a Node.js application as you would as if you were running it locally. To run a Node.js application on port 80 by using Ubuntu server does require an elevated privilege, which is why you needed to utilize the sudo command to start your application. If you had omitted this and still attempted to run on port 80, you would have encountered an error like the one shown in Listing 12-25.

Listing 12-25. Requiring Elevated Permissions for Port 80

```
ubuntu@ip:~/test$ node app.js

events.js:80
        throw er; // Unhandled 'error' event
        ^
Error: listen EACCES
    at exports._errnoException (util.js:676:11)
    at Server._listen2 (net.js:1051:19)
    at listen (net.js:1093:10)
    at Server.listen (net.js:1168:5)
    at Object.<anonymous> (/home/ubuntu/test/app.js:7:8)
    at Module._compile (module.js:449:26)
    at Object.Module._extensions..js (module.js:467:10)
    at Module.load (module.js:349:32)
    at Function.Module._load (module.js:305:12)
    at Function.Module.runMain (module.js:490:10)
ubuntu@ip:~/test$ sudo node app.js
```

12-8. Deploying Your Application Using Heroku

Problem

There are several solutions that represent platforms that you as a developer are able to utilize to deploy your code to the cloud. One of these that allows for Node.js applications is Heroku. You would like to be able to install your application to the Heroku platform as a service.

Solution

To install your Node.js application to the Heroku platform, there are essentially two steps: install the Heroku command-line tools (known as the toolbelt), and then push your code to Heroku for deployment.

In order to get started, you must first download the Heroku toolbelt from the Heroku web site, https://toolbelt.heroku.com, shown in Figure 12-5.

Figure 12-5. *Heroku toolbelt download page*

Once you have downloaded the toolbelt, you must now sign in to Heroku by using the CLI. Now would be a good time to create a Heroku account online if you have not yet done so. You can sign on to Heroku by using the toolbelt CLI, as shown in Listing 12-26.

Listing 12-26. Heroku Login

```
> heroku login
Enter your Heroku credentials.
Email: your.name@email.com
Password (typing will be hidden):
Authentication successful.
```

Next, you can go about the business of developing your Node.js application as you normally would, ensuring that dependencies are listed in your package.json file associated with the application. The subtle differences occur when you are preparing to test and deploy your application with Heroku.

When you deploy a Node.js application to Heroku, you must first create a file, called Procfile, in the root of your application. This file will tell Heroku the type of application process that you are attempting to create. In the case of a Node.js application you will generate a Procfile that will tell Heroku you intend to create a web application and the node <script> target that will be the entry for your application (see Listing 12-27).

Listing 12-27. A Node.js Procfile for Heroku

```
web: node server.js
```

You can now test your application utilizing Heroku's testing service called Foreman. This happens when you type $ `foreman start` in the directory that houses your Procfile. This will create a local web instance of your application running on port 5000 by default, allowing you to test your application before you deploy.

After testing is completed, you can deploy your application to the Heroku platform. This is done by first storing the application into a Git repository, if it is not already present in one. This Git repository is then associated with a Heroku origin with the command $ `heroku create`. This will generate a creative and unique URL for your application, and it will add a remote of Heroku to the Git repository. The Heroku remote will be the target of your deployment pushes. Once you have successfully committed your changes, you can push them to the Heroku remote and the deploy will automatically commence, showing you stdout of the process as it occurs, as shown in Listing 12-28.

Listing 12-28. Abridged Deploy Output

```
$ git push heroku master
Counting objects: 7, done.
Delta compression using up to 4 threads.
Compressing objects: 100% (4/4), done.
Writing objects: 100% (4/4), 361 bytes | 0 bytes/s, done.
Total 4 (delta 3), reused 0 (delta 0)

-----> Node.js app detected
-----> Resolving engine versions
       Using Node.js version: 0.8.21
       Using npm version: 1.1.65
-----> Fetching Node.js binaries
-----> Vendoring node into slug
-----> Installing dependencies with npm
       Dependencies installed
```

```
-----> Building runtime environment
-----> Discovering process types
       Procfile declares types -> app, restart

-----> Compiled slug size: 35.7MB
-----> Launching... done, v122
       http:// yourrepo.herokuapp.com deployed to Heroku

To git@heroku.com:yourrepo.git
   Sha...hash  master -> master
```

You will not only be able to view your application on the web, but the Heroku web interface will also give you an insight into the state of your application (see Figure 12-6).

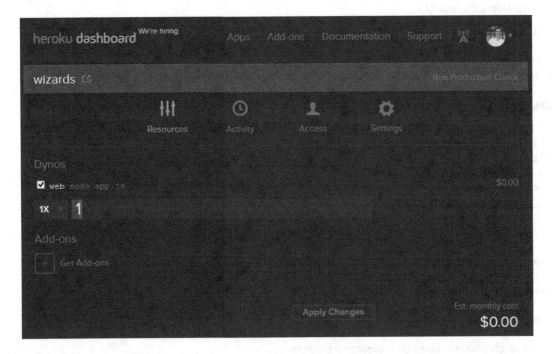

Figure 12-6. *Heroku dashboard*

How It Works

Heroku deployment for Node.js works by leveraging Git to deploy code to the appropriate technology stack in the Heroku platform.

When you first generate your Procfile, which tells Heroku which process you want to run your Node.js under, you tell it to use the web type. This means that the web stack and web-routing processes will be utilized in order to generate and run your application.

Heroku will also, during the deploy process, automatically detect a Node.js application and know that it will ensure that the prescribed versions of Node.js and npm are installed and utilized. It will then parse your package. json file and install the listed dependencies before attempting to run your application. You now have your application running on the Heroku platform.

12-9. Deploying Your Application to Nodejitsu
Problem

You want to utilize Nodejitsu in order to host your Node.js application on the cloud.

Solution

To start deploying your Node.js application with Nodejitsu, you must first create a Nodejitsu account at https://www.nodejitsu.com/signup/. Once you have an account, install the command-line tools that are utilized to deploy your Node.js application to the cloud.

To install the CLI for Nodejitsu, use npm and install it globally, as shown in Listing 12-29.

Listing 12-29. Installing the Jitsu CLI

```
$ npm install -g jitsu
```

This will then give you access to all of the features of the Nodejitsu command line. You can see what commands are available to you by typing $ jitsu, which will output all of the help documentation, as you can see in Listing 12-30.

Listing 12-30. $ jitsu Options

```
$ jitsu
info:    Welcome to Nodejitsu cgack
info:    jitsu v0.13.0, node v0.10.17
info:    It worked if it ends with Nodejitsu ok
info:    Executing command
help:
help:        __  __
help:       / / /  / _  / /
help:      _/ / / /  _/ /_/
help:
help:    Flawless deployment of Node.js apps to the cloud
help:    open-source and fully customizable.
help:    https://github.com/nodejitsu/jitsu
help:
help:    Usage:
help:
help:        jitsu <resource> <action> <param1> <param2> ...
help:
help:    Common Commands:
help:
help:    To sign up for Nodejitsu
help:       jitsu signup
help:
help:    To log into Nodejitsu
help:       jitsu login
help:
help:    To install a pre-built application
help:       jitsu install
help:
help:    Deploys current path to Nodejitsu
help:       jitsu deploy
```

```
help:
help:    Lists all applications for the current user
help:      jitsu list
help:
help:    Additional Commands
help:      jitsu apps
help:      jitsu cloud
help:      jitsu logs
help:      jitsu env
help:      jitsu conf
help:      jitsu users
help:      jitsu databases
help:      jitsu snapshots
help:      jitsu tokens
help:      jitsu logout
help:
help:    Options:
help:  --version, -v   print jitsu version and exit
[string]
help:  --localconf     search for .jitsuconf file in ./ and then parent directories
[string]
help:  --jitsuconf, -j  specify file to load configuration from
[string]
help:  --noanalyze     skip require-analyzer: do not attempt to dynamically detect dependencies
[boolean]
help:  --colors        --no-colors will disable output coloring                        [boolean]
[default: true]
help:  --confirm, -c   prevents jitsu from asking before overwriting/removing things   [boolean]
[default: false]
help:  --release, -r   specify release version number or semantic increment (build, patch, minor, major)
[string]
help:  --raw           jitsu will only output line-delimited raw JSON (useful for piping)
[boolean]
info:    Nodejitsu ok
```

You now need to log in to your Jitsu account by using the $ jitsu users login command (see Listing 12-31).

Listing 12-31. Jitsu Login

```
$ jitsu users login
info:    Welcome to Nodejitsu
info:    jitsu v0.13.0, node v0.10.17
info:    It worked if it ends with Nodejitsu ok
info:    Executing command users login
help:    An activated nodejitsu account is required to login
help:    To create a new account use the jitsu signup command
prompt: username:  you
prompt: password:
info:    Authenticated as you
info:    Nodejitsu ok
```

At this point, you can create a Nodejitsu application from your Node.js source by navigating to that source directory and using the command $ jitsu deploy. This will then prompt you for a subdomain, a start script, the version you wish to name this deploy as, and the Node.js engine version you require to run. The subdomain will then be how you identify your application. To see a list of running applications once you have deployed a Jitsu app, use the jitsu apps list command, as shown in Listing 12-32.

Listing 12-32. Listing Nodejitsu Applications

```
$ jitsu apps list
info:    Welcome to Nodejitsu cgack
info:    jitsu v0.13.0, node v0.10.17
info:    It worked if it ends with Nodejitsu ok
info:    Executing command apps list
info:    Listing all apps for user
data:    name    state    subdomain drones running snapshot
data:    wizards stopped wizards       0/1     user-wizards-0.0.1-4.tgz
data:    wsserv  stopped wsserv       0/1     user-wsserv-0.0.1-7.tgz
info:    Nodejitsu ok
```

How It Works

By using the Jitsu command line, you can deploy code to the Nodejitsu cloud platform with simple commands. This happens because Nodejitsu knows and expects a Node.js application to be deployed to the platform. When you run jitsu deploy on your source it will provision a virtual server that will host your subdomain on the server, allowing you to run your Node.js application in the cloud.

Similar to the Heroku CLI, Jitsu allows you to manage your applications and your account fully from the command line. This means that you can start, stop, restart, view, and create applications with the command line, as you can see from Listing 12-33, which outlines the Jitsu apps * procedures available.

Listing 12-33. Jitsu apps*

```
$ jitsu apps
info:    Welcome to Nodejitsu cgack
info:    jitsu v0.13.0, node v0.10.17
info:    It worked if it ends with Nodejitsu ok
info:    Executing command apps
help:    The `jitsu apps` command manages
help:    Applications on Nodejitsu. Valid commands are:
help:
help:    jitsu apps deploy
help:    jitsu apps list
help:    jitsu apps create
help:    jitsu apps cloud   [<name>]
help:    jitsu apps view    [<name>]
help:    jitsu apps update  [<name>]
help:    jitsu apps destroy [<name>]
help:    jitsu apps start   [<name>]
help:    jitsu apps restart [<name>]
help:    jitsu apps stop    [<name>]
help:    jitsu apps setdrones [<name>] <number>
```

```
help:
help:      For commands that take a <name> parameter, if no parameter
help:      is supplied, jitsu will attempt to read the package.json
help:      from the current directory.
help:
help:      Options:
help:         --version, -v     print jitsu version and exit
[string]
help:         --localconf       search for .jitsuconf file in ./ and then parent directories
[string]
help:         --jitsuconf, -j   specify file to load configuration from
[string]
help:         --noanalyze       skip require-analyzer: do not attempt to dynamically detect dependencies
[boolean]
help:         --colors          --no-colors will disable output coloring
[boolean] [default: true]
help:         --confirm, -c     prevents jitsu from asking before overwriting/removing things
[boolean] [default: false]
help:         --release, -r     specify release version number or semantic increment (build, patch,
minor, major) [string]
help:         --raw             jitsu will only output line-delimited raw JSON (useful for piping)
[boolean]
info:      Nodejitsu ok
```

12-10. Deploying to Windows Azure

Problem

You want to utilize the Windows Azure cloud platform to deploy your Node.js solution.

Solution

When Node.js was first created, running Node on Windows was an afterthought. Today Windows has become a first-class citizen in the Node.js realm and as such Microsoft has devoted a great deal of time and effort to making deploying Node.js code and managing it on their cloud platform—Azure—easy and accessible to developers.

To get started with Node.js and Azure, you must first create an account. Sign in to the Azure management portal found at https://manage.windowsazure.com. Once you have signed in, you can create a new web site. Click on the large "+ New" button and then select "web site." You will then name your subdomain and select a region before creating your web site. This process is shown in Figure 12-7.

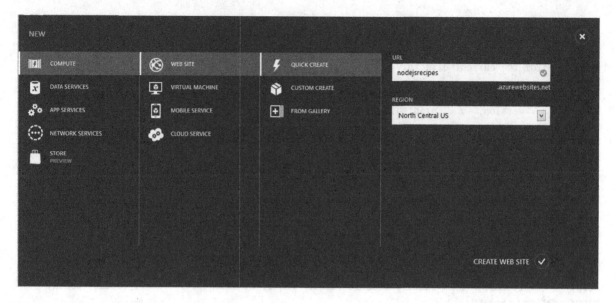

Figure 12-7. Creating an Azure web site for your Node.js application

From here, one of the easiest ways to get a Node.js application created is to go to the dashboard for your newly created application and select the "Set up deployment from source control" option. This option will then present you with the ability to choose any location in which you have stored your application source as source control, which will look similar to Figure 12-8.

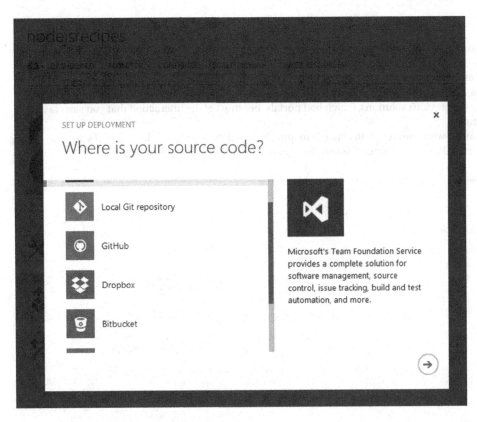

Figure 12-8. *Source of the application in Azure*

From there you can choose your repository. Azure will grab the source and dependencies and deploy the application directly, which will then show on your application's "Deployments" dashboard (see Figure 12-9).

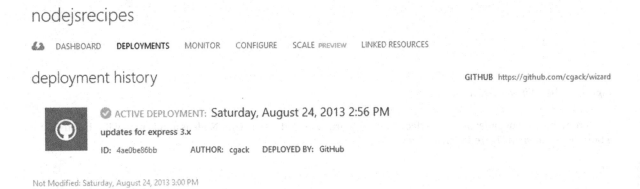

Figure 12-9. *Application deployed*

How It Works

Deploying to Windows Azure is similar to the other deployment methods that have been covered in this chapter. The source code will be located via a source control URL, which will then be uploaded to the platform in the cloud. The dependencies will then be installed and the application will start.

Windows Azure does this through a rich web portal that allows for viewing the data and interactions in real-time via the web as opposed to the previous solutions, which had portals, but most of the interaction that you saw was based in the command line.

One thing that you can do with your Azure instance is to quickly go online to monitor the status of your application and the resources that it is utilizing. This interface looks similar to that shown in Figure 12-10.

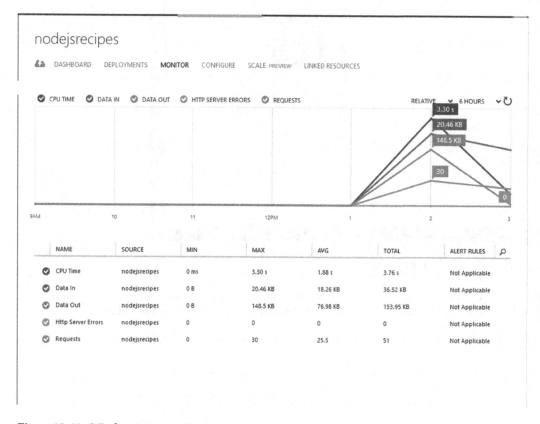

Figure 12-10. *Window Azure monitoring*

From the bottom panel of the interface, you can start, stop, and restart your Node.js application with the push of a button, as shown in Figure 12-11.

6 OPERATIONS HAVE COMPLETED
DISMISS COMPLETED
Started site 'nodejsrecipes'
OK
Stopped web site 'nodejsrecipes'
OK
Restarted site 'nodejsrecipes'
OK
NEW
BROWSE
STOP
RESTART

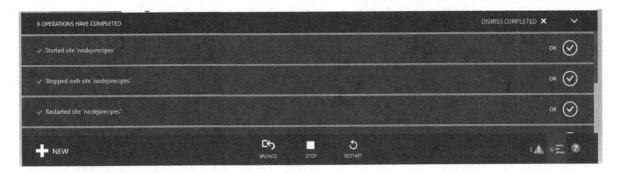

Figure 12-11. *Start, stop, and restart your Azure application*

Once you are running your application, you will also want to be able to publish changes to that application quickly. These deployments can be controlled via Azure Git URLs. To find and configure which URLs will control your future deployments, navigate to the Configure section of the Azure web portal for your application, as shown in Figure 12-12.

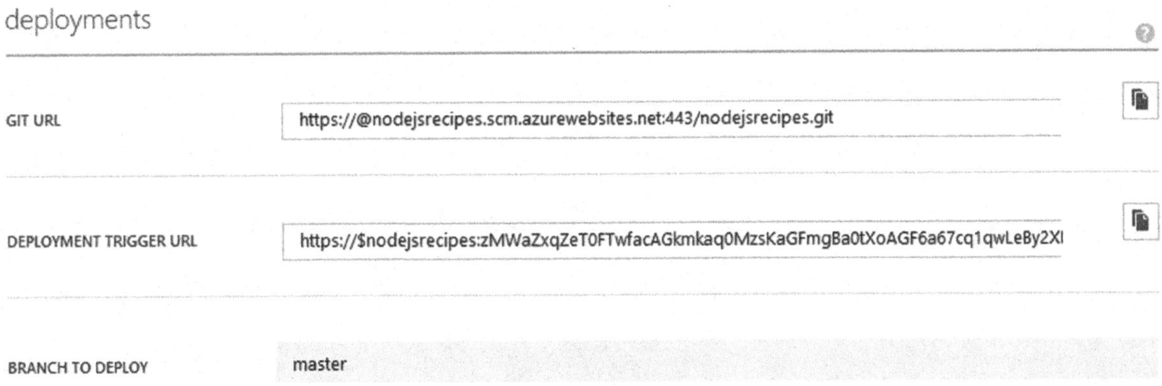

deployments
GIT URL
https://@nodejsrecipes.scm.azurewebsites.net:443/nodejsrecipes.git
DEPLOYMENT TRIGGER URL
https://$nodejsrecipes:zMWaZxqZeT0FTwfacAGkmkaq0MzsKaGFmgBa0tXoAGF6a67cq1qwLeBy2Xl
BRANCH TO DEPLOY
master

Figure 12-12. *Configure deployment URLs for your Azure Node.js application*

You now have your Node.js application running on the Microsoft Windows Azure cloud. While this solution is slightly different than the previous cloud-hosting platforms that you have seen, you have seen that all of the platforms in this chapter can be wonderful resources for deploying your Node.js applications to the web quickly and efficiently on a web-based platform as a service.

Index

Get the eBook for only $10!

Now you can take the weightless companion with you anywhere, anytime. Your purchase of this book entitles you to 3 electronic versions for only $10.

This Apress title will prove so indispensible that you'll want to carry it with you everywhere, which is why we are offering the eBook in 3 formats for only $10 if you have already purchased the print book.

Convenient and fully searchable, the PDF version enables you to easily find and copy code—or perform examples by quickly toggling between instructions and applications. The MOBI format is ideal for your Kindle, while the ePUB can be utilized on a variety of mobile devices.

Go to www.apress.com/promo/tendollars to purchase your companion eBook.